D1611545

The Black Woman in America

Books by Robert Staples:

The Lower Income Negro Family in Saint Paul (1967)
Editor, *The Black Family: Essays and Studies* (1971)
The Black Woman in America: Sex, Marriage, and the Family
    (1973)

The Black Woman in America

Sex, Marriage, and the Family

by Robert Staples

Nelson-Hall
Publishers

Chicago

Professional-Technical Series

ISBN 0–911012–55–9 (hardbound edition)
ISBN 0–911012–420–9 (paperback edition)

Library of Congress Catalog Card Number: 72–95280

To my mother
Anna Staples
in the hope that the toil and
sacrifice of her sisters will not
be unrequited by my generation.

Contents

Foreword

by Joyce A. Ladner

Over the past decade there has been an increasing amount of interest in Black women. In 1965 public attention was focused on Black women by Daniel P. Moynihan's infamous report *The Negro Family: The Case For National Action*.[1] Although Moynihan's analysis of the Black family as a "matriarchal society" is highly erroneous, it did cause an unusual amount of public debate and discussion of the definitions and roles of the Black woman in the family and the broader society.

Within the past five years a simultaneous social scientific and literary curiosity on the subject of Black women has resulted in a growing body of literature. Andrew Billingsley published the noted work, *Black Families in White America*,[2] which examines the socio-historical roles of Black women. Toni Cade's anthology *The Black Woman*,[3] Jay David and Melvin Watkins' anthology *To Be a Black Woman*,[4] Mari Evans' book of poetry entitled *I Am a Black Woman*,[5] Inez Reid's work *Together Black Woman*,[6] and my own study entitled *Tomorrow's Tomorrow: The Black Woman*,[7] comprise the bulk of literature on the subject.

ix

Books of photographs on the subject of Black woman-hood, magazines, and other literature including numerous short stories and essays are appearing regularly. There is now at least one private foundation that makes grants and technical assistance available to Black female organizations and projects.[8] Black women's caucuses and conferences have also been organized on an increasingly frequent basis. Most of these activities and groups have as one of their primary goals that of providing a positive definition and perspective to Black womanhood. One must admit that this is long overdue; for no other racial, ethnic, or religious group of females in the United States has undergone as much degradation, stereotyping, and actual punishment as Black women. The noted Black scholar W. E. B. Du Bois once reflected on this problem when he wrote:

> *No other women on earth could have emerged from the hell of force and temptation which once engulfed and still surrounds Black women in America with half the modesty and womanliness that they retain.*[9]

Hence, the blurred roles and the heavy responsibilities of Black women in America have been difficult for them to cope with. The vast majority have had womanhood thrust upon them long before their white counterparts had to experience it. Economic inequities forced many to carry the burden of responsibility for their entire families without the security offered to women of other racial and ethnic groups. At the same time, they were coerced into taking on some of the purely feminine characteristics that prevail in mainstream American society. Hence, they were expected to be the "head" of the Black family, but, to some great degree, also become a "dainty" symbol of American womanhood. Herein lies the contradiction referred to by Du Bois. It has existed as long as Africans have inhabited American soil. This then is the sordid side of the Black woman's heritage.

The more positive aspect of Black women's heritage is

that they also experienced a type of womanhood that has recently come to be viewed as desirable by white females who are seeking "liberation." Black women were allowed to be strong, independent individuals who were not perpetually being propped up by the crutches of the male dominated society. There has seemingly always existed a feeling that failure to protect white women in this manner would result in the destruction and dissolution of a "feminine mystique," whose esoteric quality could only be maintained if the revered status white women had thrust upon them were sacredly guarded. Hence, white women were protected from Black males because it was feared that sexual interaction with them would destroy the body of myths that surrounded their existence. Of course, Black women never had this protectiveness thrust upon them, nor were Black men *allowed* to play this role when they sought to do so.

The history of Black women has brought into existence dual concepts of her identity, definitions of her ideals, attitudes, behavior, roles, and responsibilities. Because of her powerless status, she has been forced to live with the racist myths that emerged from the white society about her so-called immorality. The stigmas of illegitimacy and matriarchy are two misconceptions that she has to cope with and attempt to destroy. In the latter part of the 20th century this onus still follows her in somewhat the same fashion as it did when she was a slave. Regardless of how often she has attempted to provide her own definitions of herself, she has never been able to force the dominant society to accept their validity. The other side of this duality has to do with the extent to which some of the myths have been laid to rest, and how strenuous are the attacks being waged upon those other myths that seem reluctant to "die." More and more, social scientists and creative writers are recognizing the "truth" about the myths, their functions, and the destruction that has run rampant upon the lives of the countless millions of Black women who have fallen victim to them.

Robert Staples' work on the effects of racism upon Black women belongs to the latter category. He sets forth many of the popular misconceptions, particularly regarding their sexuality, carefully examines them, and lays them to rest. Hence, *The Black Woman in America* falls within a growing body of literature that seeks to clarify the distortion and present more accurate portrayals of the enigma of the Black woman. The special insight he brings to this volume comes from his extensive knowledge of the Black family. As one of the most authoritative social scientists on this subject today, he has previously published works that have covered the vast range of Black family behavior.

Staples examines the "dual dilemma" the Black woman faces: that of being *Black* and *female*. The burdens of racism and sexism are two of America's historical traditions. Blacks have always fought against racist oppression, and so have American females. Today there are social movements that are geared toward the elimination of both. Through the use of empirical studies and literary sources of data, he examines "the Black women's sexual, marital, and familial roles." It has been within the areas of sexual attitudes and behaviors that many of the above mentioned myths have been propagated. For example, in chapter two, Staples writes:

> If there is any facet of the Black woman's role that needs to be explored, it is her sex life. In no other area is there so much speculation, so many stereotypes and myths, than that of Black female sexuality. Curiously, it is her sex life that researchers have ignored.... Consequently, the cultural beliefs about Black female sexuality run rampant while the facts remain unexamined.

The author's assessment of the harm rendered Black women in this area has enabled him to present a body of empirical data derived from a vast number of sources. He presents, perhaps for the first time, that more accurate picture for which we have so long waited. One of the important areas he has examined is the relationship of her sexuality to that of the "virility cult" of Black men. Staples recognized the strong relationship between the Black female's definitions of self and the way in which Black males define their masculinity. By definition, the two have always been intricately connected.

Although Staples has performed a remarkable service by analyzing this body of data from a Black perspective, it must be viewed as a strong beginning instead of the final product. His work should inspire other avenues of investigation that will answer some of the questions he was not prepared to deal with within the scope and intent of this work.

One of the criticisms that the author is likely to hear regarding this discussion of the Black woman's sexuality has to do with the objections and ambivalence that many Black readers will express when the subject is raised. Many feel that *too much* negative discussion (and no positive analysis) has already occurred on the topic. All of this has served to perpetuate extant myths. Others simply ponder the question, "Whose concern is it as to what kind of sex life she has, and what *relevance* does it have to the priorities of human welfare and social justice that Blacks have already established."

Although this is a very valid polemic, perhaps the time has come when a frontal attack must be waged against racist sexual myths, as well as eliminating hunger and police brutality. Ultimately, all of these injustices are interdependent.

Staples' discussion of marriage and parenthood is especially informative. He traces the development of the institution of marriage from precolonial West African societies to the American slave plantation system, pointing out similarities and differences between the two. His extensive discussion of contemporary attitudes and practices in the areas of marriage and motherhood again provides a broad view of many of the covert dynamics involved. New light is shed on such topics as common-law marriage, power relationships within the marital arrangement, child rearing practices and divorce. One of the salient characteristics of this discussion has to do with a redefinition of the marriage institution. The historical conditions of slavery and subsequent economic instability gave rise to the creation of alternative attitudes and behavior patterns in marriage. Hence, what many social scientists have observed to be a "brittle" or "fragile" arrangement based upon an assumed mutual lack of respect for the institution of marriage is an incorrect evaluation. For Staples illustrates how the appearingly "fragile" marriages are simply highly functional adaptation to negative external conditions. Hence, the common notion that welfare mothers prefer to remain on welfare rather than to be married simply means that they prefer to maintain their modest economic security (welfare) rather than risk it with being "married" to a man whose job instability prevents him from taking care of his family.

Staple's discussion of the "Black Woman's Liberation" provides much insight into the double jeopardy status to which Black women are subjected: being Black and female. His understanding of the dynamics of economic exploitation, racism, and sexism that have their impact upon Black women provides the reader with an expanded view of the societal forces that affect Black women in adverse ways. Hence, the Black woman's burden is peculiarly different from that of her counterparts in other racial and ethnic groups.

The Black Woman in America is an important contribution to our understanding the enigma of the Black woman. Let us hope that substantive works such as this will continue to appear.

Acknowledgments

It is difficult to acknowledge here my gratitude to all the people responsible for the publication of this book. I know that I am indebted to my colleagues and friends, Dr. Jacquelyn Jackson and Dr. Joyce Ladner. They read parts of my original manuscript and made many helpful suggestions for revision. Their works on Black women were essential references that I turned to many times while writing this book. As Black female sociologists they have been a constant source of inspiration to me.

Many others have helped in the formulation and development of material for this book. My thanks for their various forms of assistance go to Dr. Robert Hill, Jualynne Dodson, Roger Libby, and Johnetta Cole. I also want to acknowledge the assistance of Julianne Hau and Helen Taylor, who typed and edited the original manuscript.

Over the past years I have also benefited from my discussions with Nathan Hare, Robert Chrisman, Gerald MacWorter, and Talmadge Anderson. Each in his or her own way contributed to the formation of this book. The comments of my Black female students at Howard University helped to sensitize me to many aspects of the Black woman's subjective reality.

R. S.

Introduction

For this, their promise, and for their hard past, I honor the women of my race. Their beauty—their dark and mysterious beauty of midnight eyes, crumpled hair, and soft, full-featured faces—is perhaps more to me than to you, because I was born to its warm and subtle spell; but their worth is yours as well as mine. No other women on earth could have emerged from the hell of force and temptation which once engulfed and still surrounds Black women in America with half the modesty and womanliness that they retain. I have always felt like bowing myself before them in all abasement, searching to bring some tribute to these long-suffering victims, these burdened sisters of mine, whom the world, the wise, white world, loves to affront and ridicule and wantonly to insult. I have know the women of many lands and nations—I have known and seen and lived beside them, but none have I known more sweetly feminine, more unansweringly loyal, more desperately earnest, and more instinctively pure in body and in soul than the daughters of my Black mothers. This, then—a little thing—to their memory and inspiration.

W. E. B. Du Bois
Darkwater (1920)

1

This book is the culmination of a project that I began over six years ago: to explore all the psycho-social dimensions of the sexual, marital, and familial roles Black women play in American society. Since I began, various other matters have occupied me, including graduate school, work in the community, teaching, and the completion of two other books. If I had devoted all my time to writing this book and had completed it in 1966, it would have lacked the insights that the Black and women's movements have provided since that time.

Those two movements created in me a greater awareness of the significance of Black culture and the role of women as a national minority. The scope of this book was broadened to include these new dimensions of Black women. My discussion of the roles Black women play might otherwise have been confined to discussions of their roles on the American continent, and my analysis might not have emphasized so strongly the institutional weaknesses that exist in the United States.

Before discussing the relationship of those two movements to my writings, I must address myself to the question that inevitably will be asked: why a male took it upon himself to write a book about women. It should be understood, initially, that I approach the subject of Black womanhood as a member of the Black community and as a sociologist. I claim no detachment, but I bring to this study both my personal interest in Black women and my standards of scientific analysis. This duality of roles may leave me open to criticisms from either side, but that is a risk I must take.

When I first began the research for this study, I was strongly inclined toward a favorable view of Black women. My own life experiences had been such that I was closer to the Black women in my life than to Black men. Despite the rumblings of some Black men that Black women are hard to get along with, I myself have found that a person who is deserving cannot ask too much of them and undeserving persons usually get more from them than their actions warrant. As the readers of this book will discover for themselves, the superlatives I apply to Black women have their basis in fact.

Aside from my personal fondness for Black women, however, I am writing a book about women because I am a family sociologist, and women are usually the group we study. "Family studies" could be more accurately labeled "women studies," because by far the greatest part of our research has focused on women. Most studies of human sexual behavior, for example, have focused on the female, since the male sexual response is considered more predictable and less responsive to social stimuli.

My own interest within the field of family studies is the area of human sexual behavior. In fact, my wish to study this area was my original motivation for becoming a family sociologist. This book bears the imprint of that interest. At least two of its chapters are concerned directly with Black sexuality and others deal with it indirectly. My interest stems chiefly from the fact that sex plays such an important part in the lives of Black people. White people have generally based their view of, and behavior with, Black people on sexual inferences. This is evident in the fact that when whites are stripped of their beliefs about the inferiority of Blacks, their final resort is to ask: "Would you want your daughter to marry a Black man?"

If there is a central theme to this book, it is that Black women have been oppressed as a result of their biological characteristics—their sex and race. All dimensions of the roles they play in America are affected by the racial and sexual oppression they are subject to. One cannot understand the dynamics of the Black woman's sexual, marital, and familial roles without examining how racism affects the performance of those roles. This makes any study of the Black woman unique because she faces dual subjugation: being Black and female. It is important to understand how the Black woman copes with the duality of her oppression and with the forces that impinge on her everyday life.

This book has a somewhat pan-African perspective, since it attempts to trace the development and unity of Black female roles from their African origins through slavery to the present period. As philosophers, historians, and sociologists agree, we cannot understand the present or predict the future if we do not understand the past. The use of historical data helps us discover the constant elements of the racist conditions under which the Black woman has lived and to study the changing elements of the roles she has played.

Each role of the Black woman is viewed from a historical perspective. In each case we have gone back to precolonial African societies to see how the role of sexual consort, prostitute, wife, or mother was acted out. The historical data are scant since Africans have a tradition of oral rather than written history. Moreover, the historical literature on Blacks in America does not allow us to assume great similarities between African and Afro-American women. Pan-Africanism's central thesis is that Black people throughout the world are the same because they share the common condition of being oppressed by white people.

Although this book deals with the sexist oppression of Black women, one should be cautious about grouping it with other current books about women, particularly those about white women. I do not deal extensively with the nature of sex roles in human society. While the women's movement has highlighted the fact that woman's assigned role is sociological as well as biological, my treatment of Black women is mostly in terms of the traditional concept of woman's role in marriage and the family.

In examining the role of motherhood, for instance, I have confined myself to examining how Black women have acted out this role. I have not raised the question of whether Black women are oppressed because they are stuck with bearing and raising children instead of having a meaningful career. This is not because I do not consider motherhood one aspect of woman's oppression, but because I do not think that this aspect is particularly relevant right now to most Black women. Many of them have found their gratification in their children. To attack motherhood would be to strike at the heart of their reason for living.

I believe that I understand Black women better than most white women do, though I realize that I cannot totally grasp the subjective reality Black women face. This book is not intended as propaganda favorable to Black women. My intent is to present a balanced, objective view of Black women. Negative as well as positive features of Black women are depicted here. It was not my purpose to dichotomize the Black community into "good" Black women and "evil" Black men.

The problem of Black people must be seen as it is, not as others would like us to see it. To a certain extent, white society has created a Black subculture in which men and women come into conflict and name as the source of their oppression the members of the opposite sex. This is quite clear in the case of Black marriages. One cannot dismiss the high Black divorce rate as incidental. It reflects the subculture's conflict.

But attempting to place the blame on each other is being unable to see the forest for the trees. As a couple of Black women warn, "We are, in fact, focusing only on the trees when we expend time and energy in this senseless and debilitating family squabble while the real culprits stand laughing in the wings."[1] Once Black people are caught up in this intersexual struggle, they will once more become victims of the divide-and-conquer strategy of their real enemy—white racism and its agents. White society knows that any group struggling for liberation is weakened by dissension within its ranks.

Perhaps I should clarify here that when I use the term "white racism," I refer also to its exploitative economic system. The two are combined and are really two elements of the same mechanism. Thus, I do not refer to the masses of white people when I speak of white racism. In a very practical sense, one can easily be mislead by assuming that all white people are actively oppressing Black people. Power lies not in the hands of the average white man but in the upper levels of government and business.

The masses of white people do not have the power to oppress most Blacks, although they have become willing collaborators with those who do. Recent events reveal that mass opposition has proved incapable of halting immoral wars, political corruption, and economic trends that make the poor poorer and the rich richer.

Let us, then, be quite clear about the nature of the problem. Men and women are set in conflict with each other because of an exploitative system. Women are conditioned to believe that all that men want from them is sexual gratification and that men should be made to pay the price of marriage for that privilege. At the same time men are socialized into a concept of manhood that is based on sexual conquest and economic domination of women. Marriage only brings all these preconceived attitudes and modes of behavior into focus. The woman has identified sex as an instrument while the man has identified it as a definer of status.

The outcome, then, is a woman who becomes aware of her sexual bondage, chained to the home and family that fulfill her greatest ambitions but leave her without personal fulfillment. When she reaches old age, she becomes a social outcast whose very being is valueless. Her man loses his interest in the sexual thrill after victory is won. The "other woman" becomes his new sexual thrill and the chase is on. He begins to feel trapped in the family because it restricts his freedom to pursue his manhood. Thus, the stage is set for an attack and counterattack by the two sexes.

While all this is going on, the power elite in American society is quite happy to see men and women fighting each other. This male-dominated group has found it very profitable to have sex-linked jobs in the work world, with women occupying all the lower-paying jobs simply because they are women. Men outside the power elite comply with this scheme because it saves the better-paying jobs for them and maintains their economic control over women.

The real hope of the Black and women's movement is that people will begin to question and challenge this exercise of power by a minority. They may direct attention to the issues of immoral wars, inequitable distribution of the society's resources, and deteriorating quality of urban life. Perhaps then men and women, Blacks and whites, can begin to construct a society in which race and sex are not divisive issues, where people relate to each other as fellow humans and not as members of superordinate and subordinate groups. With that hope rests the future of all humanity.

Black Womanhood: Myth and Reality

There is little reason why Negroes should not regard contemporary social science theory and technique with anything except the most unrelenting suspicion. There is, come to think of it, no truly compelling reason at all why Negroes should not regard the use of the social science statistical survey as the most elaborate Fraud of Modern Times. In any event, they should never forget that the group in power is always likely to use every means at its disposal to create the impression that it deserves to be where it is. And it is not above suggesting that those who have been excluded have only themselves to blame.

Albert Murray
The Omni-Americans (1970)

9

In recent years there has been an increasing interest in the role of women in American society and throughout the world. The women's liberation movement has dealt a serious blow to the traditional concept of the female role as immutable, biologically fixed, and subject to the constraints of physiology. The renewed concern with women in general has brought with it a focus on the Black woman in particular. As is true of Black people in general, the role of the Black woman has been affected by the racism extant in White America. Thus she faces a unique dilemma: being Black and being female. It is important to understand the dynamics of this dual oppression and its manifestation in everyday life.

The usual cultural image of the Black woman in America is that of a domineering type who rules the family, her husband included. She is seen as a masculinized female who must be subordinated in order that the Black male may take his rightful place in society. This image of her is conveyed through the mass media, is accepted by White people, and is frequently acted on by some Black nationalist groups. Sociological studies find the matriarchal structure of the Black family a primary deterrent to Black progress. One can only wonder how the victims of a dual oppression have acquired such an image. A look at some historical antecedents may clarify this phenomenon.

Anthropologists and historians tell us that most African societies were (and still are) male dominated. One should not assume from this fact that the role of the female was unimportant. The historical deeds of Black women in the preslavery period of Africa are recorded on the tombs of ancient Egypt, enumerated by Semitic writers, and are part of Greek mythology. Women formed the economic bulwark of Nigerian society. In the Balonda tribe of southern Africa, women held a position economically superior to that of men.[1]

Women played an important role in the political organization of various tribal societies in Africa, as reported in local chronicles and the records of early travelers there. In West Africa, the ancestral home of most Afro-Americans, the women of the Ashanti tribe were reputed to have founded small states such as Mampong, Wenchi, and Juaben. Among the peoples of Niger and Chad, women reputedly founded cities, led migrations, and conquered kingdoms. There are also accounts of the courage of the female legions who fought in the armies of Monomotapa and of the privileges they enjoyed.[2]

In most of the traditional society systems of Africa, women have played important roles. Although their roles may have assumed diverse forms, there does exist a cultural continuity between the roles of African and Afro-American women. The difference is that African women were allowed opportunities by kinsmen to participate in their society whereas Afro-American women had their role fashioned out of the racial oppression they endured and the need to assume the task of Black survival.[3]

There is nothing surprising in these facts. The functions ascribed to the female have always been important to their societies. It has usually been the custom to devalue these functions simply because they are female tasks—not because they are unimportant. But upon her arrival on the shores of the Americas the Black woman acquired a role unique in the annals of mankind. It is this period we must look to for an understanding of contemporary Black women.

The development of tobacco and cotton plantations in the Americas created a need for a large labor force to cultivate them, preferably an inexpensive labor force. A captive labor force was not a new idea, having existed in earlier societies such as the Greek and Egyptian civilizations. It was simply a matter of economics. Slavery, despite the problems it posed in terms of regulating human labor through coercion, was the most profitable source of labor available. As slavery increased in importance and profit in the South, the ideology that supported it changed. The supposed inferiority of Blacks became the predominant ideology supporting the enslavement of formerly proud, and culturally distinct, African peoples.[4]

Until the middle of the eighteenth century, most of the Black slaves were male. Originally, the slavemaster's preference was for males who could perform the heavy duties required of bondsmen. Black men were encouraged to "marry" white women in order to augment the human capital of the slave-owning class. The intermarriage rate, however, became so high that unions between Black men and white women were prohibited. After that time there was a marked increase in the number of Black women. The end of the slave trade also led to an increased emphasis on the domestic breeding of slaves, a task for which Black women bore primary responsibility.[5]

Black women also had the responsibilities of laboring in the fields and in the slavemaster's house. This was the beginning of their dual oppression as a captive labor force and as breeding instruments. Although the Black man was stripped of all paternal functions except the biological one, Black women hardly fared better.

The slave woman was first a full-time worker for her owner and only incidentally a wife, mother, and homemaker. She was allowed to spend only a small fraction of her time in her quarters; she often did no cooking or sewing; and she was not allowed to nurse her children during their illnesses. If a field slave, she had to experience pregnancy and childbirth while performing daily hard labor in the fields. Since the children were the master's property and did not belong to the parents, the slave women frequently were breeding instruments for children who were later sold. There are reports of Black women who strongly resisted being separated from their children and having them put up for sale, even though their opposition subjected them to great physical violence. Occasionally the Black woman committed infanticide rather than have her child endure the oppression of slavery.[6]

During this period of slavery the Black woman's body was forcibly subjected to the carnal desires of any male who took a fancy to her, including the slavemaster, his overseer, or any male slave. If she was permitted a husband, he was not allowed to protect her. Essentially she was left defenseless against sexual onslaught by other males on the plantation. This was especially true of her relations with the white slavemaster. It appears that coercion, as well as desire, was an important element in her sexual relations with white men during that time.[7]

It has been suggested by Angela Davis that the sexual subjugation of the slave woman was the slavemaster's symbolic attempt to break her will to resist. According to her:

> *In confronting the Black woman as adversary in a sexual contest, the master would be subjecting her to the most elemental form of terrorism distinctively suited for the female: rape. Given the already terroristic texture of plantation life, it would be as potential victim of rape that the slave woman would be most unguarded. Further, she might be most conveniently manipulable if the master contrived a random system of sorts, forcing her to pay with her body for food, diminished severity in treatment, the safety of her children, etc.*[8]

The sexual exploitation of the slave woman did not derive simply from carnal desire but from the slavemaster's design to intimidate the entire slave population. He wanted to assert his control over the entirety of the slave's being. The rape of the slave woman brought home to the slave man his inability to protect his woman. Once his masculine role was undermined in this respect, he would begin to experience profound doubts about his power even to break the chains of bondage.[9]

Consequently the slave woman was the center of the family. The Black father, if present, had little authority.

Under slavery the Black man's function was fieldwork and service. The mother named the children and often had sole responsibility for their care and discipline. Whatever authority the mother did not have belonged to the slavemaster.[10] It is this fact that led to the emergence of the Black matriarchy concept. But the matriarchy concept implies some advantage for women in the society. Instead of having any particular privileges under the slave system, Black women were, in reality, burdened with the dual role of laborer and mother. Here is the origin of her two-pronged oppression, which has been labeled the notorious Black matriarchy.

The Postemancipation Era

The plight of the Black woman did not markedly improve after manumission. The aftermath of the Civil War only transformed Southern chattel slaves into impoverished, landless freedmen and then returned them to new forms of bondage. Thus, slavery gave way to sharecropping and debt peonage for the landless Blacks. Instead of slaves, they became sharecroppers; the slave barracks near the big house became dispersed wooden shacks; moneylending charged against the value of the sharecropper's share of the crops became an economic surrogate for slavery. Through constant indebtedness, the slave become tenant farmer was as tied to the land and the landlord as he was under slavery.[11]

Consequently, the Emancipation Proclamation did not free Blacks. Moreover, they were faced with the problem of adjusting to an alien society from which they had been excluded. Black men had to cope with the task of providing for and protecting their families. They found it very difficult to obtain work that would allow them to maintain any sense of pride and achievement. Black men who had held jobs as skilled craftsmen, carpenters, and other skilled workers were forced out of these occupations. In some instances, they could only find work as strikebreakers.[12] It was then left up to the Black woman to do what was necessary in order for her family to survive.

Although the Black man could not find work, the Black woman returned to her familiar job: working in the white man's kitchen. She scrubbed, cooked, and cared for another woman's children and home in addition to her own. It was supposedly her ability to obtain this kind of work that gave the Black woman such an advantage over the unemployed Black man. However, working in a white household as a domestic can endanger the individual's dignity. As W. E. B. Du Bois once said of domestic servants, "The personal degradation of their work is so great that any white man of decency would rather cut his daughter's throat than let her grow up to such a destiny."[13]

In the same essay, Du Bois described the exploitation that domestic workers are subjected to. He portrays them as prey to all sorts of indignities, such as having to enter and exit by a side door, receiving extremely low wages, and being subject to sexual exploitation by their employer.[14] An example of the latter is cited by John Dollard:

> An informant pointed out what it means to the Negro woman who gets two to four dollars a week as a cook to have the man of the house offer her five dollars for sexual intercourse. She probably has a family to support, certainly has bills to pay and needs the money.[15]

While many Black men could not find work, there were some Black women who could not find work either. This was particularly true of certain white-collar workers, such as teachers. Around 1880 the illiteracy rates were greater for Black females than for Black males, and continued to be greater until 1910. Hence, it is no surprise to find that nearly two-thirds of the Black public school teachers before the turn of the century were men. It seems that some Black men (we do not know how many) did manage to support their families. And there were Black women who were victimized as much as men were by the lack of employment opportunities.[16]

Although these were horrendous circumstances for the Black woman, she suffered these indignities because the survival of her family was at stake. For the sake of her children and of their future, she chose to go on. In many cases women did it alone. Hortense Powdermaker observed many families where there was no man in the household at all. There were instances of women in their seventies and their middle-aged daughters, with or without children, forming one household.[17] When the male was present but unemployed, the fact that the woman was the only bread-winner in the family sometimes had psychological effects on the marital relationship. Black men, who felt a loss of masculinity, were inclined to blame Black women for the oppression they suffered under a chaotic and irresponsible economic system.

Of course, in many cases the unemployment of the male actually strenghtened the marital relationship, especially when the male lost his job due to a physical illness or handicap. Black men who are rendered incapable of providing for their families do not necessarily suffer feelings of inadequacy or emasculation. They realize that if the family is to survive, alternate action must be taken. The Black woman's adaptability to several other roles may then increase the male's appreciation of her and bind them closer together.

In addition to the many difficulties the Black woman encountered due to her new role of breadwinner, she suffered as a result of her sex. The Fourteenth Amendment, adopted in 1868, granted voting rights only to free males. Although the leaders of the Republican Party sought to make use of the Black votes of former slaves to beat the Democratic Party in the South, they saw no political value in giving the franchise to women—Black or white. At any rate, Black men were also soon deprived of political rights by the same political leaders.[18]

Around the turn of the twentieth century, a combination of natural disasters in the South, increasing mechanization of agriculture, and industrial expansion in the North altered the relationship of Blacks to the means of production. There was a massive migration of Blacks from the rural South to urban industrialized areas of both the South and the North. Black migration was a result of the increasing urbanization of both North and South, along with the expansion of war industries that required cheap Black labor to be recruited.[19]

These events highlight the role of Black women as a surplus labor supply, the control of which is essential to the profitable functioning of a capitalist economic system. During periods of labor shortage, this labor supply can be tapped to correspond to fluctuations in the rate of accumulation of capital. During periods of war mobilization, Black women are mustered out of the household—where they may be either wife or servant—and drawn into industry. With the end of the conflict, they find themselves barred from jobs which they were considered capable of performing during the hostilities. In the main, Black women are systematically exploited by being paid less for doing the same work that men perform or by being consigned to low-paying jobs that offer no possibility of advancement.

If Black women constitute a reserve labor supply, then Black men are surely the lumpen proletariat of our society. The irregularity or lack of employment has contributed to the prominent role of Black women in family affairs. However, the implication drawn from this situation is that Black society is matriarchal—that the female-headed household is one of the greatest weaknesses of the Black community. Such a supposition does not stand up under closer inspection.

The Female-Headed Household

A variety of factors interact to create a disproportionate number of female-headed households in the Black community. In past years it was common to accept the facile explanation that the vicissitudes of slavery had weakened marriage as an institution among Blacks. It was believed that the lack of a legal basis for marriage among bondsmen coupled with the slavemaster's arbitrary separation of families created a casual attitude in Blacks toward the sanctity of the marital institution.[20] Yet most Black females see marriage as an ideal to which they all aspire.[21]

Events of the hundred years or so after slavery seem sufficient to explain the inordinate number of female-headed households in the Black community. While demographic, historical, and social elements enter into the breakup of families in a given society, the economic factor is the predominant reason. This is quite evident in any observation of the class character of the female-based household. It should be noted, first of all, that the bi-parental unit is the modal type of family organization among Blacks. In 1970, over 70 percent of all ever-married Black males were living with their wives.[22]

Although about 28 percent of Black families are headed by women (compared with 11 percent of white families), 90 percent of Black families with incomes above $10,000 a year are headed by males. Moreover, at every level of income above $3,000 a year, the vast majority of Black families are headed by males.[23]

If there is any such institution as the Black matriarchy, then it should surely be found in those homes where the male is absent. But instead of reflecting a group of privileged, domineering Black women, the statistics reflect the reality of their class oppression. More than half of the Black families headed by a woman live in poverty. In 1966, 60 percent of the nonwhite and 28 percent of the white families headed by a woman were poor. The comparable percentages for nonwhite and white husband-wife families were 27 percent and 8 percent, respectively. Black families headed by a woman had a median family income of $3,270 a year, less than half the $6,778 median income of Black families headed by a man.[24]

The problems of the female-based household become even more apparent if one notes that in metropolitan areas, about 86 percent of all families headed by a female included children. The percentage of impoverished families among those in which Black women head a family with one or more children was 60 percent. In 1969 only 24 percent of the Black children of families with incomes below $3,000 were living with both parents—compared with 44 percent of all white children in comparable economic circumstances.[25] Thus, the objective reality of the Black woman emerges: Black women have a significant amount of family responsibility and need for income but have a lower income than the Black male or white female.

One might ask: Where is the Black male and why is he not taking care of his family? Some have attributed his absence to the legacy of slavery. It has been said that during slavery the male's primary function was to sire children, not to provide for or raise them, and that consequently he never took his paternal responsibilities seriously.[26] The facts contradicting this belief are found, once more, in statistical data. Unemployment rates have long been twice as high among Black men as among white men. The persistent unemployment of Black men has frequently led to the breakup of their family life. In 1964, Black men constituted 34.1 percent of all unemployed males who were married but not living with their wives.[27]

The unemployment of the Black male often leads the family to depend on the welfare system to meet its needs. Some welfare departments have made it a condition for receipt of certain types of aid that the male be absent from the home—that the woman be either divorced or abandoned along with her children. This requirement places a premium on desertion. There are many Black men who would have stayed with their families but were forced to leave home so that the wife and children could receive financial assistance.[28]

Welfare in the United States is definitely linked to racist oppression. On the national level almost half the families receiving aid to dependent children are Black. But in the larger cities and in the South (where racism is a dominant ethos), the welfare rolls in 1971 were filled with Blacks: 90 percent in New York and a startling 96 percent in Washington, D.C. Welfare has become the dumping ground for the victims of unemployment, poor education, and racial oppression.[29]

Life on welfare is a ceaseless and humiliating ordeal for those who must depend on it. In many cities it means endless trips to the welfare office to establish basic claims. The money welfare recipients receive barely keeps them at the level of subsistence. Welfare diets are substandard almost by definition. The welfare administration reported in 1965 that the average income (including assistance) of the more than four million men, women, and children on welfare was $1.15 per day.[30]

The majority of Black families receiving public assistance are headed by women. A common stereotype of these women holds that they are living a life of leisure at public expense. But $1.15 a day is hardly sufficient to guarantee even bare survival. Figures recently released by the Census Bureau reveal that two-thirds of the women heading Black families work. Thus, although about half of these families are on welfare, the majority of them are not totally dependent on welfare.[31]

Another element that contributes to the large number of female-headed households among Blacks is the sex ratio. In the age range of greatest marriageability, 25 to 64, there are about 85 Black males for every 100 Black females.[32] The excess of females increases the probability of female-headed households while the scarcity of males reduces the number of possible husband-wife combinations. The imbalance between the sexes is intensified by the distribution of Black males and females to create an even greater shortage of Black males in household-forming populations, which in turn increases the number of Black female-headed households.

Historical patterns of racism and discrimination affecting health patterns and resources have created a gap between the life expectancies of Blacks and whites. Blacks can expect to live about ten years less than whites, and the percentage of Black females who are aged (65 or over) is greater than the percentage of Black males who are aged.[33] Thus the operation of the normal age specific and sex specific death rates reduces the number of males versus females in a population as age advances, modifying the sex ratio in the relevant portion of the population.

The abnormally high mortality rate for Black males of a marriageable age or younger is attributed to war mortality and the effects of ghetto living. Death rates for young Black males are much higher than for any other sex-race group. This is due in part to the large number of deaths from homicides and accidents. The pressures of ghetto life, inability to find work, and the self-inflicted violence of America's colonial subjects all combine to kill off the youth of the Black community at an alarming rate.

One unfortunate effect of living in a racist society is the development of a tendency of Blacks to kill Blacks. The highest rate of homicide involving relatives can be found among Black women. They are most likely to be defendants in homicides involving family relations. Usually the homicide represents the woman's attempt at self-preservation when attacked by a Black male, often her spouse. These homicide rates are rising.[34]

While the high homicide rates among Black females

result partly from their need to defend themselves against attack, the homicidal acts of Black males are more directly traceable to social pressures and racist influences. The traumatic experience of being a Black man in a society which does not provide avenues for Black masculine expression apparently takes its toll. This is particularly true for Black males in the 25-44 year range.[35]

American militarism has also claimed its share of Afro-American youth. The Black males drafted by the army represent the upper echelon in achievement and potential. While the more privileged white male is exempted from service—by deferment or, in many cases, medical disqualification—the more "qualified" Black male high-school graduate with no gross handicap is likely to serve.[36]

America's neocolonial wars have taken a high toll of the youth in the Black community. Because he is unable to find work, the Black teenager may enlist as a mercenary in his country's imperialist efforts. In the war in Vietnam, for instance, in 1967 reported Black casualties accounted for 23 percent of all deaths related to the war. Since Blacks comprised only 11 percent of the total population, those figures reflect the tragic effect of an exploitative economy which in its declining stages sends the most oppressed members of its population off to die at a rate double that of the advantaged members.[37]

An additional factor weighing on imbalance of the sexes is the large number of Black political prisoners in the nation's jails.[38] Most of the Black prisoners are males and most are poor. The percentage of Blacks within the prison population is more out of balance than the percentage within any other population. In cities like Chicago, as many as 90 percent of the county jail's inhabitants are Black. In California, more than 40 percent of the state's prisoners are Black. These facts are not surprising in light of the evidence showing disparities of as much as twenty years in the sentences meted out to Black men and white men for the same crime. More than half of the nation's executions for the crime of rape involve Black men. It was recently estimated that there are more Blacks in prison than in college.[39]

One other force favoring female-headed households is the wage-labor system. Since an expanding capitalist economy requires a mobile male labor force, it produces an imbalance in the sex ratio, an excess of adult females over males. Black men, who constitute an important part of the lumpen prolitariat, have to make irregular journeys of varying lengths of time to obtain wage labor. They frequently leave their wives and children behind. Some return at frequent intervals throughout the year. Others may be absent for several years.

The mobility of the Black female labor force has also contributed to the imbalance. During World War II, for instance, many Black females migrated to the West Coast for employment. This kind of geographic imbalance tends to affect the sex ratio. In industrial states, for example, females tend to migrate to large cities where they can find white collar jobs or receive a higher education. This accounts for the Black male-female ratio in cities like Washington, D.C. and New York City. There, women outnumber men three to one because they are white collar towns. Conversely, Black males outnumber females in such states as Montana, Idaho, and Arizona.[40]

These discussions have delineated a reality quite alien to the cultural beliefs about the Black female-headed household. The concept of the privileged, domineering Black woman only serves to mask the real economic and social deprivation of the Black female underclass. The economic order, in conjunction with racism and sexism, has placed the Black woman in triple jeopardy, forced to face the machinations of capitalism, racism, and sexism by herself. However, one might still believe that Black women by virtue of their education, occupation, and income are ascendent in the family. Let us look a little closer.

Education, Occupation, and Income

It is commonly believed that Black women occupy a higher and more powerful place in Black society than Black men because they have more education, can more easily find employment, and earn a higher income. The most devastating blow to this belief has been dealt by Jacquelyn Jackson. After a thorough analysis of the data, she concluded that:

> The overall status position of Black women is lower than that of Black men. While their educational levels, as measured by median years of formal education, are not significantly different from those attained by the men, their education and, hence, their occupations have been far more constricted. Their rates of unemployment have usually been higher; their income levels, consistently lower.[41]

The findings of Jackson about the educational position of Black women may shock even the most knowledgeable students of Black life in America. In 1965 Daniel Moynihan was able to state that the matriarchal pattern of Black families reinforces itself over the generations and that the process begins with education.[42] He cited figures showing that Black women had more education than Black men. But by 1971 Jackson reported that Black females were now more disadvantaged educationally than Black males or whites. By 1969 not only were Black females less likely to have completed high school or college than these groups were, but the gap between them had widened since the previous year.[43] Jackson cites two reasons for this widening educational gap: 1) Black female school dropouts due to pregnancies and 2) more recruitment and admission programs to attract whites and Black males to institutions of higher learning than to attract Black females.[44]

Historically, Black women have been more educated than Black men.[45] This situation is often explained by stating that Black mothers expressed a preference for the female child when a decision had to be made about which child to send to college. But there is little or no evidence to show that low-income Black mothers are significantly active in determining which offspring will attend college; neither do they express a sex preference. Jackson has noted that:

> *A realistic historical assessment of Black prefer-ences for more education for females, where they may have existed, should be functionally related to the greater educational requirements for obtaining an oc-cupation as a public school teacher, with almost the only visible occupation for Black females then being that of domestic employment, whereas most educa-tional requirements for occupations open to the males were not stringent. Hence, what has usually been translated as a greater preference for educating a daughter than a son may really have been translated as merely trying to keep the daughters away from "Mr. Charlie's house" as a domestic servant and as a more vulnerable sexual object.*[46]

Furthermore, higher education is not always reflected in a higher income. Despite being more educated than the Black male, the Black female in 1967 had a median salary income of $3,268; the Black male's median income was $4,837. Even among Black families with incomes of $3,000 or less, in 85 percent of the families, the husband's income surpassed the wife's.[47] This latter fact runs counter to the popular belief that in low-income Black families the wife's earnings are often greater than the husband's. It illustrates that sex discrimination in employment and income is even greater than racial discrimination and once more highlights the fact of the Black woman's dual oppression: sexism and racism.

One result of the Black woman's higher level of education has been a shortage of marriage partners at her socioeconomic level. Educational compatibility as a basis for marriage poses a special problem for Black women. In American society women rarely marry men with less education than they have. But one study of Black female college graduates revealed that 50 percent of them were married to men whose occupations placed them at a lower socioeconomic level than their wives.[48]

Although marriages involving women who are more educated than their husbands have a high rate of failure, it is not the woman's superior education that creates difficulties. The difficulties probably result from the wife's assumption of a superior status due to her higher educational level or from the husband's feelings of inadequacies with resultant jealous and destructive behavior on his part. Of course, there are also instances in which educational incompatibility has led to divergent life styles and values.

Her educational superiority has not guaranteed the Black woman any easier access to employment opportunities than to marriage partners. Contrary to popular belief, the unemployment rate is higher for Black women than for Black men or for whites—6.7 percent, compared with 4.2 percent for Black men, 3.6 percent for white women, and 2 percent for white men.[49] As we have already noted the Black woman's income is below that of the Black man. Tobia Bressler and Nampeo McKenney have shown that when you compare them by the same work category, the type of job, and amount of education, their incomes are rarely equal.[50]

Indeed, a recent report revealed that the highest unemployment rates for any group are those for Black female teenagers in low-income areas of central cities. Their unemployment rate in recent years has seldom been below 33 percent and is often as high as 50 percent. These figures really indicate the minimum level of unemployment among Black women, since large numbers have given up hope and have stopped looking for jobs.[51]

One other factor to be considered is the type of employment Black women are able to obtain. We have already mentioned the hazards of domestic work in this society. According to the United States Women's Bureau, 1,500,000 people were employed in private household work in 1970. Almost two-thirds of them were Black. The median income for full-time, year-round household workers was approximately $1,800 per year. These workers do not receive minimum wage protection from either the federal government or 48 of the 50 states. Generally they are excluded from unemployment and workmen's compensation benefits and rarely receive sick leave, holidays, or vacations with pay. Two out of three are at least partly self-supporting, and one out of eight is head of a family.[52]

It is difficult to assess the impact of the Black woman's dual household tasks. One can only speculate that the problem of running two households—her own and her employer's—takes a rather high toll of the Black woman's body and mind. In light of this and the other difficulties she faces, it is hard to believe that she plays the omnipotent role attributed to her. Since it is often asserted that she controls the Black man and her children, let us investigate the power structure of the Black family.

The Black Power Structure

In recent years the concept of the Black woman as unchallenged governor of the Black family has been reinforced by some behavioral scientists. Probably the study which gave greatest credence to this theory was the Moynihan Report of 1965. According to Moynihan, white society has forced the Black community into a matriarchal structure which, because it is so out of line with white America's patriarchal family system, retards the progress of the Black community as a whole. It is this Black female dominance—asserts Moynihan—that will lead to a host of pathologies in the next generation of Black children. As evidence for this supposition, he cited statistics showing that 21 percent of

Black families were headed by females, compared to 9 percent of white families. He also tried to demonstrate that children from such homes perform poorly in school, drop out earlier, and have higher delinquency rates.[53]

Moynihan's characterization of the Black family as matriarchal in structure is based on census figures that show that the father is absent in less than a quarter of all Black families in the nation. Since this is only a minority of Black families, one wonders about his generalization to the entire Black community. His other evidence in support of the existence of a Black matriarchy is in the form of learned opinions and speculation.

One study quoted by Moynihan was conducted by Robert Blood and Donald Wolfe. They found that the Black wife was dominant, as measured by the criterion of decision-making, in almost 50 percent of the families in their sample; the husband, in 19 percent. In 38 percent of the families, both had equal power to make decisions. However, these findings were not interpreted as evidence of Black matriarchy. Rather, the researchers reported that Black wives assumed the decision-making role because it was imposed on them.[54] Since only the wives were interviewed, it is possible that they were inclined to overstate their own power when reporting who made decisions in the family.

Moreover, decisions made because of the male's default are not valid indicators of the power alignments in the Black family. Only decisions that are made in opposition to the Black male's wishes, and carried out, would indicate a real power imbalance in the family structure. One reason Black men defer to their wives in decision-making is simply because the wives may be more competent to make them in certain areas. Black women are often better acquainted with the workings of the white world, since contacts with white society have been more readily available to Black women than to Black men.

There are other studies which show no significant

differences in dominance between Black and white families. One such study by Russel Middleton and Snell Putney concluded that:

> *We find no evidence that whites and Negroes, professors and skilled workers, differ as to which spouse dominates in the making of daily decisions. Contrary to the literature our data suggest that all these groups are predominantly equalitarian. In view of this, it would be interesting to conduct further investigations with lower class whites and Negroes to see whether they deviated from the predominant equalitarian pattern.*[55]

A major difference in the two studies quoted is that the authors of the second study did not rely on self-appraisals to determine dominance in the making of decisions. Instead, they chose to observe minor decisions in daily life. Another technique was employed by Delores Mack, who also found that there were no power-distribution differences between Black and white families. Instead of asking spouses who was the most powerful in their marriage, she observed both partners in various situations. She later combined the facts she gathered from these observations to form a composite picture of power in each family. Her conclusion: Important differences in the distribution of power in the family are functions of class, not race.[56]

Further weakening the matriarchy theory are the findings of Herbert Hyman and John Reed. They report that the actual white pattern (of female influence) is almost identical with the Black pattern, that the woman's influence surpasses the man's in a number of instances. Even in the area of politics, where male dominance has long been assumed, white and Black children are more likely to side with the mother when parents disagree about a party choice. They note that the concept of a culturally linked Black-white difference in family organization needs to be critically reexamined.[57]

Power relationships within the Black family are influenced by economic factors. Since some Black women have not been economically dependent on Black men, they have been more independent than the white female who has been more economically subservient to the male. Black women, in general, are more aggressive and independent than white women because it has historically been necessary in order for them and their children to survive in a racist society. The alleged stability of the white family is partly a function of the subordination of the white female.

There is little evidence to support the notion that patriarchal societies produce individuals who are more emotionally adjusted or intellectually capable than matriarchal societies do. Such a notion fits well into the male chauvinist model of the female's role in society. When she is in control, assumes the chauvinist, there must be a deteriorating situation. Yet it is the patriarchal family structure that is being challenged throughout the world.

The effects of the self-reliant character of the Black woman are in complete contrast to the outrages committed in the name of patriarchies, where women and children are mere pieces of property. It is also useful to distinguish self-reliance from dominance or power, as Joyce Ladner has so cogently pointed out in her study of Black women. She observed:

> The problem is that there has been a confusion of the terms "dominant" and "strong." All dominant people must necessarily be strong but all strong people are not necessarily dominant. Much of this misconception comes from the fact that women in American society are held to be the passive sex, but the majority of Black women have, perhaps, never fit this model, and have been liberated from many of the constraints the society has traditionally imposed on women. Although this has emerged from forced circumstances, it has

nevertheless allowed the Black woman the kind of emotional well-being that women's liberation groups are calling for.[58]

What has been labeled a destructive matriarchy is, in reality, nothing more than the shifting of responsibility from male to female. This situation is a consequence of the racism and sexism extant in American society. It is a cultural formation common among oppressed people throughout history. Role shifts are responses to economic exigencies. The Black woman's adoption of the role of provider for her family deserves praise, not condemnation; compassion, not opprobrium.

Summary

The travail of the Black woman has spanned two continents and four centuries. Abducted from her native land of Africa where her status, though subordinate, was honored, she fell victim to the imperatives of a nascent capitalist economic order. Her body became the property of all men. Because slaves, whether men or women, had no legal or human rights, her body was violated with impunity. Her man, if she had one, defended her honor only at the risk of his life. Thus even the physical security accorded most women in a society was denied to the Black woman under the peculiar institution of slavery.

Her role as a sex object and breeder of more slaves, while important, did not exempt her from forced labor. In the case of fieldwork, the slavemaster conveniently overlooked sex distinctions as the Black woman took on the dual role of worker and mother. His lack of concern for her welfare meant that Black women were forced to labor in the fields while pregnant. In fact, many a Black child entered this world in the tobacco and cotton fields of the plantation.

America's Civil War freed the chattel slaves owned by Southern slaveholders and began transforming them into wage slaves of the Northern and Southern economic order. During the reconstruction period, Blacks in the South were able to make substantial gains in achieving democratic rights and held important political, economic, and intellectual power in the South. However, these gains accrued to Black males only. The Black woman was confronted with the oppression of her sex role. Although the Fifteenth Amendment guaranteed voting rights to freed slaves, it did not include women. Without even the minor political rights guaranteed Black men, the Black woman in the South was often a landless peasant who had to rear her family by herself.

In the twentieth century, instead of being dispersed throughout the rural South, Blacks were concentrated in huge urban ghettos. Location in this new setting only transformed the Black woman's status from that of landless peasant to most oppressed member of the urban proletariat. A combination of economic forces have created an inordinate number of female-headed households in the Black community. Black men have been forced out of their family dwellings by the vagaries of the labor market and the forces of the politico-economic system, which decrease their number through wars, political imprisonment, and the vicissitudes of ghetto life.

Still the Black woman has managed to hold her own. Although the male chauvinist model dictates that a man, in strong control, must be head of the household, female-based Black families are quite stable. A Black female-headed family that sustains itself is stable, not unstable. Black family stability should not be measured by the presence or absence of a male head but rather by the extent to which the family meets functional obligations. And Black female-headed families have acquitted themselves well despite occupying the lowest rungs of the employment and income ladders.

Considering her heroic role in the face of negative elements which threaten her constantly, one has cause for bewilderment at the cultural image of the Black woman as a privileged, domineering segment of the Black population. How did such an image emerge? And if it is false, what is its purpose?

The image surfaced out of the necessary role shifts in the Black family. Because Black women had to be strong figures in order to ensure their family's survival, society labeled their social structure a matriarchy. There is nothing inherently wrong with such a social structure. Our patriarchies have led us into numerous wars, urban blight, and a host of other social ills. Surely women could have done no worse. However, it is precisely because Black women have not fit into the traditional passive, subordinate role ascribed to the white female that they have suffered the opprobrium of the matriarchy label. White society conveniently ignores the fact that circumstances forced Black women to be strong and self-reliant in order to achieve the survival of the Black community.

As for the purpose of the myth of the Black matriarchy, cultivated by America's image makers, it is part of the divide-and-conquer strategy that ruling classes have used throughout history. The system of racism and capitalism benefits from maintaining sexual differentials in income and status within the Black population. Blacks as a group would constitute a far more homogeneous and formidable antagonist if all discrimination and interior divisions were eliminated.

Instead, Black men who accept the myth of the Black matriarchy act on the premise that they can gain their rightful place in society by subjugating Black women. They believe that in order for the Black man to be strong the Black woman must be weak. Thus we find certain Black nationalist groups who assert their masculinity by demanding that Black women revert to a domestic, submissive role, that the subjugation of the Black woman is a sine qua non for Black liberation.

Consequently, the reality of the Black woman's oppression has come full circle. After her years of toil, her sacrifices, and her contribution to the struggle, she becomes victimized by sexism within the very group which she helped to survive. The question of whether she needs Black liberation or woman's liberation is no longer relevant. She needs both and she needs them now.

Black women must confront the white male rulers of this country who are responsible for the oppression of Blacks and women. The unified struggle of all the forces in the Black community is the key to bringing about a new birth of freedom for both women and Blacks in a humanist America in a free world. Black women must participate in the struggle to bring about the kind of society in which Black children, Black men, and Black women can grow up as free people, liberated from the pressures of racism and sexism.

2

The Sexual Life of Black Women

In her girlhood all the delicate tenderness of her sex has been rudely outraged. In the field, in the rude cabin, in the press-room, in the factory she was thrown into the companionship of coarse and ignorant men. No chance was given her for delicate reserve or tender modesty. From her childhood she was the doomed victim of the grossest passion. All the virtues of her sex were utterly ignored. If the instinct of chastity asserted itself, then she had to fight like a tiger for the ownership and possession of her own person and ofttimes had to suffer pain and lacerations for her virtuous self-assertion. When she reached maturity, all the tender instincts of her womanhood were ruthlessly violated. At the age of marriage—always prematurely anticipated under slavery—she was mated as the stock of the plantation were mated, not to be the companion of a loved and chosen husband, but to be the breeder of human cattle for the field or the auction block.

Alexander Crummell
Africa and America (1891)

If there is any facet of the Black woman's role that needs to be explored, it is her sex life. In no other area is there so much speculation, so many stereotypes and myths, than that of Black female sexuality. Curiously, it is her sex life that researchers have ignored in their study of Black women. Consequently, the cultural beliefs about Black female sexuality run rampant while the facts remain unexamined.

The image of the Black woman is that she is the most sensual of all female creatures. One Black writer has even described her as "potentially, if not already, the most sexual animal on this planet."[1] While his description was meant as a compliment, the white view of Black sexuality is rife with negative connotations. The lusty sexuality that whites impute to Blacks represents to them the most abnormal, vulgar, and base instincts of mankind. The image of the Black woman as innately sexual is a combination of fact and myth. But that image has been used as a justification for racist practices, because it suggested unrestrained sexual urges that civilized people do not possess.

A basic point that must be understood, however, is that sexual expression is determined by both physiological and sociological factors. Although the basis for sexual motivation is physiological, in no group in any society is sexual behavior determined solely by physiological factors. The white image of raw Black sexuality has its origin in the sexual repression to which whites are subjected. Because of the restraints on their own sexual expression, they conjure up fantastic images of the uncontrolled animal sexuality of Blacks. But as E. Franklin Frazier has noted, the sexual behavior of Blacks, like the sexual behavior of peoples all over the world, can only be understood when it is studied in relation to the social and cultural context in which Black sexual attitudes and behavioral patterns are shaped.[2] To do this, one needs to start at the beginning and develop an understanding of pre-slavery sexual behavior in Africa.

African Sexual Patterns

The main impression derived from most studies of African sexual behavior is that this behavior takes on protean forms, peculiar to the specific geographic and cultural contexts. The diversity of African societies makes it impossible to generalize about the sexual patterns. The available evidence indicates that sex behavior before and after marriage is traditionally under strict community and family control. In African societies sexual behavior is strictly regulated by the customs and mores of the various tribal groupings. For example, one finds rigid chastity prescribed in some societies and permissive sexuality occurring in others. The most common feature of African sexual relations is that they are institutionalized parts of the society.[3]

For example, among the Dahomeans, youths are ignorant of sexual facts until they reach late adolescence. At a particular age girls receive their sexual education and begin to hear admonitions about avoiding sex play with boys. As their sex training proceeds, the warnings both at home and at school grow more frequent until, when they reach puberty, they are definitely conscious of the negative consequences they will face if they are not virgins at the time of the marriage.[4]

Conversely, among other African tribes (such as the Masai, the Nuer, and the Zulus), sexual relations are normally expected to take place before marriage. Yet they occur within the context of the cultural values of each African society. Among the Masai, prenuptial coitus takes place with women who form a part of the village especially organized for that purpose. Girls in the Yao tribe are deflowered as part of a rite. Overall, it appears that premarital virginity is not valued significantly in most traditional African societies.[5]

An important reason for this is the difference between the African and American concept of sex. Throughout Africa south of the Sahara, there is a concept of a deity, sometimes multiple gods, but the deity issues no dicta on sexual morality. A violation of the sexual code is an offense against individuals and not against God. Also, in Black Africa the norms associated with sex are part of the religious values related to reproduction and are not related to sex itself. This is in contrast with western systems in which sex has become largely separated from procreation. Consequently, sexual relations before marriage are allowed, and under some circumstances, unmarried males have the right to engage in sexual relations with married women.[6]

The Influence of Slavery

While the African's sexual behavior was permissive vis-à-vis European sexual patterns, it was at least under group control. But under slavery that control was eliminated and the only restraint was lack of desire. In the beginning of the slavery era, however, the shortage of Black women imposed some restraints on the Afro-American's sexual impulse. After 1840, when the sex ratio of the slave population grew more equal, there were few if any restraints on the satisfaction of the slave's sexual desires. There are reports of male slaves seizing the closest female slave and satisfying their sexual appetites.[7]

Sexual promiscuity and exploitation were strongly encouraged by some slavemasters. The practice of using virile Black males to sire children by a number of female slaves indicates that many slave holders were more interested in the fertility of their slaves than in their moral conduct. In fact, the function of female slaves was to breed additional slaves, who would become organic property for the slave-owning class.[8]

Predictably, the slave woman was also subject to the carnal desires of the slavemaster and his overseers. She was used and abused, sexually, by many white males on the plantation. While there may have been some slave women who submitted voluntarily to the slavemaster's sexual advances, there is sufficient historical evidence to show that many of them were compelled to enter into various sexual associations with white males because of their captive status.[9] As one writer has noted, the American slaveholder's sexual domination never lost its openly terroristic character.[10]

The coercive character of sex relations between the slave woman and her master is poignantly illustrated by this young man's story:

> *Approximately a century and a quarter ago, a group of slaves were picking cotton on a plantation near where Troy, Alabama, is now located. Among them was a negro woman, who, despite her position as a slave, carried herself like a queen and was tall and stately. The over-seer (who was the plantation owner's son) sent her to the house on some errand. It was necessary to pass through a wooded pasture to reach the house and the over-seer intercepted her in the woods and forced her to put her head between the rails in an old stake and rider fence, and there in that position my great-great-grandfather was conceived.*[11]

There is little substance to the theory that the Black woman was the aggressor in her sexual relations with the slavemaster. Such a supposition ignores the type of existence the female slave led. As a slave she had no protection from the sexual aggressions of salacious white men. She realized that the only recourse available to her was a violent death. As one historian has noted, if the slave woman submitted it was only under coercion. Indeed, some miscegenation was little more than rape, though no such offense against a slave woman was recognized in law.[12]

Slave women were deprived of any protection against the sexual assaults of white males. Under slavery, Blacks were not permitted to be witnesses against whites in a court of law. There were no laws to protect the Black woman from assaults upon her body. For example, the North Carolina Supreme Court ruled in the nineteenth century that no white male could be convicted for fornication with a slave woman. The North Carolina Constitutional Convention of 1835 declared that any white man might go to the house of a *free* Black, mistreat and abuse him, and commit any outrage upon his family. If a white person did not witness the act, no legal remedies were available.[13]

The cultural belief about the Black female's sexuality emerged out of the experience of slavery. The sexual availability of slave women allowed white men to put white women on a pedestal, to be seen as the goddesses of virtue. In a way this became a self-fulfilling prophecy. White women were held aloof from the world of lust and passion and in many cases became more inhibited emotionally, sexually, and intellectually because of the oppressive presence of slavery. Consequently, while the white woman's experiences and status inhibited sexual expression, the Black woman's encouraged it.

While the white concept of Black female sexuality developed out of the peculiar conditions of slavery, the Black female's sexual morality was also shaped by this experience. Once she accepted the fact that she did not have control over her body, the importance of virginity to her was considerably reduced. As Calvin Hernton comments, the Black woman came to look upon herself as the South viewed and treated her. In fact, she had no other morality by which to shape her womanhood.[14]

The end of slavery did not give the Black woman any greater right to sexual integrity. What slavery began, racism and economic exploitation continued. In the postbellum South Black women were still at the mercy of the carnal desires of white men. According to W. J. Cash, Black women were forced to give up their bodies like animals to white men at random.[15] Others have noted that many Southern white men had their first sexual experience with Black women. In some cases the use of Black women as sexual objects served to maintain the double standard of sexual conduct in the white South. Many white men did not have sexual relations with white women until they married. Some Southern white men were known to jokingly remark that until they married they did not know that white women were capable of sexual intercourse. [16]

It was protection of the sexual purity of white women that partially justified the erection of racially segregated institutions in the South. The Southern white man assumed that Black men have a strong desire for intermarriage and that white women would be open to proposals from Black males if they were not guarded from meeting with them on an equal level.[17] As Jessie Bernard writes: "The white world's insistence on keeping Negro men walled up in the concentration camp (of the ghetto) was motivated in large part by its fear of their sexuality."[18]

Meanwhile, the Black woman in the South was left without any protection against the sexual assaults of white men. The Black man could not protect her unless he was prepared to lose his life in her defense. This does not mean that he did not try. After emancipation when the marriages of Black women were legally recognized, Black men began to demand that Black women be treated with respect and courtesy and that white men cease their seduction and rape of Black womanhood. In 1874 one Black congressman declared: "We want more protection from the whites invading our homes and destroying the virtue of our women than they from us."[19]

The sexual exploitation of Black women was not always accompanied by violence. White men were able to use the economic deprivation of Black women to their sexual advantage. The sexual exploitation of Black women who worked as domestic servants is legendary. According to

Calvin Hernton, even today throughout the South white men are able to sexually use Black women in the course of the woman's employment, or in the course of their seeking employment.[20]

One such example of the white male's economic advantage serving sexual ends is reported by John Howard Griffin. He quoted the following revelations of a white employer:

> He told me how all of the white men in the region crave colored girls. He said he hired a lot of them both for housework and in his business. And I guarantee you, I've had it in every one of them before they get on the payroll.
> "Surely some refuse," I suggested cautiously. "Not if they want to eat—or feed their kids," he snorted. "If they don't put out, they don't get the job."[21]

It is easy to understand why there failed to emerge in the Black culture the rigid sexual regulations so prevalent in the dominant American society. As the violation of her body became routine, Black women could not value that which was not available to her—virginity. She has been sexually used by men of both races. It has been noted that after emancipation, many Black men had a casual sexual life. Many of them wandered from town to town, seeking employment. Frequently, they were taken in by lonely women engaged in domestic service who were sympathetic to their hard luck stories of life on the road. Once their sexual hunger was satisfied, these Black men took to the road again.[22]

Only among the middle-class group did Black women have much protection against the unwelcomed sexual advances of white men. Middle-class Black males preferred that their wives stay at home.[23] This middle-class element in the Black population was very conscious of its unique position in relation to the masses of Black folk. Contrary to their lower-class brethren, they placed an exaggerated emphasis upon moral conduct and developed a puritanical restraint in contrast to the free and more liberated sexual behavior of the dominant Black population.[24]

While the legacy of slavery and the effect of white racism strongly influence the sexual practices of Black women, there are many other social forces that impinge on the sexuality of Black women. Among those forces is their socialization into sexual behavior.

Socialization into Sexual Behavior

The process of socialization is designed to condition the human organism to the behavior patterns of his society. This is the way that humans acquire their knowledge of sex and the particular values they come to hold in relation to it. Black women face a unique situation in that the sexual values inculcated into them by their parents are counteracted not only by the conditions under which they live but also by their observation of their parents' violation of the moral code they teach their daughters.[25]

There is little doubt that Black parents teach their female children to remain sexually chaste before marriage. When Lee Rainwater asked a group of fifty adults how important it was that a girl be a virgin when she marries, over 50 percent of both the men and the women answered that it was very important. Most of them admitted that this norm was honored more in the breach than in the observance.[26]

Some schools reinforce this standard by their technique of sex education for the female child. Sex is made to appear horrible and extremely dangerous. There are examples of some females being warned by their teachers that any sexual relations before marriage will result in contracting a venereal disease.[27] This type of sex education often creates severe anxiety in the female about her sexual impulses and responses. She becomes afraid to have sexual intercourse and convinced that all sexual behavior is sinful.[28]

No less harmful are those parents who maintain an awful and complete silence on the subject of sex, yet punish harshly for any form of sexual play. When the child's interest in sex becomes stronger, she frequently discovers that her parents do not wish to discuss sex in a way that is significant to her. Therefore, it is not strange to find that many Black females acquire their knowledge about sex through the folklore and myths of their age peers. Most of the Black females in the author's study learned about sex through a source other than their parents.[29]

Failure to practice what they preach contributes to Black parents' inability to control the sex conduct of their children. While the parents may warn the female child against engaging in sex relations before marriage, she is frequently presented with an example of extramarital sexual behavior. She observes at an early age that the parent's behavior is not punished and realizes that there are no serious penalties in her culture for sexual exploration.[30]

Within the lower-class Black population, the conditions of life encourage early sexual experimentation. The smaller living quarters of most poor Black families prevent adults from having any degree of privacy for their sexual activities. These conditions often allow the child to observe sexual relations. The open character of sexual intercourse sometimes leads to imitation by the child observer, an imitation that may occur at such an early age that the child is not able to critically evaluate the meaning of her behavior.[31]

Consequently, many lower-class Black females have their first sexual experience at an early age. Boone Hammond and Joyce Ladner report that many lower-class Black females have tried to have sexual intercourse by the time they reach the age of seven. At this age the meanings attached to the sex act are not clear. Much of it is simply imitative and is seen as a form of play and entertainment or recreation.[32]

The conditions of poverty mean that many Black females are subjected to the many dimensions of sex long before the middle-class white female becomes aware of its existence. It is understandable, then, to find that Black females have their first full sexual intercourse some years earlier than the typical white, middle-class female.[33] According to the Kinsey Institute, the level of exposure to premarital sexual relations is about three to four times higher for Black teen-age females than for white teen-age females. At age twenty a much larger percentage of Black grammar school educated girls report having had premarital sexual relationships than college educated white girls. In fact, at the age of fifteen more grammar school educated Black females have experienced sexual intercourse than white males of the same educational level.[34]

These statistical differences mostly indicate the earlier sexual involvement of Black females. When comparing overall percentages of females who have premarital sexual relations, the difference in the proportion of Black and white female virgins is considerably reduced. But Black females do not reach sexual maturity at an earlier age than most white females.

White females are more likely to learn about menstruation, fertilization, pregnancy, and abortion at slightly earlier ages than Black females. The Kinsey Institute also found that the white female was more likely to have learned about penis erection by first-hand observation while Black females were more likely to have learned about it through discussion with their peers.[35]

The peer group constitutes an important source of sex information for the Black female. A typical pattern is for most ghetto children to discover sex for themselves, then discuss their discovery with their close friends. Many Black females choose an older sister for this purpose. Thus, much of the Black female's socialization into sexual behavior takes place among same-sex peer groups.[36]

One reason for the importance of the peer group is the absence of the parents from the home. The prevailing marginal economic status of Black people is an important factor in the determination of their sexual behavior. A high rate of unemployment and underemployment among Black males forces many Black women into the labor market, leaving the children in many Black families without parental supervision. Thus, the present racist conditions and economic deprivation under which Black people are compelled to live creates a salient difference in the sexual socialization of Black and white women in this society.

The Loss of Innocence

In adolescence many Black women have their first sexual experience that has meaning to them. It acquires a significance at this stage of their psychosocial development because these young women have a greater understanding of sexual relations as human relations and because the consequences (pregnancy) of premarital coitus are greater.

Among lower-class Black females there is a greater chance that the first sexual experience will be a violent one. Joyce Ladner reports that an eight-year-old Black girl has a good chance of being exposed to rape and violence. Most of the Black girls she interviewed could relate directly to some form of violence. All of them were acquainted with someone involved in violence and rape. Moreover, neither parents or community leaders had the power to eliminate this violent behavior.[37]

In many cases the first sexual experience occurs as a result of a boyfriend's pressure for sex relations. The following story illustrates the dynamics of such male pressure.

I didn't know anything about sex or where babies come from because didn't nobody tell me . . . . This particular night he asked me and I refused and one thing led to another. He wanted to know why? I told him I was scared. He said it wasn't going to hurt. I told him I didn't know and I didn't want to find out. We got to wrestling and—this is sort of embarrassing—he just kept on pestering me. He told me I didn't care anything for him and things like that. He said he wouldn't let anything happen to me or something similar to that. This went on for about an hour and a half. I said "okay" and that was that. [38]

Among middle-class Black females the first sexual experience occurs at a later age but is no less emotionally painful. Perhaps the defloration process is even more traumatic because their sex training is more puritanical. In this author's study, many of our subjects remembered prominently the physical pain associated with the loss of their virginity. They admitted, however, that the pain they encountered may have been the result of the psychological guilt they felt for violating their moral standards. All of them stated that they did not expect their first sexual experience to be so traumatic.[39]

One respondent related that she was afraid that her mother would find out and her body subconsciously refused the entrance of the penis. This in turn caused more pain; the further the penis penetrated, the more her vaginal muscles contracted, and the more pain she felt. After complete penetration, the pain was reduced although still noticeable.

Most of our subjects reported that they cried after their first sexual experience. They did not know if they were emotionally distraught because they were no longer virgins or because of the pain. At any rate, once they had submitted to sexual intercourse, they overcame their guilt feelings. When the guilt feelings were gone, the pain was gone. Some state that they had intercourse again in that same night. Others were reluctant to try intercourse a second time, but after a period of time elapsed, they got over their feelings of guilt.

Unlike white females who progress into premarital intercourse after extended periods of petting, i.e., sexually stimulating behavior, the Black female faces an all-or-nothing situation. In fact, the word petting is almost unknown to Black people. For instance, many white females allow sexual intimacies other than intercourse with the male in order to preserve their virginity. Such women are known as technical virgins.

A technical virgin in the Black population is very rare. One reason is that some petting practices, such as oral-genital relations, are unacceptable to many Black women. Another factor is that sexually enticing behavior without the intention of sexual consummation can provoke the Black male into physical violence.

When a Black woman is petitioned by a Black man for sexual relations, she is virtually defenseless. Although she may have been thoroughly indoctrinated with the idea of premarital chastity, other powerful forces operate to reduce her resistance to his sexual advances. One force, of course, is her desire to maintain the relationship. She is often made aware that if she does not allow him sexual gratification, there are others who will.

Also, in the Black culture engaging in premarital sexual relations is a way of demonstrating a woman's maturity. There is the feeling that you are not a woman until you have had intercourse with a man. Sexual experience bestows a certain status on a female that she did not have before. To refuse a male sexual access is to display immaturity. The peer group of many Black women reinforces this feeling by the prestige and status they confer on girls who are sexually "sophisticated."[40]

The peer group is important in justifying premarital coitus after the act has been completed. Probably, some of the important dynamics of the ghetto sexual culture are reflected in this conversation with one of our subjects. The subject is seventeen years old and is an unwed mother.

Q: *How old is your baby?*

A: *She'll be nine months in about five days.*

Q: *What do you think your family has stressed as far as values and things?*

A: *Be a good little girl. Do everything you're supposed to do.*

Q: *What is doing what you're supposed to do?*

A: *Do what I (parents) say do and not what I do. Don't break no laws and that kind of stuff. They want me to go to school, get married, and be successful— things like that.*

Q: *What are some of your friends' attitudes on sex?*

A: *Like most of them, they like it. I don't really talk to them about it. Cynthia doesn't indulge. Leslie likes it. She has a really free attitude on sex.*

Q: *What do you consider a free attitude on sex?*

A: *She doesn't try to hide the fact that she does it.*

Q: *Does she (Leslie) ever talk about her experiences?*

A: *Yes, she likes to talk about it a lot.*

Q: *Explain a nitty-gritty experience.*

A: *She told me how she got pregnant. She liked the dude just for screwing. I think she wanted to get married, but he didn't. It was at her house. It was good to her but she didn't go into detail.*

Q: *How old were you when you had your first experience?*

A: *I think 14 years.*

Q: *Were you satisfied?*

A: *No. I was pissed off.*

Q: *Describe it in detail.*

A: *He was about 22 years. It was at his house. I was just talking to him (visiting). He just decided he wanted to screw. And he kissed me which was O.K. but he forced hisself on me.*

Q: *Did you enjoy it after he started?*

A: *I didn't enjoy it at all. It bothered me for sometime.*

> *I get scared of dudes sometimes. Plus when I was 10*
> *years old my uncle tried to rape me.*
>
> Q: *What about birth control?*
> A: *I don't use birth control. I would use an IUD*
> *(intrauterine device) if I did.*
> Q: *How often do you have sex?*
> A: *Not very often now under the circumstances but it*
> *used to be very often while having the baby and*
> *after.*
> Q: *Do you have to be madly in love?*
> A: *No. It depends on the moment, if I want to do it or*
> *not. I usually have some affection for the person.*
> Q: *What would you consider the best approach?*
> A: *It depends on how I feel. Sometimes I don't like*
> *them to beat around the bush.*

After they gain an appreciation of sex for its own sake, Black women develop standards for their sexual conduct and for the selection of their sexual partners. Like most standards, these represent ideals, not realities. However, a study of sexual standards can provide insights into the sexuality of Black women that knowledge of sexual behavior alone cannot.

Premarital Sexual Standards

One of the best known studies of Black sexual standards is that of Ira Reiss. He studied a group of Black and white college students and a Black and white adult population. Generally, he found that Blacks had a more permissive premarital sex code than whites, that Black males were the most permissive race-sex group, and that white females were the most restrictive. Black females were more likely than Black males to require affection as a basis for sex relations and were less inclined to accept kissing and petting without affection.[41]

There is very little in the Reiss study that is surprising. One finding of interest was that religiosity does not significantly affect Black sexual codes (or behavior for that matter). Among whites, being very religious is usually associated with a conservative premarital sexual code.[42] Religion has less effect in influencing or controlling premarital sexual behavior among Blacks.

As we previously stated, the African God did not issue commands relating to sexual matters among Africans. The contrary was true of religions practiced by whites. The most puritanical religions taught that sex was intrinsically evil. All religions had a formal standard of abstinence before marriage. Theoretically, the rule applied to everyone, but informally, premarital sexual experimentation was permitted for males.[43]

Although Afro-Americans adopted the religions of the Euro-Americans, the role of organized Black religion was considerably different.[44] The puritanical traditions that influenced white sexual standards were never strong among Black people. The Black church's function related more to reducing tension than to setting sexual standards. Premarital and extramarital sexual relations have never been approved by the Black church, but neither have they been strongly condemned. Possible exceptions can be found in certain middle-class and fundamentalist churches in the Black community.

Another reason for the weak moral traditions of the Black church is the poor moral example set by the Black minister. In a recently popular song, singer Roberta Flack describes a Reverend Lee who was sorely tempted by female flesh and started sanctifying his female parishioners with acts of sexual ecstasy. A writer, Calvin Hernton, is even more explicit in his description of the sexual role of the Black preacher. Hernton states that one Black man has been allowed free sexual access to a large number of Black women. He asserts:

*I am talking about the Black preacher. He has been
allowed to be as sexual as any man, Black or White,
could ever wish to be, in as well as out of the pulpit. The
common songs, myths, jokes and ditties about the sexual
activity of the Black preacher are legend. Black women
worship and love him; they will give him not only their
good loving but their hard-earned money, even the
money that their husbands and boyfriends have slaved
long hours to earn.* [45]

Considering the different history of Blacks, and the
different conditions under which they live, white sexual
standards may not be applicable to Black females. While
Blacks are influenced by the majority culture's moral code, it
does not necessarily guide their behavior, especially in the
lower class. According to Joyce Ladner, premarital sex is not
regarded as an immoral act but rather as one of those human
functions that one engages in because it is natural.[46]

The Ladner study revealed that lower-class Black
women had basically two responses to premarital sex:
indulgence or nonindulgence. These responses were motivated by pragmatic considerations. Those who did not
"indulge" in premarital coitus were concerned with avoiding
pregnancy and often did not condemn girls who would not
abstain. The abstainers were more likely to be upwardly
mobile and were worried lest a premarital pregnancy prevent
them from achieving a higher status than their parents.[47]

It is not only Black women that do not adhere to
traditional American moral standards. Black males do not
have as strong a double standard as that of white males. In
the lower-class white population, particularly, the double
standard of sexual conduct is very strong. Both sexual rights
and sexual pleasure are perceived as male prerogatives. In
many cases the sexual act is defined as satisfying only the
male. Girls are ranked severely according to the extent of
their sexual activity, with virgins being highly valued and

more permissive girls quickly put in the category of an easy lay.[48]

In contrast, Black males do not hold such rigid moral standards for Black females. Rainwater asked his Black subjects the question: Do you think it matters much if a girl has sexual relations with boys but does not get pregnant? Implied in the question was that she might have more than one sexual partner. Only 50 percent of the men responded that it matters much if a girl has sexual relations with boys, while 80 percent of the women indicated concern.[49] Nevertheless, this also shows that sexual relations before marriage lower a girl's chances of being treated as a respectable person and increase the probability that she will be viewed with suspicion and distrust by potential mates.

Black women, however, do not find themselves ranked exclusively according to whether or not they are chaste. Elliot Liebow notes the qualifications for a "nice" Black girl:

Her ethics bespake a fundamental honesty and decency. She does not say one thing to your face, another behind your back. She is not sexually promiscuous and while she may not necessarily remain wholly faithful to her husband or boyfriend, she cuts out on him "discreetly," with selected persons, and usually only after provocation, such as mistreatment or repeated and public infidelity on his part.[50]

It is not only the male who ranks the opposite sex as desirable or undesirable. Black women, too, have their standards in selecting a sexual partner and in evaluating his sexual performance. When we asked the subjects in our study what qualities they find sexually attractive in a Black male, they stated two: personality and physical appearance. Some wanted a combination of both.[51]

When questioned further on what kind of physical appearance they sought in a man, they listed a muscular physique, tall stature, nice clothes, masculine movements, and dark color. One might consider these women's interests in physical appearance as a masculinization of mate selection standards. While men have traditionally ranked women by their physique, women have usually selected men on the basis of emotional attachment, personality, or socioeconomic status.

These standards, moreover, have a sexual meaning. Muscular and tall men, for instance, are preferred because Black women assume them to have larger than average sexual organs. While there is no absolute relationship between body build and penis size, many Black women assume there is. Furthermore, penis size has little to do with giving a female sexual satisfaction. It is the male's technique that is important. But, Black women think penis size is important. It becomes important to them.

Black women expect sexual satisfaction of some sort. Unlike many white women who see sexual relations as primarily an activity designed to give men pleasure, Black women expect their sexual partner to try to satisfy them sexually. Clearly many Black women are not satisfied, but the assumption that a woman should receive pleasure from sexual relations is a normative one in the Black community.

The Black male who fails in his sexual performance is often rated by his female partner. In contrast to many white women, the Black female tends to be open about her sexual experiences. Within the peer group her participation in sexual relations does not long stay secret. Many Black females share details about their sexual intimacies with other women. Some of them do not share the definition of the male as the sexual aggressor. Sex is not necessarily something that is done *to* them. They are known to remark that "I nearly killed him in bed" or "I gave him a really good workout."

The sharing of sexual experiences with other women helps to reduce the amount of guilt or anxiety as a result of participating in premarital sexual relations. It allows Black women to possess standards of sexual conduct to which males must address themselves. It also allows peers to give advice to each other about matters that continue to plague other women who maintain a terrified silence about their sexual acitivities.

Although Black women have a great deal of sexual freedom, it still does not equal that of Black men. This remains true because men do not have to face the consequences of a premarital pregnancy. Additionally, sexual relations often have different meanings and a different function for men. One of those functions is the maintenance of a male virility cult.

The Male Virility Cult

Some people participate in sexual relations for the pure physical pleasure; others for reasons of love, economic gain, or for many other reasons. It is almost impossible to isolate one exclusive reason why people have sexual relations. One thing that seems certain, however, is that some men want more sex than they could possibly need for physiological gratification. This suggests, then, that sexuality is strongly linked to society's definition of masculinity.

In the male, virility cult status within the peer group is based on the number of women that one is able to have sexual relations with. Thus, the male who has a variety of premarital sexual experience occupies a prestigious position within his peer grouping. Sexual conquest of women becomes strongly associated with the definition of masculinity. It is sex as a symbol of manhood that supposedly motivates the male's sexual interest as well as physical desire.

It is among Black males that the virility cult is supposed to have its strong adherents. Franklin Frazier asserts that:

For the Negro male, sex has often been the means by which he has asserted and maintained his masculinity.

Much of the sexual promiscuity of Negro males has been due to this, rather than any great sexual energy or powers that overrode. Their sexual prowess has been a means of overcoming their inferior social status, not only in family relations, but in relation to the white world.[52]

One finds a great deal of agreement with Frazier in the literature. Jessie Bernard states that because the ordinary manifestations of masculine identity were all but impossible for large numbers of Black men, sex became a major instrument of power and status.[53] A similar view is held by Clement Vontress who, referring to the Black female-headed households, asserts that Black men are emasculated and must resort to emphasizing secondary aspects of masculinity such as the sexual exploitation of women.[54]

On the verbal level some Black men do see themselves alternately as lovers and exploiters of women. As Elliot Liebow found, these men are eager to present themselves as exploiters to women as well as to men. Within the lower-class group, men not only saw themselves as exploiters of women but expected the same of other men. When the behavior of other men did not meet their expectations, they could not comprehend the other men's actions.[55]

In reality, however, the tendency to use women to gain sexual and economic ends is counteracted by other feelings and goals, especially the male's need to have a meaningful relationship with a woman he loves. Despite their self-image as a user of women, many Black men are very supportive individuals to Black women, in both an emotional and an economic sense. David Schulz discovered that many of the women in female-headed households were receiving support from boyfriends.[56]

The discrepancy between the rhetoric and the reality can best be explained by the kind of image Black men wish to sustain, both within the peer group and in their community. Many males do not wish to be seen as emotionally dependent on the "weaker" sex. Thus, they counter any suspicions that they are a weakling, sucker, or patsy by their representation as a user of women, a person whose inter-personal involvement is based only on the economic and sexual gain that accrues from such a relationship.

While the gap between talk of sexual exploitation and real actions is large, many Black women do suffer some consequences from the male virility cult. One woman complained that the Black man spends too much time trying to prove that he is the great lover that he is accused of being by the white man. In the words of another, "200 years of brainwashing has forced the Black man to prove that he is a super-stud."[57]

One positive function of the Black male's virility cult is that Black women do not suffer one fate of white women: being divided into "bad" and "good" girls. Women who are virgins may be preferred by many Black men—but chastity is certainly not an essential requirement for marriage. This allows Black women to develop an appreciation of sex for its own value. It is not surprising to find that a greater proportion of premarital sex acts result in orgasm for the Black female while a larger percentage of white females report that they had not reached orgasm at all prior to marriage.[58]

The confrontation between the Black male's strong sexual orientation and the Black female's responsiveness to the social restraints placed on her sexual behavior and her fear of premarital pregnancy can create some negative results. The interplay of these two factors has a dynamic of its own. The players are most single Black men and women; the stage may vary; and it all occurs within the context of what is called the dating game.

The Dating Game

In American society dating has a number of functions. For some people dating is a form of recreation. It constitutes a form of entertainment and serves as a source of pleasure for the people involved. For others it is a way to develop social skills of learning how to get along with women.[59] But in the Black community dating behavior is ipso facto sexual behavior. It becomes sexual behavior because the male desires a sexual experience with the female. This does not mean that all Black male-female relationships are sexual ones. But the emotional involvement develops at a later stage. The Black woman usually dates a man because she sees him as a potential boyfriend or husband.

The stage is set. Boy meets girl. His motivation, initially, is sexual gratification; her motivation is courtship. While he may not be opposed to courtship nor she to sexual involvement, they are not either's primary goal. The dating relationship is, then, a conflict relationship. Many elements are involved in the kind of accommodation that eventually emerges from a situation in which each partner enters with a different set of goals.

One of the first things the Black female faces in her quest for courtship is competition. The competition for Black males is intensified by two factors. One is the tendency of white females to pursue Black mates while white males rarely date or marry Black females; the other is the low sex ratio in the Black community. According to the 1970 census there are over a million Black females in this country who are without available mates.[60] This situation has led one sociologist to state that Black women are competing for relatively scarce goods, that when Black women look forward to marriage they are buyers in a seller's market.[61]

In her relationship with the Black male, the Black woman can hardly avoid being influenced by the paucity of available Black men. While Black women apparently adjust to this situation, at least one Black female leader sees it as an albatross around the Black woman's neck. She says:

As long as she is confined to an area in which she must compete fiercely for a mate, she remains the object of sexual exploitation and the victim of all the social evils which such exploitation involves.[62]

While this is possibly an exaggeration of the obvious, the low sex ratio probably reduces the Black woman's chance for role bargaining. Some years ago Waller outlined what he called the principle of least interest. In the male-female relationship, during various phases of it, one partner is more committed to staying in the relationship than the other. The one who is least interested usually gets his/her way when a conflict emerges.[63] When a Black woman realizes that there is stiff competition for the available Black men, her alternatives when he demands sexual relations are limited, and there is a greater likelihood that she will acquiesce.

Some black women disagree that the low sex ratio affects their dating behavior. One of the subjects in our study had this to say:

> *An attitude I don't agree with is, if a Black woman does not agree with the Black man's desire for premarital sex, there are always others who will. It is too easy for Black women to take this same attitude, that there are too many fish in the sea. (Although she may be aware this isn't necessarily true.) Using this attitude probably will be in her favor because the Black man can see this threat means nothing to her. Also, by resisting the threat the Black man has posed upon her may be a reflection of her pride. I give the Black man more credit than to use this method to entice a woman to indulge in sexual relations. I believe he uses a much more subtler approach, line, or conversation to convince her to have sexual intercourse with him.*[64]

The line or conversation that she speaks of is known as "rapping." Lee Rainwater defines rapping as one of the linguistic techniques found in the Black community for manipulating sex-role interaction to get what one wants.[65] In general the rap consists of truths, exaggerations, and lies about the female's qualities, the male's intentions, or his status. There is no definite pattern in rapping language. Usually, it is everyday ghetto parlance but its effectiveness partly lies in the rapper's technique.

In rapping to a Black woman one must be able to use such words as "cool," "baby," "what's happening," and "right on" in the proper context. This shows that you are with it and worth her attention. These are unique words in that they have a special meaning in the Black community, and the use of such words is labeled "heavy talking." The tone and quality of the words is important. One uses a different rap for lower-class women than for middle-class women. Since a woman may be either attracted or repelled by the man's rap, it is important that the male use the appropriate words in the right context.

As in the rest of human society, symbols have to be mutually shared. Most Black women expect men to try and seduce them. Whether they agree to have sexual relations or not does not depend solely on the rap. It is a part of the ritual of sexual seduction and both parties usually know it. But, Black women want to feel that they are not just casual sexual partners and that the male really cares for them. The rapper has to convey a feeling of sincerity, or he fails to complete the seductive process. Although Black women enjoy the physical aspects of sex, it is still linked with an emotional meaning for many of them. It signifies that one belongs to someone and satisfies a need for a kind of human relatedness.

To the male, sexual relations takes on other dimensions, among them is the thrill of making a sexual conquest. This is illustrated in one Black male's dating pattern:

> My behavior during dating (or most common behavior), before concluding an evening or night of courtship with a female, consist of a compulsion for kissing or (tonguing) the female.
> Leading up to this event, I usually precede with

petting *and* rubbing *my hand slowly across the buttocks of my female several times.*

If I succeed in (tonguing) the female, I usually succeed in experiencing a sexual relationship with her; and very often, experience more than one "sexual trip" with her.

I personally have found the prone position to be the most common position desired by most females.

Usually, when I take a female out on two successive dates and fail in getting her to engage in sexual intercourse, I discontinue being aggressive toward her, but shy away from associating with her and usually she will finally make some excuse to engage my company again in some way or another.

When I'm successful in having intercourse with the so-called hard-to-get female, I find myself engaging extensively in various body positions, and very often, these type females are the ones who are difficult to "get rid of."

They usually attempt to go steady, and will hang on the longest.

It would appear that the more brutal *I am while engaging in various sex acts, the more difficult it is for me to get away from this particular (type of) female.*

The context of dating varies among Blacks. Since most Blacks enter into heterosexual relations at a relatively early age, there is very little formal dating. Much of the dating takes place in two places: at parties and in school. Black males and females have one of their best opportunities to meet members of the opposite sex in school. They attend school dances together, and they begin to "go out" with one another. From there they go on to sex play, which culminates in real sexual involvement.[66]

Parties provide another setting for sexual activity. In many cases they serve as substitutes for going out, picking up, and dating. Some persons have their own apartments that can be used for parties and as places of private or group sexual activities. It is at parties that the male initiates the seductive process. Many of the males and females either come to the party alone or in homogenous groups. The male selects a female that appeals to him, begins his rap and tries to persuade her to go to a more private surrounding. If she agrees, sexual relations may take place in another room of the apartment, in a car, or just in the great outdoors. Sometimes parties only function as a setting to make contacts. More formal dating may take place at a later date.

Sexual Deviations

When we look at the Black definition of sexual perversion, we see the forms of sex control that exist among Black people. In general any sexual act other than simple and direct coitus is considered a perversion. Fewer incidences of incest occur among Blacks than occur in some culturally isolated white groups. Homosexuality and other forms of "deviant" sex practices occur less frequently among Blacks because of group sanctions against such sex activities.[67]

When we asked the women in our study what sexual acts they considered abnormal or repulsive, they stated that masturbation, homosexuality, and oral-genital relations fell into those categories.[68] The Kinsey Institute found that among the subjects they interviewed, the first source of orgasm for white females was coitus in less than 1 percent, but more than a third of the Black females stated that the first source was coitus. Whites are much more likely to substitute masturbation and oral sex for coitus than Blacks.[69]

The above finding does not mean Blacks do not engage in these sexual activities at all. In fact there has been a significant increase in oral-genital relations among the Black middle class. This usually takes place at the initiative of the male and often the female consents under duress. As a result of Black folk beliefs concerning oral sex, the female may believe it to be an unsanitary and perverted practice. Additionally, she may fear the ruin of her reputation if knowledge of her participation in such an act should become publicly known.

A female also has to be more restrained in initiating oral-genital relations. Because of the strong taboos on such activity, she runs a considerable risk in commencing such an act with a male who disapproves of this kind of sexual behavior. One also finds that the male is more likely to be the receiver of oral gratification (fellatio) rather than the one who gives it (cunnilingus). This may reflect a logistical problem. Or it could represent the balance of power in the Black male-female relationship.

Homosexuality may be more or less prevalent in the Black than in the white population. There are no available data on the subject for Blacks. Some writers have claimed that Blacks have a greater incidence of male homosexuality than whites. They believe that female-headed households in the Black community have resulted in a lack of male role models for male Black children.[70] There is no evidence to support this supposition.

As part of their studies of sexual deviants, the Kinsey group investigated Black homosexuality. They found that Blacks were more comfortable around homosexuals and did not perceive them as any kind of threat to the manhood of heterosexuals. Consequently, Black homosexuals (male and female) were not as isolated from the Black heterosexual population. They were not relegated to their own bars or social cliques. Also, Blacks were more likely to be bisexual than exclusively homosexual.[71]

The Black lesbian, like her white counterpart, is a hidden figure. Lesbians are known to exist because some Black women report being approached by them. Some have even suggested that Black lesbianism is on the increase because of the shortage of Black males. Considering the strong heterosexual orientation of most Black women, this does not seem likely. The response of most Black women to the male shortage is to play at a modified form of polygyny (i.e., sharing men).

One pair of Black lesbians came into public view recently by applying to the Milwaukee county clerk for a marriage license. They stated that they were serious about their intent to marry and that they planned to have a marriage ceremony performed even if they were denied a license. Their experiences with other Blacks do not confirm the earlier observation that Blacks are more tolerant of homosexuality. This lesbian couple complained that their families were not too accepting of their relationship. They had to move from their residence because of crank calls and continuous threats. Perhaps Blacks are more critical of such a blatant display of homosexuality.[72]

Another sexual practice that is found among whites but is almost nonexistent among Blacks is group sex. In fact, if this activity is practiced among Blacks it is a well guarded secret. No group sex practice has ever come to the attention of this author or any of his acquaintances. According to one authority "group sex is essentially a middle-class phenomena and most Blacks don't have that much dough." He elaborated by noting that in order to participate in mate swapping, one must be able to rent a "pad" and afford the other accompanying luxuries. Also, he said, the Black man is willing to be promiscuous but doesn't want his wife to be.[73]

The author of a study on group sex, Gilbert Bartell, stated that he knew of no research concerning the role of Blacks in group sex life but added that there was hearsay evidence that Blacks engaged in this practice on a Blacks-only basis. It was also his belief that Black women find it easier to take part in overt sexual acts than do white women.[74]

The one sexual perversion that many Black women encounter is rape. Contrary to popular belief most rapes committed by Black men are committed against Black women, not white women. One study of 646 cases of rape in Philadelphia revealed that Black girls between the ages of ten to fifteen are most often the victims. Of the total number of rapes, 30 percent involved whites raping whites, 60 percent Blacks raping Blacks, in 10 percent whites raped Blacks and in 3 percent Blacks raped whites.[75]

The 10 percent figure for white men raping Black women is probably an underestimate. In general, white men have been able to rape Black women with impunity. In fact the punishment of a white man for raping a Black woman is so rare that one Mississippi case in which a white man received a life sentence for raping a fifteen-year-old Black girl made the national headlines.[76]

Many of the sexual assaults on Black women by Black men go unreported. A significant number of quasi rapes occur daily, especially in lower-class life. Often a girl leads a man to believe that she will have sexual relations with him but protests when he reaches the point of penetration. Sometimes she simply wants to be taken in a violent way. Other times it may be forcible intercourse. The line between the two is a thin one. Many rapes involve close friends or acquaintances of the women involved.[77]

Interracial Sex Relations

One thing should be stated about interracial sex relations from the outset. Black women are generally opposed to any sexual liaison with white men. The frequency of such sexual contacts—unlike past years—is much less than Black male-white female relationships. In order to understand how this situation has evolved, two factors have to be examined: The historical relationship of white men and Black women, and the different function and meaning of interracial sexual contacts in comparison to intraracial coitus.

Historically, Black women have been raped by white men and have been subject to all sorts of other sexual abuses from them. They have served as sexual objects, concubines, and prostitutes to white men of all classes and racial philosophies. But they have rarely been accorded the protection and legal rights of white women. White men have seldom elevated Black women to the status of a wife with all the privileges that status implies.

Even today when Black women have more freedom from the wanton desires of the white male, she is the subject of annoying, obscene approaches of white men, both on the street and at social gatherings.[78] Black women report that they are insulted by white men daily. White men slam or close doors in their faces after holding them open for white women. Others complain of being terminated from their jobs after refusing to acquiesce to white male requests for sexual favors.[79]

Because of the Black woman's historical vulnerability to white male sexual overtures, whites stereotype her as a "slut," a woman who will go to bed with anyone, especially a white man. One of the results of this myth is a hatred of white men by some Black women and a resolve to avoid any sexual contact with them. One woman reports that:

> When I was 13, living in San Diego, a white man swerved his car to miss a white woman and killed my only brother. He said it was an accident but he went all the way across the street, so I'll always believe he made some choice. They try to flirt with me sometimes now, but I shine them on because if the white woman is first in death she might as well be first and last in sex. They can kill my brother but they can't screw me to boot.[80]

Because white men have historically been interested in Black women only on a sexual basis, many Black women assume that any white man who wishes to date them is interested only in sex. When Frank Petroni asked a Black girl how easy it would be for her to accept if a white boy asked her out, she replied that she would suspect the motives of any white boy who asked her out. In her own words: "For a Negro boy to have a white girl is some sort of status symbol, but if a white asked me out, it would be a step down for him. I would think he wants something I'm not about to give him."[81]

Many Black women refuse to date white men. One such woman claimed that there is a recent tendency among Black girls to disapprove of interracial dating. She said, "I have many girl friends who won't go out with a white man and as a general rule I wouldn't except in business."[82] Of those Black women who do date white men, it is a qualitatively different type of relationship than the Black man has with the white woman.

One study comparing the interracial dating patterns of Black and white male college students found some large differences. While 90 percent of the 80 Black men studied report experiences in interracial dating, only 12 percent of the 140 white men reported such experiences. Interracial dates without any sexual intimacy are in the minority in the case of Black men. More than 50 percent of the white men report no intercourse associated with interracial dating while only 9 percent of Blacks so report. None of the white men had ever entered into a steady relationship with a Black woman while 45 percent of the Black males had "gone steady" with one or more white females.[83]

Not only are Black women less permissive with white dating partners, but their motivation for dating them is often different than when dating Black men. When we asked the women in our study about their feelings on interracial dating and sex, very few (less than 20 percent) approved of it or would participate in it. Some of them mentioned that they were not physically attracted to white men; others cited the historical abuse they had suffered from white people. Those who approved of interracial dating said they would do it but only for financial reasons. One said: "If a white man was good enough to satisfy me plus put money in my pockets, then it's all right."[84]

The economic motive along with the white male's higher status is cited by Clark as a primary reason for interracial sex relations:

> Certain Negro women of status who have married White men report that their choice was related to their discovery that the Negro men they knew were inferior in status, interests and sophistication and hence unsuitable as partners. Many problems of race and sex seem to follow this principle of the self-fulfilling prophecy. The Negro woman of status may see the Negro male as undesirable as a sexual partner precisely because of his low status in the eyes of Whites. Unlike a White female who may reassure herself that the lower the status of the male, the more satisfying he is as a sexual partner, the upper-class Negro female tends to tie sexual desirability to status and exclude many Negro males as undesirable just because their status is inferior.[85]

There are other reasons why few Black women date white men. One simple reason is that many white men do not wish to date Black women. In the interracial dating study, 77 percent of the white men expressed a preference for dating females of their own race. Some of them cite religious, moral, or family objections as their reason. A more important reason is adverse social pressures. Examples of this were hostile and disapproving stares from the public, verbal abuse, and refusal of public accommodations.[86]

A Black female is handicapped in initiating the dating relationship with an attractive white male even if she so desires. In our society women are expected to be passive while the men are aggressive and demanding. Thus, while Black men have rapped their way into the hearts of some white females, the Black woman must wait to be approached by the white male, who is often not as aggressive or as interested as his Black counterpart.

Black women also have to cope with the attitudes of Black men toward their dating white men. One study tells of many Black girls who will not date white boys because of pressures from Black young men who would object if Black girls dated whites.[88] This situation has led one sociologist to assert that some Black men are trying to imitate those white men who have had sexual access to both Black and white women. She describes instances on white college campuses where Black males date white coeds, reducing the number of dating partners for Black coeds. Then, when some Black coeds dated white men, a few Black male students have castigated and threatened them.[89]

This sort of situation reflects several forces at work. One factor involved is that in the Black male-white female relationship, it is the white female who is, theoretically, sexually exploited. The Black female is defined as the victim when she dates outside her race. Moreover, her sexual victimization is considered an extension of the historical pattern of her sexual subjugation.

Some Black males have acquired general male chauvinist values. They have a double standard of interracial dating, which allows them the freedom to date white women while simultaneously restricting the freedom of Black women to date white men. As one Black woman stated: "While our [Black] men seem thoroughly abreast of the times on every other subject, when they strike the woman question they drop back into 16th-century logic."[90]

Summary

The sexuality of the Black female has been shaped by a number of factors: the African past, experiences of slavery, racist oppression, and economic exploitation. No one factor is responsible for her sexual values and behavior since all interact to form a patterned configuration. Those who argue that African influences are nullified by the experience of slavery may be correct. Yet one cannot escape the similarities between African sexual expression and the contemporary sexual behavior of Afro-Americans. The naturalistic character of sex relations and the importance placed on the pleasurable aspects of sex form the elements of the sexual subculture in Black life.

This may possibly explain why the factors of social class and religion are not influential in controlling Black sexual practices. Of course, the various social stimuli Black women are exposed to may cancel each other out as important controls on sexual behavior. The fact that the dominant society does not provide any protection for the Black woman's virtue has left her vulnerable to the sexual advances of many men. What cannot be protected will not long remain cherished. There is little possibility that the Black church could alter this fact of the Black woman's life.

Social status has not altered Black sexuality in any meaningful way. It is true that middle-class Black females are more restrictive in their sexual relations but they are not as strict as white females. One possible reason for this phenomenon is that most middle-class Black females are recent arrivals from the lower-class group. Consequently, they may have retained the lower-class values relating to sex. Even if Black women identify with the sexual morality of middle-class America, many middle-class Black males do not. Thus, Black women must still face male pressures for premarital sexual relations with the knowledge that eligible males are even more scarce in the middle class.

The racist conditions under which Black people live also affect their socialization into sexual behavior. This is especially true of middle-class Black children who, because of residential segregation, are compelled to live adjacent to the lower-class members of their race. Hence, the middle-class Black female continues to be exposed to the sexual ethos of the lower-class culture. The lack of parental supervision and the absence of privacy for adult sexual relations lead the lower-class Black female child into a sexual involvement at a much earlier age than her white counterpart.

Fortunately, all these historical, racial, and economic influences have functioned in positive ways for the Black female. While the white female is just beginning to accept sexual relations as a normal human function and is starting to throw off the shackles of centuries of sexual repression, the Black female provides a model of sexual liberation that she might well emulate. Since retaining virginity has been a less important goal for the Black woman, she has learned to appreciate the intrinsic pleasure of sexual congress without the crippling and inhibitive emotions of guilt and anxiety.

In American society new patterns of sexual relations are beginning to emerge. Some of these new forms are manifested in unhealthy ways as a group that has been restrained in its sexual expression for years becomes obsessed with the idea of finding new sexual thrills. In the Black community the natural values associated with sex have allowed it to retain its lusty, wholesome quality.

3

Bodies for Sale: Black Prostitutes in White America

Ever since the Black woman has been in America, she has largely been forced into the role of a "whore"—not only sexually, but also as an economic and cultural "prostitute" in American society. When she has been able to escape having to surrender to sexual advances of the white man, she has not escaped having to "prostitute" her femininity, her sex, in the form of being a "domestic servant" in white people's homes, in their shops, restaurants, office buildings and elsewhere, where the qualities and labor of her sex were expropriated from her by having to nurture white babies and children, clean and take care of white homes, wash, iron and cook for white people. And, she was not respected for these things, but was demeaned by them.

Calvin Hernton
Coming Together (1971)

A shorter version of this chapter, entitled "The Black Prostitute in White America," appeared in *The Black Family: Essays and Studies*, ed. Robert Staples (Belmont, California: Wadsworth Publishing Co., 1971), pp. 366-375. It is reprinted by permission of the publisher.

Throughout the ages, all over the world, women have bestowed their sexual favors on men who were not their lawfully wedded husbands for money as well as other reasons. Primitive peoples yielded their women to transient guests. In the fifth century B.C. each Babylonian woman was required once in her lifetime to yield herself to a stranger in the temple of Mylitta for money, which she contributed to the wealth of the temple. In those days the role of prostitute was an honorable one; or at least a tolerable occupation. Later the functions of prostitute were assigned to wretched castes who were segregated in ghettos or in restricted quarters. They were forced to wear distinctive signs on their clothing and were vulnerable to the capricious whims of the police.[1]

Prostitution in Africa began as a religious ritual, as it did in Western societies. In the local Zimbawe temple, "The House of the Great Lady," the king's daughters were offered as sacred prostitutes. They practiced hierogamy (the coupling of man and God) with a snake, which represented the incarnation of the God. Hierogamy was also practiced by the Kikuyu of East Africa who offered young virgins to a sacred snake. This ritual transpired in a special hut, and the priest, symbolizing the snake, deflowered the virgin. The children of such unions were considered to be of divine origin and entitled to special privileges.[2]

Many of these acts of sacred prostitution were associated with fertility rites. They were likely to take place when the barley began to bloom and were designed to insure the fertility of the livestock and a bountiful harvest. In African folklore, the snake, especially the serpent, is considered a phallic fecundative symbol. Being a prostitute in this context was a high honor. Among the Lele, about 10 percent of the women were sacred prostitutes, one of the highest ranks in the village, and were called village wives.[3]

Due to the sexual freedom extant in many African societies, the kind of prostitution that existed in Europe was a rare phenomenon. The era of colonialism and industrialization has brought about an increase in prostitution of the commercialized Western variety. Often the customers of African prostitutes are foreigners from European countries. One report of prostitution in Ghana disclosed that when a man goes from the rural village into town, a woman is one of the things he wants most.[4]

In some parts of Africa the prostitutes wear gaudy clothes and reside in special locations which are supervised by the local authorities. Nandi women become prostitutes in order to escape from their husbands' brutality. Usually they ply their trade in the larger cities, where they acquire a quasi independence that brings to them a certain respect on returning to their villages. Many widows become prostitutes. In the Niger Delta women charge a certain fee to their lovers, and their mothers transact the financial part of the arrangement. The wives of Dan tribesmen are encouraged by their husbands to engage in prostitution for economic gain.[5]

Prostitution has arisen in Western society because of our hypocritical attitude toward sexual behavior. Theoretically, we have a single code of sexual conduct that states that sexual relations are to take place only between a man and a woman married to each other. In reality, men are permitted premarital and extramarital sexual activity. Since the male's violation of the sex code cannot take place without a female partner, prostitutes traditionally provided them with their illicit sexual pleasures. For performing this service, women usually receive money or its equivalent. In turn, they are denied community respect and make themselves ineligible for a "respected" marriage.

Because these disadvantages attend the role of prostitute, most women reject the job. Women who become prostitutes have usually done so because of their impoverished circumstances or because they were forced to do so. Black women who became prostitutes originally did so for the latter reason. As slaves they had to submit to their masters and received no compensation. However, some white slavemasters saw the opportunity for commercial profit in peddling the bodies of their female slaves. As a result, there was in the South a considerable traffic in Black women for prostitution. Particularly desirable was the mulatto woman, herself a result of earlier miscegenation between a white man and a Black woman.

In the antebellum South, large numbers of mulatto girls were carried to the cities and sold at enormous prices into private prostitution. Little respect was shown for kinship ties, as some white men even sold their Black daughters to other men for prostitution. In one such case:

> *A planter had two beautiful daughters by a slave. They were educated in England and introduced as his daughters, but he failed to emancipate them; so that on his death they were snatched away by the creditors and sold to a purchaser who was to reap his gain from their prostitution.*[6]

Although the dual elements of bondage and force impelled most Black women into prostitution, some Black females were brought up by their mothers for the career of concubine. If the white men had wealth or standing, Black girls frequently preferred such an arrangement rather than marriage to a Black male. In the role of concubine to wealthy white men, she received not only greater social status but protection from the unwanted attentions of other white men.[7]

One disadvantage in becoming a concubine to a white man, particularly a married white man, was the resentment of white women. A man who was having his sexual needs satisfied by a Black concubine was less likely to want a wife. During this period of widespread concubinage, the South had an inordinate number of bachelors. This meant that some white women, who desperately desired marriage, had to remain single. One white woman, decrying the sexual relationship between white men and Black women, wrote: "Like the patriarchs of old, our men live all in one house with their wives and their concubines, and the mulattos one sees in every family partly resemble the white children. Any lady is ready to tell you who is the father of all the mulatto children in everybody's household but her own."[8]

With reason some white women feared the competition of Black females for their husbands' affection. Frazier notes that a white woman often saw in the Black woman not only a rival for her husband's affection but also a possible competitor for a share in his property. Some white men became so enamoured of their Black mistresses that they disinherited their wives and children.[9] White women who faced this problem were known to vent their jealousy in savage ways. One such white woman had slaves hold a Black girl down while she cut off the forepart of the victim's feet. Then the girl was thrown into the woods to die.[10]

Most Black women did not represent a threat to the marital status of white women. White men rarely considered marriage with their dark sexual companions. In fact, men of the master class often justified their sexual excursions with Black women with the reasoning that doing so preserved the virginity of white women for marriage. Whether they accepted this explanation or not, most Southern white women endured their husbands' infidelity because they had no choice. Economically dependent on the males for support, few white females refused to marry a man who possessed a goodly number of slaves, though they were sure his affections would be shared by the best looking of the females.[11]

After emancipation, the flagrant sexual abuse of Black women by white men decreased. However, the amount of organized prostitution among Black women increased because it was the only means that some Black women had of supporting their families.[12] And, these Black women met a need of white men. As one writer asserted:

> For the young white man, Negro or mulatto girls existed to initiate him into sexual experience. Later he might set up one such girl as a concubine and produce a family. Or he might continue to indulge himself throughout life whenever opportunity presented itself. The point to bear in mind is that despite legislation, official sexual propriety, and Christianity itself, the Southern white had embarked upon the systematic prostitution of Negro women.[13]

Although many factors compelled Black women to become prostitutes, the most important one was the need for money. As an economically deprived group they were subject to enticement into sexual relations with white men of considerable means. While they may have disliked the idea of intercourse with the oppressor, their family could not be supported with high moral values. Some domestic servants, for instance, supplemented their low incomes by having intercourse with the man of the house.[14]

But other variables enter into the Black woman's decision to become a prostitute, assuming that she does decide and is not forced into the role. Included in her reasons may be a desire to get back at white women. A woman with this motive revealed: "Well, these white women may high hat us, but we sleep with their men just the same. We may have to cook for them, but we get back at them in this way."[15] If their vengeance is not directed toward white women, it may be aimed at what they consider pulling the white man down. Sex relations, it is said, strip the male of any claim to immortality.[16]

It is, also, quite possible that some Black women enjoy their sexual liaisons with white men. With the cultural restrictions on their sexual behavior very weak, Black women may receive transitory gratification from their sexual relations with white men. Unlike white women in the South, for whom chastity is a cultural imperative, Black females can yield to their sexual impulses more freely. Prostitution, although socially degrading, may thus give some Black women sexual pleasure as well as money.[17]

Whatever advantage the Black prostitute may have gained is cancelled out by the loss of social esteem. Women who play-for-pay are looked down on everywhere. Although she often performs a service for chaste white women by allowing white men to release their prenuptial sexual urges upon her, she receives opprobrium. Universally despised, she makes herself ineligible for marriage by her sale of passion. A tragic example of her plight is recorded thus:

> *A Negro told me of a childhood sweetheart whom he had once wanted to marry. He left town for a time and when he returned met this girl again. She had become a prostitute. He asked her if she had known what was in his mind when they were boy and girl together, and told her he thought then that she would make a good wife for some man someday. The girl regretted that she had gone too far now ever to be able to marry, and said it was the fault of her godmother who turned her over to men before she was grown up.[18]*

The disrespect that the Black male has for prostitutes of his own race is frequently reciprocated by dusky ladies of the streets. One Black prostitute stated to an observer:

> *A nigger don't treat you with as much respect as a white man. The white man treats you courteous like, and leaves you free to yourself most of the time. Those white men will pay you five and ten dollars and likely*

won't bother you but once a week. That's all they want, and they don't think they have the right to beat you when they want to.[19]

Black women who perform the role of concubine fare somewhat better than streetwalkers. The bond between the concubine and her lover is closer because their relationship is more permanent. While such associations are few, and getting rarer each day, they were part and parcel of the postbellum South. This is particularly true of Louisiana, where they had formal balls to acquaint white men with Black women for whom they could bargain. Children born of such relationships were often treated with affection by their father as though they were his legitimate children. In some cases, the men clothed their children and even provided for them in their wills.[20]

In one Southern town a number of white men had Black mistresses. Most of these men were racial segregationists who believed that Blacks were inferior and preached that Blacks should have their own life, separate from that of whites.[21] Although this may seem paradoxical in view of their sexual liaison with Black women, it is no more paradoxical than the violation of their marriage vows. What is more confusing is the affectionate relationship so often emerging from this type of relationship.

But, as Frazier noted, the human relations between the Black and the white race tended to dissolve the formal and legal principles upon which segregation was based. Sexual relations broke down caste barriers and paved the way for a relationship based on individual merit and not racial membership. Sexual attraction produced at times genuine affection and the protracted relationship created between the white racist and Black mistress an enduring sentiment. To Frazier, the intimacies of sex relations and the birth of children symbolized the ultimate triumph of the deepest feeling of human solidarity.[22]

In most cases, the women had no real choice in the formation of these unions. Thus, the real losers in this situation were the women of the South—Black and white alike—who were the unwilling victims of a Southern value system that demeaned their humanity and subjected them to exploitation by the white male.

The Prostitute Moves North

Most authorities agree that around the turn of the century most prostitutes in the South were Black, while the prostitutes of the North were white. As one writer states, "In the North, prostitutes were a social and professional group, while in the South they were a racial group."[23] In other words, even lower-class white women of the South were allowed to retain their virginity until marriage whereas even some middle-class Black women were sacrificed to the white man's lust.

Along with the general immigration of Blacks from the South to the urban areas of the North went large numbers of Black prostitutes. This is reflected in the statistics of arrests for prostitution by racial ancestry. In 1914, Black women constituted 16 percent of the total number appearing in the morals court in Chicago. In 1929, Black women totaled 70 percent of the women arraigned before the morals court. Viewing these figures, one writer concluded that "if the percentage of colored women in the total load of the morals court continues to increase, the court will in a few years become practically an agency dealing with Negro female sex delinquents."[24] Although we do not know the exact figures, one could speculate that some years later this is precisely what has happened.

The increased number of Black women involved in prostitution is reflected in a number of studies. One survey found that 54 percent of the arrests of all women for prostitution in New York City were of Black women and that the rate for Black women was ten times that for white women.[25] When the Kinsey group interviewed 390 Black female prisoners, they discovered that 56 percent of these women admitted to or had been convicted for prostitution prior to their confinement.[26]

Racist oppression and problems of poverty have made prostitution more common among Black women than among white women. But differences in the degree of prostitution among Black and white women tend to be hidden by their different sphere of activity. With suffecent accuracy, we can designate the typical Black prostitute as a streetwalker and the white prostitute as a call girl.

Call girls are described by one writer as the "aristocrats of prostitution." They live in the most expensive residential section of our large cities, they dress in rich, good taste and charge a minimum of twenty dollars per sexual contact. Unlike the streetwalker they are selective about customers, entertain clients in their homes or apartments, and assid-uously avoid bars and restaurants patronized by other prostitutes.[27]

Black prostitutes are much more subject to arrest than the white call girls. As one observer comments:

> Since it is easier to observe immoral conditions among poor and unprotected people, colored prostitutes are much more liable for arrest than white prostitutes. White women may use the big hotels or private apartments for their illicit trade, but the colored women are more commonly forced to walk the streets.[28]

The low status of Black women generally prevents them from becoming call girls. The clients of call girls are usually white men who want the call girl to be a part of their social life. Often these clients require an entire night of a girl's time, maybe taking her out to a nightclub as part of the arrangement.[29] Most call girls are found in the better cocktail lounges and restaurants where the presence of a

Black woman would be suspect. Police officers have been known to arrest Black females solely because they are in the company of white men. Ordinarily a white woman can approach white men without having her motives suspect.[30]

Life as a prostitute in a society with a rigid moral code is difficult enough, but Black women have additional difficulties imposed on them by racist attitudes. A morals court official states, "I think that Negro women as a class are dealt with more harshly in the court than the whites."[31] Restricted to a certain area of the city, the Black prostitute is forced to compete with other Black women for customers. Because she is in an overcrowded profession in her particular area, she must charge less than her white counterpart. Some years ago a report revealed that prices for Black prostitutes ranged from twenty-five cents to two dollars while prices for white prostitutes ranged from one to five dollars.[32] The price differential probably has not changed since that time.

One of the greatest problems faced by the Black prostitute is the racial character of her clientele. Usually she must sell her body to white men, as Black men frequently cannot afford to pay for her sexual services, nor in many cases do they need to. Judge Murtagh describes the case of Melissa Jane, a Black prostitute in New York City. She walks the streets of Harlem praying to find a Black customer or two. But Black men do not seem to like her, and so she goes with white tricks against her will. He goes on to report Melissa Jane's feeling of shame when she undresses before a white man, the feeling of remorse when he touches her dusky skin, fearing what perverted sexual urges he will vent on her compliant body.[33]

Another of Judge Murtagh's examples is Jean Ford, a tall, slender Black girl. She explains the desirability of Black prostitutes for white men by saying:

> *A colored girl who plays her cards right and isn't*
> *too bad looking can practically write their own tickets*

with them. They seem to feel that, because some of us have remote ancestors who lived in Africa once, we are primitives at heart when it comes to sex. Actually, most of them are a lot more primitive than we are.[34]

This remark reflects the belief that the sexual tastes of white men are uncommon among her own group. This is frequently a class difference as Kinsey noted: "Both the high school and college boy want something that is usually foreign to the prostitute's background. For the sake of her trade, she may agree to such overt activity as these males desire but, interesting to note, she still would refuse to use such techniques with her husband or boyfriend."[35] Usually this involves unusual positions in intercourse, oral manipulation of the man's genitals, or stripping to the buff. When asked about her attitude toward "pervert" practices, a Black prostitute responded that "girls showed her the easiest way but you never get used to it."[36]

In many cases these "perverted" practices referred to are oral-genital relations. As stated in the previous chapter, Black women, especially in the lower class, consider any substitution for simple and direct coitus a perversion. Even the terms referring to oral-genital sex are avoided. Instead, they refer to it as an unnatural sex act. The feelings against it are so strong, according to Elliot Liebow, that when a Black woman killed her husband for trying to force her to engage in such an act, she received the support of the community and was never brought to trial for her deed.[37]

Contrary to popular belief, prostitutes are not always sophisticated in matters relating to sex. As Charles Winick and Paul Kinsie found, a prostitute may not be a sex expert.[38] Moreover, she may be more sexually modest than nonprofessional women. A former member of the Kinsey Institute related the following ancedote. He was taking the history of a very jolly, delightful two-hundred-and-fifty-pound Black female prostitute. She had essentially done everything including homosexual and heterosexual relations, exhibitions, intercourse with animals, etc. At the end of the interview she confessed that she had omitted one thing she had done—having intercourse in the nude. Complete nudity, as we stated before, is much more taboo among Black women than white women.[39]

Men with perverted sexual tastes often seek out prostitutes to satisfy their tastes. Sadists and masochists form a part of the prostitute's clientele and their peculiar needs must be catered to. Beatings administered by the sadist are a common activity of the prostitute though sometimes the beating is purely symbolic and not carried to the extent of causing pain.[40] A Black prostitute remarked that men only tried to hurt her once in a while and usually it was the white men who did it.[41]

Beatings bring a higher price, and some impoverished Black women are forced to undergo such treatment for their bread and butter. One Black hustler explained that white tricks pay a hundred dollars to beat a prostitute. Sometimes, she says, they hit you so hard you land in the hospital.[42] Other men who attain sexual gratification in bizarre ways that defy description usually have a need to degrade the woman before they can enjoy her.[43] And it is probably easier for them to vent their pernicious sexual urges upon Black women because they consider these women to be less than human. As one white man told a Black prostitute, "Gal, there's two places where niggers is as good as white folks—the bedroom and the graveyard."[44]

Sometimes there is a thin line between a prostitute and a good-time girl. The Black community does make distinctions between a hard-core professional prostitute and casual pickups available for a good time. Often the dividing line is based on the customer. One who caters to white men and middle-class Blacks would be considered a professional. Those who deal only with lower-class Blacks are held to be nonprofessionals. The exchange of money for sexual services is seen not so much as a commercial transaction but as a token of appreciation for a good time.[45]

In Soulside, for example, there are bars where more than drinking takes place. One important reason for frequenting these bars is to meet members of the opposite sex. In essence, these bars are pickup places where any woman may be approached for sexual relations. Most of the women in these places are prostitutes or semiprostitutes. But they are not strictly out for money. One of them, named Ruby, occasionally lives with one man or another for a time. Men also use her apartment as a lounge, particularly during the winter when it is too cold to be outside much.[46]

Most often, Black men have their only relationships with a prostitute when they act as her pimp. The pimp is a paid companion to whom the prostitute gives her earnings. Sometimes the pimp provides the only human relationship with continuity and meaning for her. Prostitutes, like all women, have their affectional needs, and the pimp provides them with all that they get. In addition, her status in the in-group of prostitutes often depends on the way she keeps her pimp. Whether he drives a Cadillac or a Ford is important to how the prostitute is regarded by her fellow street-walkers.[47] In return for his stylish way of living, the pimp provides the prostitute with protection, banking for jail bond and savings purposes, and fix procurement in the case of legal action.[48]

His conspicuous life style makes the pimp one of the most admired men in the lower-class Black community. Iceberg Slim, a famous Black pimp, says that he became one because of the well-heeled pimps in his midst.[49] One might note that although there are other successful Blacks in well-paying jobs, they rarely live in the heart of the Black ghetto. Thus, the pimp is the most visible sign of material success to many youth in the lower class.

Black men serve as pimps to white prostitutes as well. Judge Murtagh describes pimping as a Black man's occupation. Like domestic service, he says, the job of pimping is so low that the white men do not want it.[50]

Without the pimp, few Black prostitutes would receive any affection. Their customers look down upon them, and they have the lowest status of any group in the Black community. So it is not surprising to hear a prostitute say: "Pimps are always handy and you fall for that sugar somehow. I guess I liked the notoriety of being a pimp's woman. . . . They'd take you around in big cars and show you off and introduce you as their woman. That was exciting and you think you are somebody."[51]

But a pimp also represents a destructive influence on the prostitute. He may put pressure on his girl to accept beatings from customers so that she can give him more money. Moreover, in many instances, it is the pimp who beats the prostitutes. A great number of these girls have suffered beatings or have been knifed at the hands of their pimp. One girl said about her pimp: "He used to beat me up bad all the time. I loved him at first, but I got to hate him after a while. One day I decided to work for him no more. When I told him, he got his knife and began slashing me all over my arms and face."[52]

Despite the hardships encountered by the Black prostitute, does she at least achieve sexual satisfaction from her pimp or even her customers? The evidence available indicates that she does not. Greenwald's prostitutes received more satisfaction from their pimps than their clients, but few of them spoke of their pimps as being great lovers.[53] According to most studies, the prostitute is not sexually gratified by her clients. One psychoanalyst has even stated that frigidity is an indispensable element in prostitution.[54]

Many men believe prostitutes to be oversexed women who are thrilled at the sexual prowess of their clients. One prostitute, who admitted to rarely receiving sexual satisfaction, had this to say about the act she uses to make her clients believe she is experiencing sexual pleasure with them:

"I don't let the men know it though. I make them think they're hell on wheels. I act wooooo! As though they're doing something. But they really ain't doing nothing. I never get no kicks out of it."[55]

Even though they receive little besides money for being a prostitute, thousands of Black women are attracted annually to the world's oldest profession. While poverty is a key factor, discrimination against Black women in employment plays its part. High school graduates have gone into prostitution because the only work that they could get was as domestics or waitresses. One young woman, who lost her white collar job during the depression, explained that she could not tolerate scrubbing floors and so turned to prostitution.[56]

The effect of poverty on the Black woman's decision to become a prostitute should not be underestimated. A man familar with prostitution, a captain on the vice squad, observed that:

> There are a lot of women here who are trying to make a dollar and will take a chance and "turn a trick." But, for the most part these people are just poor women who are out of a job and can't make it any other way. If they could just get a job scrubbing floors you wouldn't see them trying to be whores very long. They are for the most part just unfortunate women who have to do anything to get something to eat.[57]

An unstable family life is a common background of many Black prostitutes. Lack of a bi-parental home or failure to receive love and acceptance from parents sometimes pushes Black girls into prostitution. The case histories of most Black prostitutes show unhappy backgrounds. Such was the case of one Black woman whose father died when she was three years old. Her mother later died when she was only nine. After her stepfather deserted her, she went to live with her married sister. This woman blames her unhappy childhood for her career choice and believes that life would have been different if her father had lived.[58]

Some authorities have asserted that prostitutes safeguard the sanctity of the home and the innocence of other men's wives and daughters. One sociologist has even declared that prostitutes receive money not only for their sexual services but also for their loss of status in the community.[59] They fail to consider that prostitution is a crime punishable by imprisonment in this country and that in most cases only the woman is arrested.

The only open prostitution left in the United States is frequently found in the Black ghetto. *Fortune* once described Harlem as: "Reefer pads, gambling houses, and countless houses of prostitution. Most hotels are brothels, and it is a usual sight to see a dozen streetwalkers on every corner in lower Harlem."[60]

One reason for this situation is the dual standard of law enforcement in this country. The police maintain a much less rigorous standard of law enforcement in the Black community, tolerating there illegal activities such as drug addiction, prostitution, and street violence that they would not tolerate elsewhere. Moreover, recent investigations of the police force in certain large cities have revealed a close collaboration between the men in blue and the peddlers of vice in ghetto communities.[61]

When not providing protection for Black prostitutes, policemen are busy discriminating against them. In Oklahoma City, a state legislator declared that either prostitution should be stopped altogether or the police should stop discriminating against prostitutes on the basis of race. It seems that the police were filing state charges, which call for a possible $500 fine and a prison sentence, against Black prostitutes but were only filing municipal charges, which call for a $200 fine, against white prostitutes.[62] In another locale, Washington, D.C., eight policemen were suspended for conspiring to illegally entrap Black prostitutes.[63]

In the past couple of years New York City has "allowed" Black prostitutes to expand their base of operation. A reporter wrote that Black prostitutes have taken over the streets. They have chased the white prostitutes off the streets. A thousand or more Black prostitutes walk the streets of mid-Manhattan. "In the area of a famous downtown hotel they are so numerous they appear to be holding nightly conventions."[64] Violence and drugs have become a common part of the prostitution scene.

Allowance of open prostitution has made the Black ghettos of America a frequent haunt of sex-seeking white men. Recently Detroit Attorney Lawrence Massey appeared on behalf of Black prostitutes who were arrested on charges of accosting and soliciting. He filed a motion with the court that alleged that the police used discriminatory practices in arresting the prostitutes but refusing to arrest the white men who invade Black neighborhoods looking for prostitutes.[65]

Because open prostitution is only allowed in Black neighborhoods, white men are frequently found in these areas seeking to buy some passion. In Los Angeles Black ghettos, it is known that white men driving around certain areas are looking for the pay-for-play girls. Often they accost Black women who are not prostitutes and make walking the streets at night unsafe for "respectable" Black women.

Some young Black men in San Francisco have formed patrols to keep white men seeking sexual services out of the Black community. After dusk, any white man seen patrolling Black neighborhoods is warned with a certain forcefulness against conducting any illegal activity in this area. Predictably, the official reaction to their activity was a warning that they would be arrested if they broke any laws. Nothing was said about increasing police vigilance against the white pursuers of Black sex who annoy Black women walking the street at night.

The recent increase in crime in the streets has made prostitution an unsafe trade. One woman who dropped out of the profession said that it had become a holy hell. Many women have been mugged or killed by criminals who roam the streets at night. With the recent reluctance of ordinary citizens to venture into the inner cities at night, prostitutes have become the victims of muggings and killings. Sometimes the trick takes her money after the act of coitus, adding insult to injury.

Women who become prostitutes face a multitude of problems. Men have been known to say that females never face starvation because they can always sell sex if they cannot do anything else. Such statements ignore the realities of the prostitute's life. Not infrequently, it is the male pimp who gets the greatest monetary gain from the sale of the prostitute's body. And even though prostitution may be lucrative for awhile, the passage of time takes its toll on the pulchritude of most prostitutes, as it does all women. When she reaches a certain age, the prostitute becomes less desirable as a sex object to most men. If she stays in the hustler's underworld, she then resorts to performing degrading services for emotionally disturbed men that all other women refuse to perform.

What happens to the prostitute in her declining years? According to Iceberg Slim, many of them become lesbians and some become the pimp of lesbians. In some cases they become the operators of bordellos. But in too many cases prostitutes have become hooked on narcotics. Many of them wind up in mental institutions.[66] A recent study of prostitution in the United States revealed that prostitutes have a very high suicide rate. Another finding of this study was that prostitutes, in general, do not earn very much ($5,000 to $6,000 a year).[67]

A woman who shares her body with all types of men inevitably encounters the occupational hazard of promiscuity, venereal disease. It has been authoritatively reported that one out of every six women appearing in New York City's Woman's Court is infected with a venereal disease.[68] Some 58 percent of the Black prison women in the Kinsey sample, many of whom were former prostitutes, had syphilis.[69]

The more recent increase in venereal disease can hardly be attributed to prostitution. Indeed, most public health authorities agree that prostitutes are usually conscientious about avoiding venereal disease and seeking treatment if they do contract it. Only 2 percent of the VD patients treated in St. Louis are prostitutes. Most cases of veneral disease are contracted by young people and homosexuals.

Summary

Our treatment of the Black prostitute runs counter to certain trends among Black writers and spokesmen to glorify or legitimize the roles of the pimp and prostitute. But we see nothing in these roles to boast about. Regardless of the social factors that socialize Black men into the role of pimp, that role represents nothing more than capitalism on-the-make. Pimping is nothing more than the exploitation of Black womanhood in the crudest fashion. As an ex-pimp, Malcolm X spoke often of the degradation of this occupation.

There is very little glamor in the Black prostitute's life. Prostitution is a miserable occupation that exposes the Black woman to every sordid side of the human personality and to all the social ills that exist in human society. Prostitutes are unusually prey to the problems of drug addiction, alcoholism, mental illness, and venereal disease. They are exploited sexually and economically, by the pimp, the customer, and the police. Their entire lives are not the carefree and happy ones depicted in the motion pictures and books. Instead, they live in a constant state of insecurity and most of them wind up penniless. They represent the epitome of womanhood abused to the level of a thing.

Our condemnation of prostitution is not based on any moral principle, except one that opposes economic exploitation. In an economic sense the prostitute's role is not that different from the married woman's, a point often pointed out by women who are struggling to liberate themselves from the oppression of sexist institutions such as marriage. As one such woman wrote: "The only difference between women who sell themselves in prostitution and those who sell themselves in marriage is in the price and the length of time the contract runs."[71] Probably the greatest difference between the two is that the married woman is respected as a human being and has some legal rights. The prostitute's humanity is not recognized and she thus represents all the forms of female slavery.

A recent book has characterized all women as prostitutes. Ester Vilar declares that women do not employ their intellectual capacities for anything except to con males into supporting them. According to her, by the age of twelve at the latest, every girl has decided to become a lifelong prostitute, i.e., she wants to get married. Men, she asserts, have been trained and conditioned by women, not unlike the way Pavlov conditioned his dogs, into becoming their slaves. As compensation for their labors, men are given the periodic use of women's vaginas.[72]

While there is much truth in her analysis, she ignores the fact that women are socialized into these roles by strong environmental and educational forces that are under the control of men. The economic system under which we live teaches us that an item of value is sold for a profit or exploited for some value within the context of supply and demand. It is this fact that has inculcated in women the belief that sex is a commodity to be sold rather than enjoyed or shared. But, as women have belatedly found, the benefits received in return for giving their bodies are outweighed by the disadvantages of their enforced chastity.

The sexual liberation of women has cut into the trade of the prostitute. Although prostitution is more open in certain cities, organized prostitution is on the decline in the United

States. Brothels are fewer in number, while free lancing is on the rise. Because women will no longer accept the double standard of sexual conduct, the prostitute must compete with amateurs who engage in sexual relations for its intrinsic satisfaction and not for financial rewards. The greater sexual freedom of contemporary women means that men cohabit with girl friends rather than with prostitutes.

Although the racist and economic pressures of white society have probably forced a greater proportion of Black women into prostitution than white women, it should be understood that the vast majority of Black women are not prostitutes. The number of white prostitutes in this country is underestimated because white policemen ignore call girls with prestigious white clientele in respectable clubs and hotels. There is some indication of a large increase in prostitution among white runaway teen-age girls who are taking drugs. The extent of prostitution among Black and white women is based on the power to control one's body. Considerable sexual restraints have been imposed upon both Black and white females, but in opposite directions. In that regard, neither was free.

Prostitution has been called the world's oldest profession. From time immemorial women have lacked the sexual freedom of men. In a society that allows men sexual expression before marriage and outside marriage yet relegates the majority of women to chastity and marital fidelity there must be some women who make their bodies available to men. Prostitutes have long played this role. Who becomes a prostitute and why? Impoverished women of all races have historically played this role. More and more, the role of prostitute in the United States is synonymous with the word Black. Although white women still become prostitutes, they are paid more and persecuted less. In all endeavors, the Black woman must face the forces of white racism. It is just as true in the prostitute's world as anywhere else.

4

Being Married— and Black

I think Negro wives, no matter what their age or background or even their understanding of the problem, have to be terribly strong—much stronger than their white counterparts. They cannot relax, they cannot simply be loving wives waiting for the man of the house to come home. They have to be spiritual sponges, absorbing the racially inflicted hurts of their men. Yet at the same time they have to give him courage, to make him know that it is worth it to go on, to go back day after day to the humiliation and discouragement of trying to make it in the white man's world for the sake of their families. It's hard enough for a poor working white man, but a hundred times harder for a Negro.

Lena Horne
in the *New York Post*
September 29, 1963

When one reviews the marital life of the Black woman, it becomes obvious that marriage has few positive functions for her. To put this in proper perspective, it is necessary to point out that the institution of marriage is under attack from many quarters today. Marriage, in the legal sense, is being rejected by people of all races because it has not demonstrated that it is a viable arrangement for promoting individual or group happiness.

Marriage in most societies is potentially a fragile relationship because it brings together a pair of persons who are, comparatively speaking, unknown quantities to each other. It involves a continuous and intimate association between two people who vary in personality traits and other social characteristics. Therefore, we find some degree of marital conflict in all societies. The degree, of course, differs from one society to another and is contingent upon a variety of factors that impinge on the marital relationship. As one sociologist has noted, "Most people in all cultures will achieve at best a life of quiet desperation in their family relationships."[1]

Rather than attempting to find weaknesses in Black culture or Black women that account for the marital conflict in the Black community, one might best concentrate on the problems inherent in marriage itself and the elements in the society that make it such a tentative condition. The chances of any marriage working out are not good. If one takes into account the marriages that end in divorce, annulment, and desertion, almost half of American marriages are failures. When marriages of convenience are added, where a woman and a man may continue to live together for the sake of appearance, it appears that only about 25 percent of marriages are really happy.

The figure is probably lower for Black marriages. Whites who have managed to achieve some degree of rapprochement in marriage are not hampered by the legacy of slavery, the vicissitudes of racism, and economic deprivation as Blacks are. Thus, the Black woman's chances for getting married, staying married, or remarrying are considerably reduced by all the negative forces she must overcome.

Historical Background

In African societies, marital stability has traditionally been an incorporated part of the social structure. Marriage was not just a matter between individuals but was the concern of all the members of both families. Divorce seldom took place because the marriage contract was commonly taken very seriously by all the parties involved. When a difficult case of marital conflict arose, both sides of the family intervened in order to resolve the disagreement. A woman was not merely a man's wife but "the wife of the family." Within this network of community control, divorce was taken very seriously and only used as a last resort.[2]

The family was the basis of social organization in traditional African society. After marriage a woman remained a part of her own family. Since her family retained a sincere interest in her well-being, the bride's husband's family was expected to pay a bride price to compensate the family for the loss of her services and to guarantee her good treatment. This bride price did not mean that the woman was being purchased as has been commonly believed. A woman did not legally belong to her husband but to her own family.[3]

Polygyny was allowed in almost all parts of Africa, although it was not a universal practice in any society. It was the custom for the head of the family to help with the expenses involved in the first marriage of a male member of the family. However, the husband had to pay all expenses connected with the second marriage. This custom compelled all but the wealthy to be content with one wife in a lifetime. Marriages that involved multiple spouses did not have an inordinate amount of conflict. Usually there were rules governing the relationship of wives to their husband, and separate dwellings reduced interaction and conflicts between the wives. Frequently, having sisters as the co-wives and treating each wife equally alleviated conflict.[4]

The character of marriage changed significantly under the era of slavery. There occasionally was a continuity between African marriage customs and marital practices during this period.[5] E. Franklin Frazier reports the case of a male slave who was required to ask the permission of every member of the girl's family before he was allowed to marry her.[6] But authority over marriage in most cases was transferred from the married couple's family to that of the slavemaster.

Marriage between slaves was only permitted by the slaveholder under his conditions. To be married two slaves would hold hands and jump over a broomstick held by two other slaves. All the slaves would then pray that their union would be happy and that their children would not be sold away from them. This ceremony was as binding for a slave as being joined by an ordained clergyman.[7] Yet slaves preferred being married by a minister. Sometimes two slaves would request the right to be married, but more often the slavemaster would simply select couples for each other and buy extra women if needed. The slaves had little choice in the selection of their mates. They were mated just like cattle and just as easily separated again.[8]

In a legal sense there was no such thing as marriage between slaves. As one historian noted, that most ancient and intimate of institutional arrangements had been destroyed by law. Slaves had no legal rights. The law did not recognize their humanity nor their marriages. In every state, white marriages were recognized as civil contracts that bound both parties to certain obligations and provided penalties for their violation. Slave marriages had no such recognition in the state marriage statutes; instead, they were regulated by whatever laws the slaveowners saw fit to enforce.[9]

The sanctioning for slave marriages derived from the

slaveholder's physical control over his bondsmen. The marital arrangements of slaves were left to the slavemaster's discretion. Since the profit gain was his primary motive and because the slavewoman was perceived as a reproductive force, the mating of two slaves was often an involuntary relationship. The profit-hungry slaveowners ignored the slave woman's choice of a mate and demanded that she mate with a partner he chose.[10]

The response of some slave women to a forced marriage was to resist such a union by running away. Harriet Tubman tells of Tilly, a slave woman, whose slavemaster was about to force her into an unwanted union.

> *She was engaged to a young man from another plantation, but he had joined one of Harriet's parties, and gone north. Tilly was to have gone also at the time but had found it impossible to get away. Now, she had learned that it was her master's intention to give her to a Negro of his own for his wife; and in fear and desperation, she made a strike for freedom.*[11]

After emancipation the question of legalized marriage for the freed slaves was still an issue. During the reconstruction period Southern legislatures had to debate whether to permit marriages between Black men and women. Finally, the right to "legal" marriage was granted by decree of the federal government. This decree did not derive from the government's recognition of the Black man's humanity but rather from an attempt to reduce the flow of homeless Blacks.[12]

At one point the legislators sought to declare that marriage consummated under slavery would be legally recognized. But this law would have left many of the freed slaves vulnerable to prosecution for desertion, bigamy, and adultery since many had more than one spouse under slavery. Some states compromised by recognizing marriages dating from the passage of the Reconstruction Acts. In other states the freedmen were allowed to select the partner they wanted to be married to.[13]

It was this past history of marriage among Blacks that led Frazier to the theory that Blacks had no social institution of marriage supported by their own folkways and mores. The indiscriminate mating of Blacks meant that the value of marriage was never that strong among the Black freedmen. Consequently, other forms of family organization took root in the Black community, especially in the rural South[14] after emancipation. One such form was the consensual union, also known as a common-law marriage.

A common-law marriage is an agreement between a man and woman to become husband and wife without benefit of ecclesiastical or civil ceremony, the agreement being provable by the conduct of the parties. Such marriages are legal in many Southern states. Another possible explanation of why the license and wedding are dispensed with by many Black people is that the expense may not seem justified to people with low incomes.

It is conceivable that the economic independence of Black women and the possibility of mistreatment by a husband restrain some of them from forming legal unions. This attitude is expressed in the statement of one Black woman: "He's nice all right but I ain't thinking about marrying soon. Soon as you marry a man he starts mistreating you, and I'm not going to be mistreated no more."[15]

Although ceremonial marriage was a status symbol for some Black women in the rural South, many of them rejected the idea of a legal union. But the acceptability of common-law marriages did not mean promiscuous behavior. For example, one widow who was "slipping up the hill" to see the father of her unborn child bragged that she never tampered with other women's husbands and declared quite forthrightly that she wanted no marriage ceremony. She was glad that her first husband was dead and did not want to be bothered with another one.[16]

Occasionally, the common-law father feels the same as the mother about the responsibilities involved in a legal marriage. One researcher cited the case of a tubercular Black thirty-nine year old man, who was himself the child of a common-law union.

> *The marital status is confusing in so far as records are concerned. He interchanged the terms "girlfriend" and "wife" with no intent of misrepresentation. He lived with the mother of his two little girls for some time, but they were not legally married. He gives her money and supports the children. The latter meant a great deal to him and he speaks of the children lovingly, individualizes them, and plans for them. Since he feels that his illness incapacitates him as a "husband," and there are no legal ties, this "wife" is now apparently being a "girlfriend" again.*[17]

These attitudes toward marriage are partly an outgrowth of the cultural pattern of slavery that was retained during the Afro-American's tenure in the rural South. Marriages sometimes took place by mere public declaration but without a marriage license. It was also commonly believed that divorce could occur by public declaration or simply by crossing state or county lines. Desertion was sometimes interpreted as separation.[18]

Another important factor is the economic independence of Black women. The power base of the patriarchal white family is based, in large part, on the economic dependence of the female member.[19] In the Black family, many women are independent of the Black male for support and assume a type of role in their families not found in the patriarchal family. At one point, for instance, the Black woman was just as likely to desert the family as the male. Instead of being economically dependent on her husband, she supported him, and her economic burden was lightened by his absence.[20]

While the above may have been immediate postslavery

marital patterns, legal marriage has apparently taken on a greater importance for the contemporary Black woman. Most Black women eventually get married because they believe that love and companionship are within the capacity of any well-intentioned man.[21] One sociologist states that the Black woman gains status from having been married at one time and being married at the present time is significant only in proclaiming the married status. The emphasis is placed on the title of "Mrs." rather than the accompanying surname.[22]

Such a supposition can hardly be proved. Black women take marriage seriously, perhaps not as seriously as white women because life in the ghetto makes achieving a happy marriage difficult and changing the conditions of her life is beyond her control. Moreover, marital stability is not always consistent with marital happiness. The nonconforming nature of Black women, along with their greater independence from the male's economic dominance, allows them to reject the idea of achieving marital respectability at the cost of their personal welfare and, often, the welfare of their children.

Mate Selection Standards

Most Black women have some concept of the ideal man they would like to marry. But these aspirations are tempered by the reality of their lives. Since it is lower-class Black women who suffer the most from racist oppression, they must modify their standards for a husband to reflect the availability of such men in their environment.

Black lower-class women, like all women, have emotional and sexual needs. Since they are primarily working class women of limited education and are unable to spend time or money in "beautifying" themselves, they cannot expect to get husbands from the middle and upper classes. Therefore, most lower-income Black women have to accept love on male terms. The husband's shortcomings are tolerated for the sake of affection and companionship.[23]

This predicament of lower-class Black women in selecting a mate is pointed out by St. Clair Drake and Horace Cayton, who note that:

> *Lower-class women don't expect much from their husbands in terms of either sexual fidelity or economic security. Like most women in America they fantasy about romantic love and the ideal husband who has a steady job, brings his money home, and makes possible a life of leisure and comfort.*[24]

But, as they found, a lower-class Black woman will believe herself to have a "good old man" if he will work when he can and does not squander all of his money on gambling and drinking. If he does get involved with other women, he will avoid emotional attachments and will not spend much money on his extramarital affairs. A "good old man" may act in a violent way with his wife if he is angry but definitely will not slap her around all the time when he is sober nor risk her life when intoxicated. If they have children, he will attempt to provide them with the necessities of life. And if he expects her to remain with him, she requires that he give her sexual satisfaction.[25]

Despite the dilution of her mate-selection standards, most Black women prefer the state of matrimony to a life of solitude. As Rainwater notes, a lower-class Black woman expects a life of celibacy to be even more ungratifying. Even an imperfect marital relationship is better than a life that lacks love and companionship. Moreover, most of the wives Rainwater studied received some satisfaction in their relationship with their husbands.[26]

Within the Black middle-class, women have a greater opportunity for realizing their ideal standard for a marital partner. In selecting a mate, the middle-class Black woman is more likely to follow middle-class norms. There is more emphasis on romantic love and less on economic security. However, romantic love is not the only basis for marriage among the Black middle class. It may be that they make an a priori assumption that their husband can provide for them and seek to maximize the emotional gratification they will receive from a potential husband.

When Jualynne Dodson asked her single Black graduate females their preferences in Black men, the majority of them stated that they had a preference for "tall" men and none of them wanted a man whose skin was lighter than theirs. In fact most of them stated that dark men were definitely preferred over fair-skinned Black males. Some of their other standards were self-assurance, older age group, and an education at least equivalent to theirs but preferably better.[27]

Their preference for a dark-skinned male is an interesting one. Even among lower-class Black women, darker males are preferred to fair-skinned ones. It appears that lighter-skinned males are considered less physically attractive. Perhaps their physical similarity to white men invokes some unpleasant historical memories for Black women. Also, fair-skinned Black males have the image of being egocentric and unreliable in their relationships with Black women.

What is strange about the low prestige value of fair-skinned Black males is that the position of light-skinned Black women has, traditionally, been the reverse. For the longest time light skin pigmentation was considered an important requirement for marriage in the Black middle class. A man who had achieved success in his occupation and had a good income would often marry a fair-skinned daughter of one of the old mulatto families in order to consolidate his social status.[28]

In the past, many Black people associated light skin color with high social status. Fair-skin pigmentation, particularly in women, was favored in mate selection. Since men usually had the power of choice, they often chose wives who had lighter skin than themselves. One study confirmed this condition by finding that the wives of middle-class Black men were significantly lighter than the wives of lower-class Black men. Men with fair-skinned wives also tended to hold more positive attitudes toward whites.[29]

Nevertheless, skin color no longer appears to be an important factor in mate selection. Indeed, the Black prestige structure is beginning to approximate the white one. Education is becoming more important as a basis for Black status. In one study of Black college students, light complexion ranked twenty-second out of twenty-eight values in dating, far below internal personality traits and social skills.[30]

As has already been mentioned, there is a serious shortage of available Black marriage partners. The excess of a million Black women tends to curtail the Black woman's chances for a good marriage. It is during the age of marriageability that the male shortage is greatest. In 1970 there were less than 84.6 Black males for every 100 Black females in the age range of twenty-five to sixty-four.[31]

There are other dimensions of the low sex ratio among Blacks that should be mentioned. The fact that men tend to marry women who are two or three years younger than they are reduces even further the available pool of eligible bachelors for Black women. The increase in the birth rate after World War II created a disparity between the number of prospective brides and grooms. For example, for every 100 Black men born in 1945, there were 130 Black women born in 1948. Hence, there was a surplus of women born in the postwar years. Consequently, Black women born in the years 1946 through 1949 will have to remain single or wait to marry men who are no older than themselves.[32]

Another factor to consider is that the male shortage does not have equal effect on all Black women. The very desirable Black woman is not as likely to feel the pinch of the male shortage. In our society a female's desirability is often derived from her sex appeal, especially at the younger ages. Black women who possess less sex appeal or lack youth will be less likely to be chosen. The available Black males will be inclined to cluster around the more attractive Black women.

The negative attitudes toward marriage held by many Black males could further reduce Black females' opportunity for matrimony. When Carlfred Broderick queried the Black adolescents in his study, he found that by the age of fourteen more Black girls wanted to marry someday than Black males. By age sixteen, less than 75 percent of the Black males in his study said they ever wanted to marry.[33]

Considering the shortage of available Black men for marriage that finding is somewhat significant. Elliot Liebow also noted a pervasive disenchantment with marriage among a group of lower-class Black men. Marriage was seen as a series of problems: public and private fights between spouses; how to feed, clothe, and house a wife; anxiety about being able to ward off attacks on the health and safety of their children. These men could not recollect a single marriage in their community that they recognized as a "good marriage."[34]

The negative attitudes of Black males toward marriage may be a negligible factor in whether they get married or not. Apparently most of them eventually do take on a wife. The reasons why vary although many do not enter marriage with a great deal of optimism. Lee Rainwater asserts that Black men see marriage as a means of attaining manhood. It means regular sexual relations without a struggle and freedom from venereal disease. In some cases, the marriage is forced upon the male by the pregnancy of the female.[35]

Whatever the reason Black men and women enter into a contractual marriage relationship, the success of the marriage is contingent on a number of factors, and its dissolution is influenced very much by the same variables. The marital relationship has pretty much a dynamic of its own.

The Dynamics of Marital Interaction

One of the most popular images of the Black wife is the Sapphire concept. Sapphire was a popular character on the

Amos and Andy television show. She was domineering, ego deflating and just hard to get along with. This image of Black women is reinforced by the folklore that Black women are difficult creatures to live with and that they lack feminine qualities that make men want to marry them or remain married to them.

Are Black women really incompatible mates because they do not cater to building up the ego of their men? One might question, in this day of women's liberation, whether women have to subordinate their individuality to the support of male ego needs. It is only in a male-dominant society that women must suffer all sorts of indignities and psychological abuses at the hand of a male and remain quiet so they won't upset his delicate ego.

Nonetheless, this lack of male-ego support is cited as a primary cause of tension in Black marriages. Some Black women who have become concerned about the encroachment of white women on the Black male supply admit that in general it is probably easier for many Black men to interact on a day-to-day basis with white women. One such Black woman states that: "White women don't challenge as much, or in the same way. White women also know more subtle tricks of boosting a man's ego, making him do what she wants without his knowing she is doing it."[36]

This tendency to use white wives as the ideal for Black wives to emulate may be based on the Black person's ignorance of what really occurs in white marriages. Calvin Hernton very aptly notes that Black men are known to disparage Black women without having associated with, let alone having been married to, a white woman. This is one of the reasons, he says, why Black women encounter so much frustration with their men. They exist in a society where the objective social position and the reputed virtues of white women obscure whatever worth Black women may have. Thus, the Black male resorts to evaluating the Black woman by what he sees and imagines the white woman to be.[37]

Many Black women do not see in the white woman a model for imitation. In fact, they feel that the white woman who is striving for liberation would do well to follow the Black woman's example. Some see the contemporary white woman as being socialized to be dependent. This trait of dependence appears to deprive many white women of character strengths. As Joyce Ladner observed, the Black woman's greater liberation has given her a peculiar humanistic quality and a quiet courage that can be seen as the epitome of what the American model of feminity should be.[38]

In many marriages the power of the spouse determines the quality of marital interaction. It is assumed that the balance of power in marriage belongs to the partner bringing the most resources to the marriage. These resources are often economic contributions, personal attractiveness, and the ability to fulfill roles adequately. In general, money has been the source of power that sustains male dominance in the family.[39] One pair of family sociologists comments that money belongs to him who earns it, not to her who spends it, since he who earns it may withhold it.[40]

Her economic contributions supposedly give the Black woman more power in the family. One of the most salient differences between Black and white role expectations is that Black husbands expect their wives to work regularly. For some men, their expectation that the wife would work is contingent on whether the children were of school age or not. Among younger Black males, there is a greater inclination to believe that the wife should work anytime she pleases.[41]

Consequently, one finds that, in 1970, 63 percent of younger Black wives worked, 52 percent full time. By comparison, 54 percent of younger white wives worked, only 36 percent full time. Since the wife is most likely to work in Black families, a common belief is that her earnings exceed those of her husband. However, in reality wives in poor Black families contribute less to the total family income than do wives in nonpoor Black families because they are much less likely to be employed. Among the low-income group, only 44 percent of the wives work.[42]

Still the fiction persists that the Black woman's economic contributions provide her with a strong power base in the family. Abram Kardiner and Lionel Ovesey point out that the entire marital relationship of Blacks is more often than not taken up with a power struggle between husband and wife, with the husband usually in a submissive role and the female holding dominance by virtue of her actual or potential capacity as a provider.[43] Of course, the Black woman's economic role cannot, by any means, be ignored. It is her financial contribution that keeps many Black families out of poverty and retains others in the middle class.

But power in a marriage is based on more than money. In the lower classes, for instance, the threat of physical abuse is a form of control exercised by the male over the female. The breakdown of communication in lower-class Black households is often accompanied by violence. Knifings and wife beatings occur frequently during domestic quarrels. Many wives do not see their homes as a sanctuary from the violence of the streets. The policeman is usually called in as a mediator when arguments reach the physical level.[44]

Among middle-class Blacks the prospect of physical violence during a domestic conflict is remote. The economic factor is more an instrument of power for the middle-class Black husband. Unlike his lower-class counterpart, the middle-class husband can more effectively use the threat of withdrawal from the marriage as a way of manipulating his wife. His higher income, for instance, enables him to pay for many services that his wife provides. He can eat out in restaurants, send his shirts to the laundry, and take on a mistress for sexual gratification. Thus, he is less dependent on his wife and has greater bargaining power in the event of a marital conflict.

In many marriages the wife uses the withdrawal of sexual gratification to gain her way. The availability of so many other women to her husband largely cancels out this advantage for many Black wives. Besides, many Black wives see sexual relations as one of the more pleasant aspects of the marriage. Charles King reports that satisfactory sex relations are positively correlated with successful marital adjustment, and conversely, unsatisfactory sex relations are directly associated with marital maladjustment.[45]

If this is true, then marriages between Black men and Black women should be quite happy. The few studies on the subject show that Black women consider marital sexual relations as extremely important. In one such study it was concluded that:

> *Negro women communicated a sense of the acceptability of a woman's interest in sex that is different from the way white wives speak of their sexual roles. They communicate a sense of wanting to enjoy sexual relations.*
>
> *The main difference between Negroes and whites is that among Negroes, rejecting attitudes toward sexual relations are somewhat less frequent. . . . Negro women are more interested in sexuality than their white counterparts. . . . Negro husbands do not as often moderate their enthusiasm for sexual relations as white husbands.*[46]

The fact is, however, that many Black marriages are not happy. Despite their greater interest in marital sexual relations most Black women find that interpersonal difficulties in other areas have ramifications for the enjoyment of sexual intercourse. Black women complain that their husbands do not help them with the housework and fail to provide them with companionship.[47] Hence, most studies show many Black women are dissatisfied with their marriages.

The Source of Marital Conflict

There can hardly be any doubt that many Black marriages, perhaps most, do not provide a great deal of satisfaction for the people involved. When Robert Bell interviewed Black wives with less than a ninth grade education, 64 percent of these women replied that they would not marry if they had to do it over.[48] In this same study of Black mothers in Philadelphia he found that these women had negative attitudes toward their husbands and toward marriage in general. When they were asked what they liked about marriage, a large proportion answered "nothing." These women rejected both marriage as an institution and their own particular marriages.[49]

Even a higher social status does not create much of a positive attitude toward marriage. Bell found that higher status Black wives were more accepting of the concept of marriage but were dissatisfied with their own specific marriage.[50] The findings of Karen Renne were similar. Younger Black women, particularly, are much more likely than white women of the same age, income, and educational level to express unhappiness with their marriage.[51]

The dissatisfaction of Black women, across class lines, with their marriages reflects the unique situation that they face in American society. Their racial oppression leads to economic deprivation, and the two elements interact to make marriage an untenable institution for them. The level of dissatisfaction seems to be greater for Black women than for Black men. Since for many women their marriage and family life form the center of their lives, the wife's dissatisfaction may be attributed to the severity of the problems she encounters.

One of the major problems is economic, especially in the lower class. Despite the knowledge of their parent's marital difficulties, many Black women marry with the expectation that their husbands will be able to provide them with some aspects of the American dream, such as appliances, clothes, trips, etc. The reality of the economic circumstances of many lower-class Black families is that many married men cannot, in fact, provide for their families all of the time. Money is rarely available in an adequate quantity and its shortage is continually a source of conflict within the household.

This situation has led Lee Rainwater to speculate that the break up of a Black marriage is often due to the husband's inability to supply the family with its economic needs. Once the husband ceases to bring money into the house, the wife withdraws her commitment to him and to the marriage.[52] While this undoubtedly happens, it assumes some rather weak emotional ties between Black mates to generate such a serious response to the male's temporary job dislocation.

Indeed, the Black male with a steady income is so rare that many Black women could not sustain a marriage without other sources of income. Joyce Ladner cites many instances where many women risked losing their welfare allowances by retaining a close relationship with their husband or their boyfriend. Furthermore, she says, many Black women do not place the blame on their husbands for their economic deprivation so much as they do on the racist society that has organized itself to suppress their men's obligations and responsibilities.[53]

One such example is how the welfare system undermines the male's role in the family. American society has placed Black males in the fragile position of underemployment and has devised a welfare system where it makes more sense—that is, it is more rational in terms of daily economic security—to be on welfare than to have an unreliable provider in the home.

This case illustrates how the welfare system can disrupt the family. One lady refused to permit her husband back into the family after he got a job. She said:

Not me, with him away I've got security. I know when my welfare check is coming and I know I can take him to court if he doesn't pay me child support. But as soon as he comes back in, then I don't know if he's going to keep his job; or if he's going to start "acting up" and staying out drinking and spending his pay away from home. This way I might be poor but at least I know how much I got.[54]

We must look to racial oppression for another source of marital conflict among Blacks. There are many Black male-female conflicts that are a result of the psychological problems generated by their racist victimization. Under the burden of racist oppression, the victims often turn their frustrations, their wrath, toward each other rather than toward their oppressor. Being constantly confronted with problems of survival, Blacks become more psychologically abusive toward their spouses than they might be under other circumstances.

Many lower-class white males face the problem of unemployment and underemployment. But the combination of employment problems and racism may have a different effect on the Black male. This may account for the problems caused by heavy drinking in many Black marriages. Drinking as such is not related to an unhappy marriage but rather the behavior associated with it. A drunken husband is more inclined to be physically violent against his wife. Conflicts also arise because the wife resents her husband's squandering the family's meager resources on liquor.

A man who is out drinking and gambling is also more likely to get involved with other women, another major source of marital dissatisfaction. Although an occasional case of adultery is not a serious threat to the marriage, a more prolonged sexual liaison is seen as an emotional attachment to the other woman that could lead to the abandonment of the legal wife.

Extramarital affairs appear to be very common in the Black community. When Robert Bell asked his Black female subjects if a wife should expect running around, 56 percent of them answered "yes."[55] Lee Rainwater discovered that Black men felt that a wife would also search for sexual gratification elsewhere if relations did not go well.[56] Whether they do or not, almost half of the Black women in Bell's study believed that a married woman would be justified in running around.[57]

Other sources of marital conflict probably fall into a nondescript category. Elliot Liebow found that many Black males attributed their marital failures to a personal inability or unwillingness to adjust to the built-in demands of the marriage relationship.[58] Another interesting cause of conflict is cited by St. Clair Drake and Horace Cayton.

> *This business of not having supper ready when the old man gets home was a frequent source of conflict in lower-class households during the depression. The wives of men who worked on the WPA often took "day work" to supplement the family income or spent time at the policy stations hoping for a lucky hit. When these activities interfered with the prompt preparation of meals, there was likely to be an explosion. The lower-class man seemed to view such "excuses" with suspicion, especially if the woman had no money to show in evidence.[59]*

Among the middle class, economic factors are not so preeminent in marital conflict. One of the biggest problems middle-class Black women face is educational incompatibility. In 1960, 53 percent of all Blacks 25 years of age or older who had graduated from college were women. This gap was even wider in the past. In 1956 Black women received 62.4 percent of all college degrees granted to Blacks.[60] Educational compatibility as a basis for marriage poses a particular problem for the Black woman. In one study of Black college women it was discovered that over 50 percent of them were married to men employed at a lower socioeconomic level than their wives.[61]

The fact that the Black college woman is not free to choose from among a large number of men who have completed college means that she must accept a mate for other values. Many of them will, therefore, have to marry a man who has not had the cultural and educational advantages they have enjoyed. One result of this educational incompatibility is a high degree of marital conflict. Studies show a much higher probability of family dissolution in the case of females who marry down occupationally.[62]

One consequence of the higher educational rank of Black college women was noted by a female Black leader. She stated that: "The Negro woman's educational superiority has created feelings of guilt in some Negro women and . . . some have even failed to go on to higher degrees in order to preserve the marital relationship from the destructive effects of envy and jealousy on the part of their husbands."[63]

More recent figures show that the educational gap between Black men and women is closing. There were slightly more Black men graduating from college in the past decade than women.[64] However, educational incompatibility is not the only source of conflict in middle-class Black marriages. Sexual satisfaction is probably less frequent among women of the middle class than the lower class. Abram Kardiner and Lionel Ovesey report that the rigidly puritanical sex education of the middle-class Black female has forced her to pay a high price in frigidity and other sexual disorders.[65]

While many Black marriages are unhappy, not all end in divorce. The main cause of divorce is that people are willing to use the divorce courts as an instrument to alleviate their marital unhappiness.

Divorce

A commonly used barometer of marital satisfaction is the divorce rate. The problems created by marital dissolution are probably greater for women in general, and greatest for Black women in particular. Black divorcees face the same problems as white divorcees, but their predicament is compounded by other factors such as the lack of money available to fatherless households and the shortage of eligible Black males, which reduces their chances of remarriage.

A unique element in the divorce rate among Blacks is that it was formerly highest in the middle-class group. In one of the early, most comprehensive studies of divorce, William Goode found that the higher the level of education among Blacks, the higher the divorce rate. After reanalyzing this data further, he suggested that the divorce rate of Blacks who actually finish college is almost as low as that of those who have very little education. Finally, unable to interpret these data satisfactorily, he concluded that poorly educated Blacks do not use the divorce courts as much.[66]

Most divorce statistics do not allow us to make social class divisions.[67] However, the divorce rate is higher among Blacks than whites, even among those of the same educational and income level. The fact, for instance, that Blacks tend to marry at a slightly earlier age than whites increases the probability of their getting divorced. Within twenty years, divorce ended 46 percent of marriages involving Black men who married before the age of 22 and 47 percent of the marriages of Black women who were under 20 years of age at the time they married. This compares with a divorce rate of 13 percent for men and 14 percent for women who married at a later age. The comparable figures for white men who married before the age of 22 was 26 percent, for white females 25 percent.[68]

In general, the statistics show that of Black men between the ages of 14 and 69 years that have been married, 27.5 percent had been divorced. For Black women of the same age bracket, the proportion divorced was 31.4. In the white group the equivalent rates were 13.7 and 15.1. In other words, the Black divorce rate is approximately double that of the white rate. If one considers the differential separation rate, i.e., persons living apart but not legally divorced, the gap is even higher between the two groups. In fact, only 52.2 percent of Black males had been married only once and had their wives living with them.[69]

The implications of divorce for Black women are so ominous that they take a longer time to consider divorce before actually filing for one than whites. William Goode found that the median time was 15.6 months for Blacks, 11.7 for whites.[70] This is understandable considering the Black woman's prospect for finding another husband in the low dating pool of eligible Black men. Although remarriages constituted 24 percent of all marriages for white women, only 18 percent of Black women remarry.[71]

In the lower class, women are often not anxious to take on another husband. They are frequently ambivalent about getting married again. Only a slight majority of the lower class Black women answered "yes" when Lee Rainwater asked them if a woman was worse off if she did not remarry.[72] Of course their answer may reflect the belief that they have few opportunities for obtaining another husband. Many of those women who have children realize that men are reluctant to take on the responsibility of raising another man's children.

Among middle-class Black women there is a greater concern about remarriage. Many of them maintained a middle-class life style only with the combined income of their husbands. In Los Angeles, for instance, there is an area known as the jungle, which has a large number of divorced women with children who live there and are always hunting for men.

Even within the middle-class group, Black women are plagued with financial problems. One Black woman, herself a divorcee, studied ten Black divorcees and found economic factors to be the basic cause of their marital disruption. She listed three major complaint themes of her subjects.

(1) A Black woman cannot be completely submissive to her husband even if she wants to be. She has to do certain things because he will not or cannot. At first the husband feels admiration at her ability to carry out family matters, but subsequently he begins to feel that she is overbearing.

(2) In financial matters the man wants to handle the money but leaves his wife to face the creditors when fiscal mismanagement occurs. The wife then must become the mediator.

(3) The Black man is easily discouraged, and the Black woman is unable to reassure him so that he can still maintain his manhood. In most households, Black women are incapable of achieving a balance. She always feels like she is head of the household.

One of the most persistent frustrations the Black woman must cope with is the constant drain on the low supply of Black males by white females. Therefore, the dynamics of interracial relations are a fruitful area of investigation.

Interracial Marriages

In the past decade there appears to have been a radical increase in interracial dating. Although there are still many social sanctions against this practice, other forces of social change have muted the social disapproval of interracial unions. Among those forces is the recent Supreme Court decision of 1967 declaring all laws against interracial marriages invalid. The fact that large numbers of interracial couples meet on college campuses away from home reduced the amount of parental and community control over the choice of an individual's dating partners. The young people's revolt against traditional institutions and values have led them to reject the taboos on dating across racial lines.

The increase in interracial dating has as a logical result an increase in interracial marriages. Using selective data David Heer found definite evidence of an upward trend in the percentage of Blacks marrying whites. The interracial marriage rate was particularly high in those areas where residential segregation by race is low and where there are minimal status differences between the white and Black population. However, he also discovered that marriages between Black men and white women are much more common than those between white men and Black women. In California, for example, the interracial marriage rate of Black grooms was 3.96 percent and of Black brides 1.16 percent.[73]

Since the largest increase in intermarriage has occurred within the Black middle class, many middle-class Black women fear the competition of white women for the scarce number of Black mates. Of course, this fear of the white woman is not a recent one. E. Franklin Frazier observed some years ago an intense fear among women of the Black bourgeoisie of the competition of white women for Black men. He noted that they often attempt to justify their fear by stating that the Black man always has an inferior position in relation to the white woman or that he marries much below his social status. But Frazier speculated that the basis of their fear was that there are not many eligible Black men and that these few should marry Black women.[74]

With the advent of increased interracial dating, the fear of white competition for Black men has been intensified. Nathan and Julia Hare comment that only a minority of Black women are able to take a nonchalant approach to a union of a white woman and a Black man.[75] One Black female leader in New York even circulated a statement that many Black women are alarmed at their suspected abandonment in social intercourse by large numbers of Black men in favor of social intercourse with and, frequently, marriage to white women.[76]

The competition of white women has been particularly disadvantageous for the fair-skinned Black woman. Her light skin has given her a decided advantage over more dark-skinned women in the past. With the white women also vying for Black mates, they realize that Black males of higher status will no longer have to settle for light-skinned Black women when they can get the real thing. As Calvin Hernton says, these women will have to stop "playing white" in the Black community and prove themselves as desirable females.[77]

In all fairness, however, the competition of white women is often invidious. Frequently, the Black woman is competing with American, white beauty standards. Since these standards were created by whites, the white woman more easily meets them. In addition, most beauty aids, such as cosmetics and skin preparations and even hair dryers and curlers, are geared toward white women. The Black woman is handicapped in meeting standards of beauty for which she is not physically equipped.

Probably the best reason against interracial dating and marriage is that it has become a divisive force among Blacks and threatens to disrupt their cultural unity. Nathan Hare put it this way:

> *All over this land, the Black college movement is being torn apart by the "infiltration" of the white female, who, because of centuries on a queenly pedestal, is able to take away from the small supply of Black male students. This pains the Black female student deeply, and she recoils in anger and indignation, refusing to match the sexual favors being offered the Black male student by the "liberated" white female who may find it relatively easy to reject sexual mores along with her rejection of the racial norms of the society which alienates her. The Black male thus is inclined to retort, when concerned and confronted by the Black female student, that she is, unlike his white lover, not "taking*

*care of business." The Black female in her rejection of
the white female, then clings all the more to her
obstinancy and abstinence, feeling that that is about all
that she has left.*[78]

While the proportion of Black men dating interracially is
much higher than Black women, the difference is not so great
when it comes to interracial marriages. While Black women
are deprived of many dates by white women, the vast
majority of Black males are still available to them for
matrimony. Moreover, a great number of Black women marry
white men themselves, perhaps an even larger percentage of
those who date persons of other races than Black males.

In the past, many of the Black men who married white
women were of a higher social status than their wives. In fact
this marrying down was so common that sociologists formu-
lated a theory about it. They hypothesized that the Black
groom was trading his class advantage for the racial caste
advantage of the white bride.[79] But contemporary interracial
marriages are more likely to involve spouses from the same
social class.[80] Furthermore, when intermarriages involved
members of different social classes, there was a pronounced
tendency for Black women to marry up rather than to marry
down.[81]

Consequently, one reason that Black women marry
white men is to increase their station in life. Of course, this is
true of many marriages. One exception, however, are the
Black female entertainers. Because they are closely associated
with white males in the course of their jobs, many of them
form interracial unions. Most of the celebrated cases in recent
years involved famous Black women who married white men
who were not equally famous or wealthy. One such marriage
ended after the woman declared herself broke because of
what she said was exploitation by her white husband.

Various motives have been suggested for Black women
who marry white men. One reason is their hostility toward

Black men. One Black woman wrote a letter to a newspaper editor about her sympathies with the rich and popular Black women entertainers who marry white men. At one point she says: "In those 'Barefoot in the Park' love scenes on TV with Scoey Mitchell and Tracey Reed, I suspected a white person wrote it, because no Black man I've ever known has been that solicitous, tender, gentle, and constantly lovey-dovey in the real life."[82]

Other forces can propel people into an interracial marriage. Some students of the subject assert that uneven sex ratios are a basic cause. Wherever a group in nearness to another group has an imbalance in sex ratio, there is a greater likelihood of intermarriage. If the groups have a relatively well-balanced distribution of the sexes, members will marry more within their own group.[83]

In interracial marriages, one always looks for ulterior motives. It is said that people marry interracially because of rebellion against their parents, sexual curiosity, and other psychological reasons. But many marriages that are homogeneous take place for the same reasons. There are kinds of unconscious variances that attract individuals in many marriages. So, in the words of Joseph Washington, people may marry "their own kind" for the most weird reasons, yet these reasons do not make each marriage suspect. Perhaps, he says, the imputation of ulterior motives to interracial couples says more about the individual making these interpretations and about the society we live in than about the couple who intermarry.[84]

While the motivation for an interracial marriage may, or may not, differ from that of an intraracial marriage, certain problems are unique to this type of marriage. When Joseph Golden studied interracially married couples in Philadelphia in 1949 and 1950, he discovered that the courtship of most of them had been carried on clandestinely and, further, that many of them were isolated from their families following the marriage. The white families, in particular, frequently refused to have anything to do with children who entered into interracial marriages.[85]

In the past, Black families were more inclined to meet with the white person who had married their son or daughter, but they were not too eager to welcome the white spouse until he or she had, in their opinion, exhibited some feeling of understanding and even appreciation of Black people. Among Black peers, however, the sentiment today is clearly against interracial marriages. Many interracial couples are shut out of any social life in Black circles. They are forced to seek friends and social intercourse in all white or other interracial environments.

A more recent study of interracial marriages revealed that the outstanding social problems encountered by the couples centered around such factors as housing, occupation, and relationships with family and peers. Several of the spouses lost their jobs because of intermarriage, while others felt it necessary to conceal their marriages from their employers. The children born of such marriages identified themselves with and were accepted by the Black community. In sum, the couples had to rely upon themselves and their own power of determination to continue the marriage.[86]

A Black woman who marries a white man faces an even greater problem. Traditionally, the society has permitted white men to enter into clandestine sexual liaisons with Black women but never to take one into a marital relationship. Today, a white man who is enchanted with the exotic and sexual qualities of a Black woman may find that marriage is the only avenue of access to those qualities. Once they are married, however, the Black wife lives with the constant fear that when he becomes used to her, she will lose her appeal for him and he will abandon her.

The fact that a woman takes on the status of her husband is especially problematical in Black female-white male marriages. It is the major breadwinner's job that is endangered by such a marriage. Also, she must enter into his world, he does not enter hers. Such a prospect encourages many white men to think twice about intermarrying. Some cannot face it. For example:

> *One of them was Bob. He came to New York to be an actor. Destitute and drunk, he was picked up by June, a twenty-three-year-old Negro girl. When he attempted suicide, she arranged for therapy for him at her expense. Recovered at the age of twenty-six, he started to work and proved to be rather efficient as a salesman. But now that he had money, he tried to break free from June. He couldn't get anywhere, he explained with a Negro wife, and he would lose his job if he lived with a mistress.*[87]

Since interracial marriages constitute less than 2 percent of all the marriages involving Black brides, the problems in such a union are not of great concern to most Black women. Considering the problems large numbers of them encounter with Black men, it is surprising that more of them have not resorted to relationships with white men. But, as they say, Black men are their preference despite the conflicts in the Black woman-Black man relationship.

Merely using the term marriage when we talk of interracial relationships indicates the changes taking place in our society. At least Black women are no longer beyond the pale of respectability, as marriage lifts their status from that of the white man's sexual object or concubine to wife. Yet, the problems of interracial marriage are those of marriage in general multiplied and magnified many times by social opposition.

Summary

Attitudes toward marriage in the Black community are as varied as the people who hold them. Any segment of a population, regardless of common bonds and heritage, is likely to encompass a variety of personalities and values. Since people are individuals with a particular set of values and ideals, marriages have esoteric characteristics. One finds stable and unstable, loving and unloving, violent and unviolent, happy and unhappy, and male-dominated and female-dominated marriages. All of these marriages exist to a greater or lesser extent in the Black community.

Their attitudes on marriage can be as different as those of Chuck Stone and Francis Black. In an open letter to his wife on their fifth wedding anniversary, Chuck Stone wrote: "No five years of my life have been more meaningful or more happy than these past five. Probably the only reason I've approached a reasonable degree of success is because of my wife."[88] But Mrs. Francis Black, a welfare mother with fourteen children and no husband, has this opinion of marriage. She says, "My whole life, my whole childhood, was good up until I got married when I was fourteen."[89]

Both of these attitudes are valid. The problems of marriage are not confined to Blacks. What was once a viable institution because women were a subservient group has lost its value for some people in these days of women's liberation. The stability of marriage was contingent on the woman accepting her place in the home and not creating dissension by challenging the male's prerogatives. In an era where both husband and wife seek to fulfill individual desires, marriage has faltered.

The Black woman marries with the expectation that her husband will be the breadwinner for the family. But, in a society of monopoly capitalism and white racism, the Black male finds it difficult to obtain employment. The jobs that are available to him are seasonal and usually pay less. Often the wife is forced to supplement the family income by taking on a job. She is put in the unnatural position (as defined by her standards of the ideal family) of breadwinner and wife-mother. Moreover, she often has a husband who does not help out with household chores, even if he is unemployed, because he considers housework a woman's job.

Consequently, the resentments of the Black wife accumulate. She becomes bitter and often resentful toward the situation. Under such conditions, she is hardly inclined to be a congenial wife who can relate to her husband's problems. Both husband and wife begin to see themselves in perpetual conflict, with different values and interests. The Black male demands the rights and status of being the head of the household while rejecting the responsibilities. The Black woman may not try to hide the fact that he is not fulfilling her expectations of a husband and a father. Such a situation frequently leads to marital discord, divorce, and female-headed households.

While Afro-American marriages dissolve in large numbers, the marriages of African society remain stable. In considering the problems of Black spouses in American society, Blacks might take more seriously the alternative forms of marriage that their ancestors had. Although the African form of marriage may not be transferable to American shores, it could hardly be worse than the present state of marriage among the Black population in America.

5

The Joy and Pain of Motherhood

I can see no reason why the mother who produces the children should have less say in their upbringing than the man whose role is only that of initiator. And, after the fertilization for nine months, the period of gestation, goes on inside the woman. The period of caring for the youth is taken by the woman. And this role is extremely crucial, in fact it is the most crucial factor in the reproduction of the species and the maintenance of society. But for some reason this most crucial work performed by woman is the basis for woman's position of inferiority. And, if anything was rational this should be the basis for the respect of women.

Kathleen Cleaver
in *The Black Scholar*
December 1971

Once upon a time the institution of motherhood was sacrosanct. A national day honoring mothers was established, politicians extolled the virtues of motherhood, and the bearing of children was a woman's highest aspiration. But times have changed, and motherhood has become one of the victims of changing times. The thrust of women's liberation from the restraints of their biology has singled out motherhood as a tool of sexist oppression. We read such feminist declarations as: "The heart of woman's oppression is her childbearing and childrearing roles."[1] A program for women's liberation includes the option of women to decide whether they will bear children or not. If they choose to have children, these women want their husbands to share in the responsibility of caring for them.[2]

While there are some Black women who have become disenchanted with the maternal role, the pervasiveness and the magnitude of their rejection of motherhood differs significantly from that of white women. In part, they differ because of the unique position they hold as caretakers of the Black race. To understand the reasons why this is so, we must again look to the past.

The Traditions of Mothering

Although many people assume that motherhood took on its importance for Black women during the slave era, there are indications that the maternal role was also emphasized strongly by African women. The available historical evidence reveals that antedating the slave experience, Black women in Africa had an unbreakable bond with their children. The universal testimony of travelers and missionaries was that the African mother's love for her children was unsurpassed in any part of the world.[3] Other examples of the Black woman's sacrifice for her children could be found in East Africa where mothers offered themselves to slave traders in exchange for their sons. Hottentot women were known to refuse food during famines until their children had eaten.[4]

The African social structure patterned the mother's attitude toward her child. Tribal customs emphasized the importance of the maternal role in the social organization of the group. Certain cultural artifacts, such as art, conveyed the place of motherhood in tribal life. In Waja, Nigeria, the fertility doll and other child-bearing figurines were employed during initiation ceremonies (rituals used to confer adulthood on the boys and girls in the tribe) to insure that the women would be capable of bearing children. It was a symbol of the continuity of life. Among the Yoruba of Nigeria, a pair of twin figurines were carved when twins were born to African mothers. It was believed that twins shared a common soul.[5]

The Ashanti tribe of Ghana (located in West Africa where most slaves came from) views the ties between mother and child as the keystone of all social relationships. A woman who is childless is pitied and feels disgraced. The Ashanti mother looks upon her relationship with her child as an absolutely binding moral relationship. No amount of labor or self-sacrifice was too great for the sake of her children. It is mainly to provide them with food, clothing, and schooling that she works so hard, importunes her husband, and jealously watches her brother to insure that he carries out his duties of legal guardian (the father has no legal right over or to his children) faithfully.[6]

An Ashanti woman expects obedience and respect as well as affection from her children. The children always speak to or address her as mother. Any demonstration of disrespect toward one's mother is akin to blasphemy. One Ashanti saying is that throughout the life of a woman her primary attachment is to her mother who will always serve as her benefactor and protector. Also, a man's foremost ambition is to earn enough money to build a house for his mother. The Ashanti woman's greatest aspiration is to achieve the high dignity of living as a mistress in her own home, with her children and her daughter's children.[7]

In African societies children are symbols of the continuity of life. They are carefully protected by the extended family system of most African tribes. During their formative years, children enjoy an idyllic life. They begin to learn their role requirements and responsibilities to the tribe. Until they reach the ages of nine or ten, children have no responsibilities. After that time they begin to take on the responsibilities of their sex role. The boys will build small huts and hunt fierce game. Girls play house and care for babies (often a younger sister). Around the age of fifteen, the child is considered an adult and will soon begin a family.[8]

Each of the examples represents the strong maternalistic feelings African women held toward children before pregnancy, during pregnancy, and after birth. Moreover, African society placed a high esteem on the mother's role as child bearer and guardian of the tribal legacy.[9] The Black mother's removal to the shores of the New World affected her ability to be a mother and to exact the initial respect and dependence of her child. But her transplantation from Africa to the Americas did not eliminate any of the fundamental impulses and instinctive maternal feelings she had toward her child. None of the brutalities suffered, the humiliation encountered, the destruction of her cultural mores altered in any basic way the mother-child relationship.

The Slave Mother

When she arrived on this continent in chains, there was no ceremony to commemorate her role as a mother. Her task was primarily to labor in the fields of the plantation with the men. Producing children was important only in that they constituted future slaves or capital for the slave-holding class. Hence, the development of maternal feelings were dependent largely on physiological and emotional responses of mother to child.

The conditions for a positive mother-child relationship were notably absent under slavery. First, in bearing the child the slave mother had to undergo the ordeal of pregnancy and childbirth while performing hard labor in the fields. As soon as possible after childbirth, the mother was compelled to return to the fields, frequently taking her unweaned child with her.[10] Since the slave mother was primarily a full-time laborer for her owner, and only incidentally a mother, she spent only a small portion of her time in the house.[11]

The slave mother's burden began in childbearing. Other slave women served as midwives for the delivery of her child. The slaveowners believed that slave women needed very little care during this period, which may partly account for the high rate of infant mortality. After bearing her child, the slave mother was unable to care for it because of her obligations as a worker.[12] Thus the slave child, in contrast to his African counterpart, had no protected childhood.

The children of slave mothers had to bear with the absence of their parent(s). A former slave child described his experience:

> *I began to feel another evil of slavery. I mean the absence of parental care and attention. My parents were not able to give any attention to their children during the day. I often suffered much from hunger and other similar causes. To estimate the sad state of a slave child, you must look upon it as a helpless human being thrown upon the world without the benefit of its natural guardians.*[13]

Lack of attention from his parents was not the only misfortune of a slave child. Often he was denied any childhood at all. Like his parents he was pressed into service in the fields as early as age seven. By the time he reached puberty, he was taken away from his mother and sold on the auction block. Thus, while white children were enjoying the carefree times of adolescence, Black children were thrust into adulthood and the continuation of their involuntary servitude.[14]

It was this practice of selling away their children that provoked the most courageous acts of Black mothers. There were numerous cases of slave mothers killing their children to prevent their sale. B. A. Botkin cites the case of one slave mother who was distraught at the prospect of having her fourth child sold away from her. She declared, "I just decided I'm not going to let old master sell this baby, he just ain't going to do it . . . she got up and give it something out of a bottle and pretty soon it was dead."[15]

The heroic acts of the slave mother are legendary. Frederick Douglass, the great abolitionist, recounts how his mother walked twelve miles to see him and had to return the same distance before the morning sunrise.[16] Even the children of the slavemaster received her devotion. The slave woman attended her mistress during pregnancy and took care of the infant as soon as it was born. Frequently she, in place of the mother, weaned the child. If the child was female, the slave was never separated from her until she was an adult.[17]

Slave mothers seized upon any opportunity they had to be with their children and to give them love and affection. After a hard day's labor in the field, they could find warmth and sympathy among their children and their kinsmen. It was in this environment that the slave mother could vent her tender feelings and kindly impulses. Booker T. Washington writes: "One of my earliest recollections is that of my mother cooking chicken late at nite and awakening her children for the purpose of feeding them."[18]

The effects of her past experiences in Africa undoubtedly play a part in the enactment of the Black woman's maternal role. Melville Herskovits saw the centrality of the mother as an African vestige, typical of the polygynous marriage in which every woman, with her offspring, formed a separate unit.[19] The Herskovits theory is not as widely accepted today as that of Frazier who ascribed to the institution of slavery the strongest influence on the mother-child relationship.[20]

One influence of slavery was that the slave father's role was institutionally obliterated. The practice of using male slaves as breeding instruments meant that their role was biological, not sociological or economic. The slave father, if present, had little authority. His function was fieldwork and service. The mother named the children and had sole responsibility for their care. Many times the father's name was not indicated on plantation birth records; the children were listed as belonging to the mother. Whatever authority the mother did not have belonged to the slavemaster.[21]

Consequently, the slave mother was the most consistent person in the young child's life. Within this environment she played a strategic role. Due to the inability of the slave father to play a sustained role in the life of his family, the mother was more often left with the ongoing care of the children. This also meant that Black women were expected to serve the vital function of providers for their families in the absence of a consistent husband-father figure.[22]

Thus all the child's familial ties were traced to the mother. Since many slaves never knew their fathers, the mother role took on a stronger image. Even slavemasters respected the bond between the mother and her younger children because of her strong attachment to them and the dependence of the child upon her for survival. Although motherhood was clothed in scant dignity due to the vicissitudes of slavery, the slave mother represented the highest ideals of motherhood in any epoch or culture.[23]

After the demise of slavery, Black women were still faced with the challenges of motherhood. The cumulative effects of slavery had left the Black family in disarray. Fathers had been sold away from their families, paternity was sometimes unknown, and countless numbers of Black children had white slavemasters as unacknowledged fathers. These factors, along with the problems of Reconstruction, left many Black mothers with unilateral responsibility for the care of their children.

Black mothers met their maternal responsibilities faithfully. Often a household was composed of two generations of female adults and their children. During the immediate postslavery period, many of these extended matricentric families were located in the rural South. They tilled the land and provided subsistence for themselves and their children. Some Black men, due to their lack of socialization into the paternal role, failed to take any responsibility for their children. Many others were forced to travel from town to town seeking work and could not stay with their families.

The extended matricentric family may have been a minority of all families. Since many Blacks did not get legally married, there are no accurate records that tell us how many Black families had the father present. At least one historian estimates that over 70 percent of Black women were married in the latter part of the nineteenth century and the father was present.[24] However, the female-headed households were functional units, as they managed to sustain themselves under the harshest of conditions.

One anthropologist studied the conditions of life in the Black community. She reported that:

> Even where husband and wife share responsibility for maintaining and directing the family, the woman is likely to contribute the larger share of the income and to assume the larger share of the family responsibility. The economic disparity is most evident in town, where employment is so much more available to the women than to the men. The matriarchal nature of the family obtains equally on the plantations. In many cases the woman is the sole breadwinner. Often, there is no man in the household at all.[25]

In a number of instances she found elderly women in their seventies living with their middle-aged daughters, with or without children, and frequently without husbands. These women composed one household with the elder woman in charge. According to Hortense Powdermaker, these female-centered households have been perpetuated by the legacy of slavery, and the widespread unemployment of Black men has helped to sustain it.[26]

Although she faced problems maintaining her family in the rural South, the Black woman supposedly encountered greater and different problems when she moved to the city. Because of the different environment, the reduced effectiveness of kinship ties, and her greater economic dependency on public institutions, she lost control of her children. Many Black women had to seek work outside the home, leaving their children without parental supervision. The children in some of these families filled the ranks of juvenile delinquents. Women who did not work were forced to turn to public assistance agencies to help support their families.[27]

We shall look at some of these factors that influence the Black mother-child relationship later. A sequential analysis of Black motherhood will first consider the process of child-bearing itself.

Childbearing

From an estimated sixty persons in 1630, the Black population has expanded to over twenty-three million in 1969. By the time of the American revolution in 1776, there were almost 750,000 Blacks in this country, about 20 percent of the population at that time. The Black fertility rate before the revolutionary period can only be estimated because no census of Blacks was taken until 1820.[28]

Among the more interesting historical facts about Black fertility is that Black women who bore children in the decade before the Civil War had an average of almost seven children. Less than 10 percent had no children and more than 30 percent had ten or more children. It was almost biologically impossible for Black women to produce more children during this period. In the period between the Civil War and the years of the depression, the Black birthrate was reduced by one-half and the average family size reduced by about four children.[29]

Around 1940 there was a large increase in the Black population. During the forties the Black birthrate was twice that of the thirties. Between 1950 and 1960, the Black fertility rate increased at a rate of 2 percent each year. Around 1961 the Black birthrate went into a state of decline (as did the white birthrate). In 1968 birthrates reached their lowest level in the past twenty-five years. During the sixties the annual birthrates for Black and white women declined at about the same rate.[30]

The Black birthrate is not a monolithic phenomenon. Regional, rural-urban, and social class factors strongly influence Black fertility rates. In 1967, Black women who lived in the South had higher fertility rates than those who resided in the North. Black women in rural areas have more children than those in urban areas. These same differences in fertility can be found among white women.[31]

One of the most significant variances in Black fertility rates is that of social class. In fact, almost all differences in Black and white total fertility can be accounted for by differences in social class membership. Various studies of postwar trends in birthrates show that when various measures of socioeconomic status are held constant, Black-white differences in fertility are either reduced very significantly, eliminated entirely, or, in some cases, even reversed.[32] For example, not only do college educated Black women have a lower fertility rate than lesser educated Black women, but they also have a lower fertility rate than college educated white women.[33]

The fertility differential between Black women of different educational levels is quite striking. While the high fertility of poorly educated Black women is understandable, the low fertility of college educated Black women is not. This is not a recent trend. In 1937 Frazier studied 114 Black faculty members at Howard University. He found that they had come from families averaging 5.1 children but they had an average of 0.8 children.[34]   Another study of Black college educated women in 1956 revealed that 41 percent of the married women in this group were childless.[35]

In a recent investigation of the factors associated with the low fertility rate of Black college educated women, Clyde Kiser and Myrna Frank found that among married women twenty-five years of age and over the fertility rate of Black women surpassed that of white women except at upper socioeconomic levels.[36]

The 1960 census probed for the reasons behind the fertility rate differential between Black and white college educated women. For some unexplained reason the delay in marriage occasioned by college attendance tended to lower the fertility of Black women more than white women. The higher divorce rate of Black women contributed slightly to the difference. With the husband absent, there are reduced probabilities for childbearing among middle-class Black women. A more significant factor was the larger proportion of college educated Black women in the labor force. Educated Black women may reject the role of mother because they feel the financial need to participate in a remunerative occupation.[37]

In general, however, the Black birthrate is much higher than the white birthrate. If 1960 birthrates are used to project future population, the amount of time needed to double the Black population is thirty years as compared to fifty years for whites. The 1970 Census shows an observed rate of 3,649 children per 1,000 Black women, 35-44 years old, compared to a rate of 2,923 for their white counterpart.[38]   Birthrates in the sixties, as we mentioned before, show a leveling off pattern in racial differences in fertility, resulting from decreases in both Black and white fertility.

Other factors serve to reduce the Black birthrate that are not so influential on the white birthrate. Despite the cultural belief that white couples have a higher amount of childlessness than Black couples, the percentage of childless couples is much higher among Blacks. Among Black women born after 1925, over 13 percent have never borne children compared to 8 percent of all ever married white women. The Black childlessness rates are higher than the white ones even when age, husband's education, and age at marriage are controlled.[39]

The Black birthrate is also reduced by the greater infant mortality rate in this group. The infant mortality rate for Blacks is about twice as high as for whites. More Black babies (2.4 percent) less than one month old died than month-old white babies (1.5 percent). In the first year after birth, 1.2 percent of Black infants die compared with 0.5 percent of white infants.[40] While these figures are for 1967, the average rate of Black infant mortality in 1967 was attained by whites in the early thirties.[41] One has to look to underdeveloped countries in Asia, Africa, and Latin America to find comparable rates of infant mortality. Of course, the United States ranks no higher than eleventh among all nations in infant mortality rates.[42]

The high rate of infant deaths among Blacks can only be attributed to the racist conditions under which Blacks are compelled to live. Most infant mortality is traceable to premature births among Black women. While other factors enter into it, the primary reason for this is the poor state of health of Black mothers due to their low incomes, resulting in a poor diet and inadequate prenatal care. Moreover, in 1967, about three times as many Black women died in childbirth as did white women.[43]

Birth Control or Genocide

Probably no aspect of Black motherhood is more controversial than the issue of birth control for Black women. No issue seems to have polarized Blacks as much, or to be as complex, as this one. To briefly state the matter, birth control was initially urged for the Black population by such race leaders as W. E. B. Du Bois and Martin Luther King. They believed that by using birth control, Blacks could improve their lot and better care for their children. In more recent days some Black leaders have viewed Black birth control as a white genocidal plot designed to keep Blacks weak and dependent, if not eliminate them entirely. The counterresponse to this has come from Black women, some of whom are involved in the women's liberation movement. They declared that women should have the right to control their own bodies and that they (women) reserve the right to have children or not.

Historically, birth control has been an important issue to the Black community. In 1933, Frazier speculated that birth control use among Blacks would only decrease the number of educated Blacks.[44] He was probably thinking of the low fertility of highly educated Blacks, a fertility rate so low that they failed to replace themselves. On the other hand, W. E. B. Du Bois argued that birth control was necessary so that Black youth could marry, have companionship and natural health, and yet postpone children until they were capable of taking care of them.[45]

Some of the following comments indicate the concern of Blacks about this issue:

> *Blacks are crying out for jobs and education and the government is pushing the pill. They want jobs and they get the pill.*[46]
>
> *A national population policy must demonstrate that it is more concerned about the health and wealth of Black people than it is about the number of children they have.*[47]
>
> *The government has been promoting family planning for the poor at the expense of maternal and child health services.*[48]

> *For us to speak in favor of birth control for Afro-Americans would be comparable to speaking in favor of genocide. If Black people are to survive, one of our best guarantees would be a more vigorous effort on our part to reproduce our own.*[49]

The charge of genocide has some basis in the historical experiences of other minority groups. The native Indian population was reduced from 750,000 to 250,000 in the span of two hundred years through systematic annihilation by white settlers. In the past, birth control was used to considerably reduce the Eskimo and Indian populations.[50]

Blacks are concerned about birth control because historically it has been imposed on them and has not been a matter of free choice. Various states have attempted to force Black women on welfare to accept sterilization as a condition to continuing to receive welfare benefits. Welfare workers and medical personnel are known to "encourage" Black women to use contraceptives, even after the first child. In a recent speech, Andrew Billingsley chided the Planned Parenthood Organization for concentrating so much of its population control efforts on the Black community, which is only 15 percent of the population. Only through Black community control and comprehensive health care, he said, would birth control programs have any benefit for Blacks.[51]

Some Blacks simply distrust the use of the term birth control. Malcolm X, for instance, believed that Blacks did not need to be controlled. He would accept the term family planning.[52] Comedian Dick Gregory states that he never trusted anything white folks tried to give Blacks with the word "control" in it. He says: "Anything good with the word control in it, white folks don't want us to have. As soon as we started talking about community control, white folks went crazy." Gregory's personal answer to Black genocide is eight Black children.[53]

Curiously enough, most of these Black spokesmen have

been men. How do Black women feel about the subject? When Joyce Ladner questioned her lower-class Black females on the subject of contraception, they expressed moral opposition to using contraceptive methods. It was their belief, supported by years of tradition, that nothing should be done to prevent the birth of a child except abstinence from sexual involvement. Some of them believed that contraceptives could cause deformity and stillbirths. Others opposed it because of their religious beliefs.[54]

One study was specifically designed to elicit Black beliefs about family planning practices and a race genocide conspiracy against Black Americans. The total sample was 160 households, and females composed 66 percent of the subjects. Over one-third of this group rejected all birth control methods, 71 percent rejected abortion, and 90 percent sterilization. Also, 62 percent agreed that birth control clinics operated by Blacks in Black neighborhoods would be more acceptable to Blacks than if operated by whites. The investigators concluded that there was a relationship between fears of racial genocide and the use of family planning methods.[55]

The unity of Black opposition to birth control is broken by the words of Toni Cade. She says:

> *It is a noble thing, the rearing of warriors for the revolution. I can find no fault with the idea. I do find fault with the notion that dumping the pill is the way to do it. You don't prepare yourself for the raising of super-people by making yourself vulnerable—chance fertilization, chance support, chance tomorrow—nor by being celibate until you run across the right stock to breed with. You prepare yourself by being healthy and confident, by having options that give you confidence, by getting yourself together enough to attract a together cat whose notions of fatherhood rise above the Disney caliber of man-in-the-world and woman-in-the-home, by being committed to a new consciousness, by being*

intellectually and spiritually and financially self-sufficient to do the thing right. You prepare youself by being in control of yourself. The pill gives the woman, as well as the man, some control, simple as that.[56]

This response is mild, and reasoned, in comparison to that of one Linda Larue. She claims that many Black children stand abandoned in orphanages while Black male spokesmen rhetorically denounce birth control as a conspiracy of whites to halt the growth of the Black population. She wants to know why there are not more revolutionary couples adopting Black children. Her solution is to declare a five year moratorium on Black births until every Black baby in an American orphanage is adopted by one or more Black parents. Then, Blacks would really have a valid reason for continuing to give birth.[57]

Linda Larue's response descends to the level of rhetoric. Few children, Black or white, languish in orphanges today. Homeless children, if not adopted, are usually placed in foster homes. Moreover, the truth is that thousands of financially successful Blacks have adopted children. Because white adoption agencies in the past were not sensitive to the needs of Black parents, Blacks have devised an informal system for adopting children. Relatives simply take in abandoned and dependent children. There is no legal process to go through, just the desire to take care of helpless children.

For one reason or another there are Black women who do not want an unlimited number of children. Therefore, they do use some means to either prevent conception or, failing to do that, to abort the unwanted child. We might call them the reluctant mothers.

The Reluctant Mothers

Despite the public rhetoric about birth control for Blacks being a white conspiracy to wipe out the Black population, the Black woman has increasingly used contraception to prevent an unwanted child. The National Fertility Study of 1965 reported that 78 percent of Blacks and 80 percent of white women living in cities had used contraception of some type. Among younger Blacks (under thirty years of age) more of them (87 percent) have actually employed some method of contraception than whites (83 percent). Indeed, young Blacks who reside in large Northern states have almost universally accepted birth control in comparison to their white counterparts. Ninety-two percent of young Blacks under thirty have tried some form of contraception in comparison to seventy-nine percent of comparable whites.[58]

These rather startling figures represent certain changes taking place among the Black population. In the decade of the sixties, many Blacks moved from the rural South to the cities of the North (and South). Many of them are upwardly mobile and trying to improve their class position. Consequently, it is among these Blacks that birth control has been almost universally adopted as a result of their new life style and economic position. Within the rural and lower-class group there continues to be opposition to birth control. In rural areas only 59 percent of the Black poor compared to 72 percent of the white poor have ever tried any form of contraception.[59]

Looking at the proportion of Blacks that are currently using birth control methods, we find that among Black couples under forty-five, about 50 percent are currently using contraceptives in comparison to 57 percent of white couples. In the age group under thirty there are almost no racial differences—58 percent of Blacks are presently involved in birth control in comparison to 60 percent of whites.[60]

When we use the term birth control, it applies to both men and women. But in the Black community women are almost exclusively responsible for preventing a pregnancy. Black men are quite frank in stating that they do not care

how effective the condom is, they are not willing to use it.[61]
The reasons they give are that condoms are too expensive,
they detract from the pleasure of sexual intercourse, and the
woman is supposed to accommodate her man.

Further evidence for the Black male's refusal to participate in family planning is revealed in the figures on
sterilization. Although either the male or female can be
sterilized to prevent pregnancies, the operation is less
complicated for the man. But, while white couples participate about equally in sterlization, among Black couples the
man is sterilized in only a tiny percentage of such operations.
It appears that many Blacks believe that such an operation
might affect a man's ability to have intercourse. Thus, the
Black woman usually volunteers for a tubal ligation.[62]

Exceptions to this custom happened recently in Hous-
ton, Texas. The Black men in that city flocked to the Ben
Taub vasectomy free clinic to be sterilized. One twenty-nine-
year-old father of eight children said that he had fathered
enough children and that if he and his wife had any more,
they would be unable to make it. This particular clinic
provided psychologists and social workers who talked to both
the husband and wife. They explained to the couple that
although the man would be sterile following the operation,
he could still engage in normal sexual relations.

When the Black woman is responsible for using a
contraceptive method, she usually selects the pill. But the
second most popular method is the comparatively ineffective
douche. Even younger Black women use this method,
although not to the same extent as older Black women. Black
women have a greater preference for the intrauterine device
than white women. Because there are few Catholics in the
Black population, one finds that the rhythm method is less
popular among Black women.[63]

In comparison to white women, however, Black women
are notably less effective in the use of contraceptive
techniques. In one particular year over half the Black women

using some form of contraception failed to be protected and became pregnant. Among whites about one-third became pregnant while using contraception. This may partly be attributed to the greater use of ineffective methods such as the douche among Black women.[64] Rainwater also found that among lower-class Blacks a high degree of conjugal role segregation, i.e., husband and wife participating in separate activities, tended to discourage communication between married couples that could promote more effective contraceptive practice.[65]

When contraception attempts fail and the woman becomes pregnant, abortion is another alternative. In an earlier study we cited it was reported that a large majority of Blacks opposed abortion as a means of terminating pregnancy. Ladner noted that the same negative attitudes that Black women hold toward contraception were even stronger in regard to abortion. The lower-class Black women in her study believed that once a woman had conceived, the inborn fetus was an organic being that should be preserved. They placed a strong value on life, particularly that of the young and "innocent" child. Health reasons were the only significant factors that would make an abortion morally justifiable.[66]

One of the earlier studies of pregnancy, birth, and abortion by the Kinsey Institute for Sex Research disclosed that few premarital conceptions among lower-class Black females were aborted. However, among middle-class Black females, a vast majority of their premarital conceptions were terminated by induced abortion. Among white college girls there was an even higher rate of induced abortions.[67]

Until recently, abortions were against the law in all states. But this did not prevent many women from obtaining abortions. Before some of the state abortion laws were abolished or liberalized, it was estimated that as many as a million illegal abortions were performed on pregnant women each year. A high percentage of women who had abortions were white and middle class. The cost of these illegal operations was often prohibitive for Black women.

The problems involved in obtaining an abortion did not dissuade many Black women. For them the choice was very clear, abortion was very cheap compared with the price a woman pays watching the slow destruction of her child. In the ghetto to be little, to be economically unviable, and to be definitely unarmed is to be valueless. The pregnant Black woman looks ahead to that living death that she and her child face if it enters the world. It is a reality that only women must face.

Hence, the pregnant Black woman often has the heartbeat within her stilled. Often she has to rely on incompetent and unconcerned butchers. In New York, before the law permitting abortions was passed, Black and Puerto Rican women suffered ten times the maternal death rate of white women, mostly due to the dangers inherent in illegal abortions. In fact 80 percent of the women in New York who died from illegal botched abortions were Black or Puerto Rican.[68]

After abortions were legalized in New York, about one-half of the abortions were performed on Black and Puerto Rican women. A nationwide study prepared by the Population Council reported that 24 percent of the women who seek legal abortions are Black.[69] The publicly stated attitudes by Black women are also beginning to change. When the *Michigan Chronicle* asked a dozen Black women if they favored the reform of laws banning abortion, only one was against legalized abortions and one was in favor of it only for the poor.[70]

The case for legalized abortions for Black women is fairly clear. They are more likely to incur an unwanted pregnancy. A number of studies show that many Black women have more children than they desire. While the average number of children desired by Black women is 2.6, they expect to have an average of 4.2 children. Thus, they normally expect to be unable to control their fertility. Abortion becomes the only viable way to determine the size of their families.[71]

Some Black leaders call abortions a form of genocide, a device to limit the Black population.[72] Such a charge ignores the plight of many Black women who, when denied a legal abortion, will be driven into the hands of quacks whose ministrations may result in death. As one Black woman states: "This concept of revolutionaries rather than revolution is appropriate in a society where old people do the voting and the youngsters do the fighting and dying . . . breeding revolutionaries is not too far removed from a cultural past where Black women were encouraged to be breeding machines for their slavemasters."[73]

Many Black women have organized groups to campaign for the repeal of abortion laws. Throughout the country they have joined with white women's groups to protest against laws prohibiting abortion. The basic issue, they say, is not whether abortions are a genocidal plot but the Black woman's right to control her own body, to decide for herself whether or not she wants to bear children, when, and how many. To Black men concerned with the welfare of their women, such a right should be considered an inalienable part of the Black liberation struggle.

The Parent-Child Relationship

Although having children has never been as simple for Black women as for white women, children have traditionally been regarded as a value in themselves, whether they were economic assets or liabilities. The attitude of Black women toward motherhood may have its roots in Black history when the social status and value of slave women largely depended on their breeding capacity. Charles Johnson observed that among plantation Blacks the assertion that a woman could not have children constituted a slur.[74] Becoming a mother in

America today is still of great importance to the Black woman, especially the lower-class Black female.

While the importance Black women attach to motherhood may derive from the set of traditions which Blacks have retained from precolonial Africa, there are other factors that enter into the emphasis on the maternal role. One factor appears to be their dissatisfaction with the role of wife. Robert Bell found that Black women believed the role of mother to be of high significance to them. Furthermore, they saw marriage as potentially dangerous because of the possibility that economic resources that could be used for taking care of their children might be squandered by the male. The role of mother was much more important to them than the role of wife.[75]

Hence, the Black woman's dissatisfaction with the role of wife is one element in the importance she attaches to her maternal role. Also, few Black women have the choice, or desire, to become career women. There is little artistic or creative ability involved in housework and other menial tasks that Black women have traditionally been relegated to. Thus, there is only the role of mother for many of them to relate to. Perhaps this accounts, in part, for the greater interest in their maternal role performance.

Black women may be the only group that ever had to raise children and support them too. Their need to work outside the home can create special problems in the socialization of the Black child, especially in light of the fact that Black husbands do not help their wives with household tasks that often.[76] According to some studies, lower-class Black children are trained to be of little bother to their parents and are expected to mature early. These children that are freed earlier for productive activity are also liberated from parental control. Hence, much of their socialization takes place within the peer group rather than the family environment.[77]

Frequently, Black children are taken care of by older

women who are unable to find other work. Consequently, the children are separated from other children because these women are unable to take care of more than one or two children at a time. The mother has to hurry home to relieve the older woman of her child. Child care facilities are rare in the Black community and few people are qualified to teach the child in a progressive manner.

The child rearing practices of lower-class Black mothers are often in conflict with contemporary theories about fostering the positive personality development of the growing child. One reason for this is that Black mothers are exposed less than white mothers to the literature on child rearing. Since there were few Black women in the middle class a generation ago, the middle-class modes of child rearing are practically unknown to recent Black entrants into the middle-class group. Thus, the Black woman frequently raises her child in the same manner as her mother or grand-mother.[78]

One example of lower-class socialization techniques is the practice of expecting children to be obedient because they have been told to behave in a certain way by their mother. In middle-class families children are more likely to receive explanations from the mother about why they are expected to behave in a certain way. In the lower-class setting, the motivation for child obedience derives from the authority of the role of parent.[79] The following case is typical of the assumption of many Black mothers that obviously their children will obey them because they are the heads of the household and they expect obedience:

> *One night Warren stayed out later than he should have and I made him stay in his room for a week and wouldn't permit the other children to even talk to him. Till today he hates that kind of punishment. Once when my father was here he marveled at how I was able to handle these boys and he wanted to know how I*

managed to make them stay in their room. I said, "I don't make them, I'm their mother."[80]

Since the Black mother often works and has more children than the average middle-class white mother, she has little time to be the careful and provident mother. She is often tired and irritable which explains her impatience and insistence on immediate obedience. Furthermore, the Black mother has little authority in the environment in which she operates. There is, consequently, a strong temptation for her to exercise authority in the only place she can, namely in the home.

One unique problem the lower-class Black mother encounters is that the child is subject to her discipline but she often cannot give him any rewards except her unbounded love and devotion. She cannot offer the more effective status rewards to her children because their educational and social opportunities are circumscribed by a racist social order and there are few available rewards in the society to which the lower-class child has access. Hence, the child is expected to renounce direct impulse gratification without the rewards given middle-class children for their obedience and conformity.[81]

It is usually the mother who disciplines the child, although in the extended family the source of discipline often alternates from mother to father, to aunt, to grandmother, to uncle, or to an older child. Regardless of the disciplinarian's identity, the typical punishment is physical not verbal. Confining a child to his room or stripping him of his play privileges may be employed, but whipping is inevitable, no matter what other forms of punishment the child may be subject to.[82]

The Black father-child relationship is not a close one as a rule. The role of the father is strongly contingent on his ability to earn a living and his willingness to share that living with his family. Fatherhood, then, is a precarious role in light of all the negative forces in this society that affect the Black man's ability to fulfill this position.[83] Children often do not understand the reasons why their fathers cannot provide adequately for them. One example is this young girl who hates her father and her home as well. She says: "Just looks like I oughta be getting a little more out of life than I do. ... These clothes, they're all rags. I don't ask for any good clothes since my mother can't give them to me. What's the use asking her. It worries her too."[84]

There are many Black fathers who have excellent relationships with their children. The home and family constitute their major interests and they represent the middle-class image of the ideal father. But, paradoxically, the Black father who most accurately conforms to the middle-class norm of desirable fatherly behavior may be doing his children a disservice by teaching the child middle-class values and skills. Ignoring the coping mechanisms needed in the ghetto, he handicaps his child who, unable to move out of the ghetto, becomes marginal to both worlds, unable to participate in either.[85]

Some of the socialization practices of Black parents are common to all lower-class groups and are traceable to the tensions and stresses associated with conditions of poverty. As the most important socializing agent, the Black mother must insure that the child receives material and emotional support and that he is encouraged to learn the educational and job skills necessary for success in the world. But, in a society where the cards are stacked against him, her task is a formidable one.

Yet, Black mothers for generations have raised their children effectively, in spite of many hardships they had to endure. While their child-rearing practices may be seen as undesirable, the love they have for their children buttresses much of their effect. Actually, Black mothers raise their children with a greater ease than white mothers. Black children are seldom inculcated with the neurotic traits of middle-class white children and they escape the status anxieties associated with some rigid middle-class child-rearing practices. It has been observed that neglect and abuse of children on welfare are more frequent among whites than Blacks and that Black mothers are more accepting of retarded children than white mothers.[86]

There are, of course, class variations in the Black community in child-rearing practices. Over twenty-five years ago a pair of researchers discovered that differences in child-rearing practices between middle- and lower-class Black mothers were similar to those between middle-class and lower-class white mothers. Besides the social class differences they found that Black mothers are more permissive than white mothers in the feeding and weaning of their children but are much more rigorous than white mothers in toilet training.[87]

The conditions of their environment create other salient differences between lower- and middle-class Black mothers. As with white middle-class mothers, the middle-class Black mother exerts a powerful and continuous pressure on her child to study, to repress aggression at school, to inhibit sexual impulses, and to avoid lower-class playmates. She sets before her child the goals of a high school or college diploma, a skilled or white collar job, and a good marriage.[88]

In the middle-class group, the woman usually has the help of her husband in the socialization of their children. One study found that Black middle-class husbands participate more in the child care area than do white middle-class husbands.[89] Within middle-class Black families, supervision of the child's activities is primarily the responsibility of the mother but violations of discipline are punished by the father. Physical punishment is rather infrequent. A child is usually disciplined by being confined to his room, compelled to miss his class meetings, or deprived of some recreational activity.[90]

The socialization techniques of the Black middle-class mother are appropriate for her class. Children are taught pride in their class as the highest in Black culture. The techniques of training that middle-class Black mothers use are designed to inculcate in the child a fear of the loss of status if he is not a good child. Often, the anxiety emerging from this type of training is adequate enough to maintain his middle-class habits.[91]

While the child-rearing practices of Black mothers vary according to their class position, this reflects the conditions of life they face. Lower-class Black mothers must prepare their children for the harsh vicissitudes of ghetto life. The middle-class Black mother requires her children to take on those values and habits necessary for achieving the goals of education and material success.

Growing Up Black

When a child is born to a Black woman, this is the high point of her life. Motherhood represents maturity and the fulfillment of one's function as a woman. The newborn baby is received into a household of warmth, humor, and love, whether it is a boy or girl. If the baby is a girl, she is cared for by a host of people who are interested in and enthusiastic toward her. She is usually the center of attention of the entire family. An older sibling may attend to her needs, and if the mother is young, the major caretaker may be the grandmother.[92]

The grandmother is frequently an important figure in the Black child's life. In West Africa, for example, the relationship between a child and his grandparents was the most revered in tribal society. The grandmothers on both sides were the most honored of all the relatives on either side of the family. Among the Yoruba, it was the duty and privilege of grandparents to name newborn children. Grandparents were a rich source of family history, folklore, proverbs and other traditional lore. They were believed to be living links with the past.[93]

A Black child is much more likely to have a grand-mother in the same household with her. In many cases the grandmother is more likely to take children into her own household than to be taken into the household of younger kinfolk. When a grandmother lives with one of her children, it is more likely to be a daughter than a son. These women play important roles in many Black families such as babysit-ting with grandchildren and providing warm affection for them.[94] Frazier's classic description of the Black grand-mother still is valid: The guardian of the generations.[95]

Young Black females are usually socialized in different ways than the males. Probably one of the most salient differences is in their sexual education. Since some Black mothers realize that the avenue to sexual gratification will be open for their children, they instruct them early in matters of pregnancy and "social" diseases. Dollard relates the case of one Black woman who reported:

> That her mother was not strict or petty with her, but more like a sister. When she was eleven, her mother told her the facts of life in order to avoid what her mother had gotten into. Her mother had not been crabby with her about going out with boys, but warned her for her own good; if she got into trouble after that, it was her own affair.[96]

It is alleged that Black girls are socialized to be more independent, disciplined, and puritanical than Black boys. There is some evidence that there are fewer social conform-ists among Black females at a fairly early age.[97] One reason for this differential socialization is that this pattern has emerged out of the belief that Black men are basically worthless and irresponsible and consequently less is expected of them. The other side of this theory is that Black women are morally and intellectually superior to Black men, and hence one can expect more from them.

A more plausible reason historically has been the Black

mother's fear for the safety of her son. The Black male with too much ambition and too much temper would have had his life shortened if he acted too aggressively towards whites. Thus, the Black mother had to teach her sons to be docile, obedient, and compliant. The white society would tolerate the independence of Black women but not that of Black men. Today, the Black mother teaches her child pride in his race and culture and defiance toward white racism.

The Black child is more fully integrated into the total family structure than the same-age white children. Rainwater noted that Black children are allowed to view most adult-centered activities although they may be disciplined if their behavior becomes too distracting.[98] It is common for Black children to participate fully in family activities at a very early age. The children are encouraged to join the adults in dancing (and sometimes drinking). What whites call the natural rhythm of Blacks actually derives from the Black child's early socialization into Black dancing patterns.

As Black children enter the grade school years, they leave the center of parental attention. When they enter school they are liberated from many of the household responsibilities that older children have. The school-age child grows up with a great degree of freedom, influenced mainly by his peers and siblings. Between the ages of six and ten, children are the least trouble to their parents. During this period, the child begins to question his parents' teachings and controls and commences to find the outside world more stimulating than his home environment.[99]

The school-age child gradually becomes more involved with his peers, and the parents define his behavior as "good" or "bad" on the basis of whether he stays out of trouble. Because there are so many possibilities for trouble in the ghetto, parents rank a child more by what he does not do than by what he does. They realize that they will probably be incapable of shielding their children from the racism and violence of the outside world. However, self-respect forces parents to believe that their children are well behaved.[100]

Young Black girls, especially, have a close relationship with their mothers. At a fairly young age they assume heavy household responsibilities such as cooking, cleaning, and child care. Many of them, by the age of nine, are given the charge of their younger siblings. The sharing of household responsibilities builds a positive relationship between mother and daughter. It is in the home where the young Black female acquires her feminine identity.

The close relationship Black mothers have with their daughters has led to the charge that Black mothers express a preference for the female child over the son. But such allegations are unsupported by any evidence. There is often a close emotional tie between the Black mother and her son. Indeed, the Black mother's overprotection of her son may be somewhat more common. One negative aspect of her desire to protect her son is that she fosters dependency in him and hinders his ability to make those decisions which affect his life as well as erode his sense of manliness and the ability to achieve and accomplish.

A key problem in growing up Black is the problem of racism. In the past a Black child's first knowledge of his caste problem occurred in subtle, indirect ways. Whereas a child was accustomed to his mother being called Mrs. in her own neighborhood, he heard a white clerk downtown call her by her first name. Another time he heard his father being addressed as boy. The child began to question his parents about what it all means. Hortense Powdermaker reported that a mother's response to the question of why white and Black children did not play together might be an embarrassed "I don't know, that's just the way things are."[101]

Although some lower-class Black parents taught their children to accept an inferior status in society, they did not leave them without tools for dealing with white people. Lower-class Black children were taught techniques like clowning, lying, and other deceptions for coping with whites.

These same children also learned to distrust whites and that no genuine intimacy between the two races was possible. One Black mother commented: "I guess we don't like white people too much, deep inside. You could hardly expect us to after what's happened all these years."[102]

Despite the hostile world outside, a strong, stable mother can still serve as an emotional support for the child in taking on the problem of racism. A good example is the support Ruby received from her mother while attending a volatile, newly integrated school.

> *Her mother reassured her, taking her to school, telling her daily of her family's support. She never denied Ruby's observations that they don't like me. But told her that her family, all of them, loved her. Most important her mother and father are strong affectionate people, and it is this intimacy between basically sound parents and child which disperses the natural fears in the young. Under such family protection harsh words and scowls are ineffective.*[103]

The young Black female must learn survival techniques in the ghetto as well. At an early age she learns how to jive, how to unmask a weak line, and how to obtain information on sexual matters from her peers. Mothers may teach their daughters to be wary of men, or the girl may have already witnessed the exploitation of women by men from her girlfriends' early pregnancies. Her whole feminine role may be shaped by her mother's attitude toward men. Soon the girl earns her own reputation in the ghetto by becoming pregnant, thereby signifying her own maturity and fulfillment as a mother.[104]

Summary

In this chapter we have examined the historical forces that have shaped the Black woman's acceptance, and performance, of the maternal role. In precolonial Africa, the role of mother was an esteemed and important position in the tribal social organization. The fact that slavery perpetuated the importance of motherhood by its emphasis on the production of children, who would be future slaves or capital, only consolidated the Black woman's attitude toward this role.

Despite the slave holder's desire for the future slaves that the Black woman would produce, he made no concession to the pregnant slave woman. She continued to labor in the fields until the child was born and returned shortly afterwards. She might later be forced to witness the sale of her child away from her.

At least the slave woman had some continuity in her maternal role. The Black man was stripped of all paternal functions and authority except one—fertilizing the egg. Moreover, the racism in society was to continue to deny him the opportunity for fulfillment of the role of father. Since fatherhood is often interpreted as the economic support and physical protection of the family, white racism and economic exploitation coalesced to keep him from doing either.

The Black mother's adaptation to the suppression of Black men has been the acceptance of the idea that she will care for and support her children. Even in the area of pregnancy and contraception, the Black woman is assigned primary responsibility. Today she even has to tolerate the exhortations of certain Black male spokesmen to abdicate whatever control she has over her body by relinquishing all forms of birth control.

Whatever the future of motherhood in this society, Black women have left their imprint on the history of maternal role performance throughout the world. The fact that this is not their only contribution makes it all the more commendable. They have often carried on familial and extrafamilial tasks—with and without the aid of men. As Erik Erikson once stated, "If it were not for the magnificent strength of low-income Negro mothers, surely the family would have disintegrated by now."[105]

Perhaps the future will bring to Black women the control over their bodies that they ask. If not, then one can only hope that the responsibilities of parenthood will not be so heavily placed on her shoulders. Men may come to share more in the tasks of rearing children and, with the demise of white racism, participate more fully in the economic maintenance of those children. A society which is committed to insuring the future well-being of its children will also provide day care facilities that are more than places where children are physically located for a period of time.

People who advocate the use of birth control by Black women so that children already born may have a chance can demonstrate their sincerity by providing comprehensive health care and education for the children in day care centers. This collective care of children can free many women from the burdens of motherhood. Then the institution of motherhood can be something that we all can take pride in, not as a condition forced on women by the nature of their biology, but as a voluntary choice based on the value children have to the society and to their mothers.

6

Black Women and Women's Liberation

Many Black women who have traditionally accepted the white models of femininity are now rejecting them for the same general reasons that we should reject the white middle-class lifestyle. Black women in this society are the only ethnic or radical group which has had the opportunity to be women. By this I simply mean that much of the current focus on being liberated from the constraints and protectiveness of the society which is proposed by women's liberation groups has never applied to Black women, and in that sense, we have always been "free," and able to develop as individuals even under the most harsh circumstances. This freedom, as well as the tremendous hardships from which Black women suffered, allowed for the development of a personality that is rarely described in the scholarly journals for its obstinate strength and ability to survive. Neither is its peculiar humanistic character and quiet courage viewed as the epitome of what the American model of feminity should be.

Joyce Ladner
Tomorrow's Tomorrow (1971)

161

Some years ago the socialist theoretician, Karl Marx, stated that the history of human society was a history of class oppression. Throughout the ages, he said, there was a segment of society that was the oppressor and a group that constituted the oppressed. Marx saw these groups as economic classes whose relationship to the means of production determined what class they belonged to. Basically, those who owned the means of production, i.e., banks, factories, etc., were the ruling class and the workers who provided raw labor were the exploited class. He said that when the working class realized the nature of its oppression, society would undergo a social revolution.[1]

While the Marxist thesis seems valid on an international basis, the United States seems to be an exception—at least up to the present time. The challenges to the prevailing order have come from groups other than the working class. Instead, the most significant social movements in the past decade have been peopled by women and Blacks. Both groups have protested against their oppression by white racism and male chauvinism. Black women relate to both of these social movements—being both female and Black.

The ascendancy of the women's liberation movement has been one of the most surprising developments taking place in this country. Only a couple of years ago most Americans would never have believed that such a movement would have any significance in American life. Indeed, the prevailing cultural belief was that women were pampered, that they controlled the economics of the society, and that "momism" was a threat to the masculine fiber of American life.

But the late sixties and early seventies saw the emergence of a rising consciousness in women. Thousands of women began marching and shouting to protest the oppression of women. Women's liberation groups sprang up all over the country—on the campuses, in high schools, in communities, in professional organizations, in churches, and in unions.

They all had one common theme: Women are second-class citizens.

Although the aims of the women's liberation movement may differ from group to group, the major goals of the movement are:

—Establishment of child care centers so that women will be free to work outside the home.

—Equal pay for equal work and the same employment benefits as men.

—Elimination of discrimination in employment.

—Classes in self-defense so that women will be less vulnerable to rape and other assaults by men.

—Adequate welfare allowances for those women in need of public assistance.

—Legal recognition of the right of every woman to determine whether she shall bear a child by the repeal of all laws against abortion, birth control, and sterilization.

—Free birth control to all women who want it.

—Institution of educational programs dealing with women, their history, psychology, sociology, and literature.

—The elimination of the generally derogatory image of women as sex objects by the media.

—Opening of all public facilities to people without regard to sex.

These goals reflect a variety of ideologies. Some women have been concerned about the way women are depicted as sex objects in magazines, movies, etc. Others have focused on breaking down the barriers to entering male-only settings such as bars and athletic teams. While these activities cover only a minority of the women's liberation efforts, the male-dominated mass media has played up these activities, leading the public to believe that what women's liberation is all about is frivolities such as burning bras and getting into men's bars.

But the women's liberation movement is but part of the broader disenchantment with American society that is occurring among many other groups, Blacks, youth, etc. Women are simply beginning to realize that people are conditioned to internalize individual troubles that are really public problems. Women have been one of the greatest victims of this form of self-blame. Women were completely indoctrinated with the idea that if they could not find happiness through marriage and the family, they were psychologically dislocated—they had failed as women and committed the ultimate crime of not living up to society's standard of femininity.

In forging the women's liberation movement, many techniques were borrowed from the Black movement—all-Black organizations, creation of Black consciousness and identity, the changing of names that signified their oppression, etc. Women took these tools from the Black movement, in part, because they had been successfully used by Blacks. But they also asserted that their situation was very similar to that of Blacks.

Women as Niggers

It is to be expected that any group that defines itself as the object of oppression will share similar traits with other oppressed groups. The same is true of women. One of the most obvious similarities between women and Blacks is that both are discriminated against on the basis of their physical characteristics. Blacks suffer because of their skin color and women encounter discrimination because of their sex. Both are said to be innately inferior, less intelligent, more emotional, dependent, etc. With both groups, their physical traits are said to represent certain limitations in their social achievement. This fact, then, becomes the explanation for their unequal status in the society.

Many parallels have been drawn between women and

Blacks. For example, women are socialized to fit into certain occupational roles in the society such as secretaries, waitresses, school teachers, etc. They are discouraged from entering traditionally masculine jobs and denied training for those jobs. As with Blacks, women are then deprived of employment in certain fields on the grounds that they are not skilled. Both groups are consigned to low-paying, monotonous jobs where a high rate of absenteeism and turnover is typical. It is then said that both groups are too unstable to trust with more responsibility.[2]

As Blacks did for a long time, women accepted the concept of their inferiority. As some observers noted, they inevitably collaborated in their own exploitation. Women frequently distrusted other women. They believed that men were more inherently capable of being leaders. Ellen and Kenneth Keniston concluded that women would never obtain their rights until they, too, refused to collaborate in their own exploitation.[3]

One can make an analogy between the different terms applied to women and the words applying to Blacks in relationship to whites. Women are frequently called "girls" while Black adult males are referred to as "boy." In both cases, the term implies that the individuals under discussion are not capable of full adulthood.[4] The same reasoning applies in distinguishing women by their marital status (Miss or Mrs.) while men are not so differentiated. Blacks were the only racial nationality referred to by a Spanish word for their color while others were known by their land of origin.

Probably one of the most interesting similarities between women and Blacks is that membership in their group may transcend all other attributes they possess. Among Blacks, for example, their skin color is the one bond that ties them together. Even the wealthiest Black man faces some problems because of his blackness. With women, the different definition of age in men and women represents an obvious liability for all women. Older women in America represent the lowest prestige group in this society.[5] Since the value of women is closely associated with their sex appeal, the aging process gradually diminishes their worth, both socially and personally. A result of this is that middle-aged and menopausal years are much more stressful for women than men.

Older women find much more difficulty in securing employment than older men. Many of the jobs women have are based on their sex appeal. As one perceptive male columnist noted: "Unemployment lines are full of women who, if their features were more regular, would be working full time. And even among the employed, the lower-paid jobs are loaded disproportionately with the bad-lookers."[6]

The source of their oppression is considered to be the same as Blacks. A white female sociologist posits an analogy between sexism and racism. Both, she says, are practiced by men of good will with the best of intentions but the barriers to equality are built into the structure. These obstacles are standards, procedures and credentials reflecting the values of white male society. By those standards, Black people were considered inferior. In the same vein, it is supposedly not discrimination that makes it difficult for women to get jobs. They just don't measure up. They are unprofessional.[7]

There is some disagreement among women on whether sexists are men of good will. Another white female asserts that over the last century Blacks and women have had the same friends and enemies. Their opponents were conservatives, Southerners, male legislators, literal interpreters of the Bible, and establishment politicians fearful of upsetting the known balance of power. Conversely, the supporters of equal rights for Blacks and women have been Marxists, intellectuals, the urban dweller, ministers of the social gospel, and politicians seeking new votes.[8]

While this list of friends and enemies may or may not be acceptable to Blacks, there is probably one thing they can agree on: the nature of their oppression is considerably different from that of women. Blacks are, as a group, confined to separate quarters where they suffer the worst of social ills. Women may be the only minority in history that lives with the oppressor. Yet, because of their close ties to men, they do not share the severe deprivation of Blacks.[9] The problems of substandard housing, poor nutrition, inadequate services, and lack of basic needs that affect Blacks do not affect women.

Although it does not diminish the effect of women's oppression, the exploitation of women is a matter of historical interpretation, whereas racial oppression is a matter of fact. The roles of men and women have generally been assumed to be different but equal, but the roles of Blacks have always been clearly unequal. The discrimination experienced by Black women and men has been on the basis of race first, sex second. Some years ago, the abolitionist Frederick Douglass argued that Black suffrage should take priority over woman's suffrage. He stated that "when women because they are women are dragged from their homes and hung upon lamp posts—when their children are torn from their arms ... then they will have an urgency to obtain the ballot equal to the Black man."[10]

The Liberation of Black Women

Whether women's liberation is relevant to Black women is a subject of considerable controversy in the Black community. The white women assert that Black and white women share a common oppression: that Blacks cannot be free until women are free. As Linda Larue comments on this analogy: "Any attempt to analogize Black oppression with the plight of the American white woman has all the validity of comparing the neck of a hanging man with the rope-burned hands of an amateur mountain climber."[11]

The greatest difference between the goals of white women and the needs of Black women are succinctly summed up by Larue:

Common oppression is fine for rhetoric but it does not reflect the actual distance between the oppression of the Black man and woman who are unemployed and the white woman who is sick and tired of Playboy foldouts, of Christian Dior lowering hemlines or adding ruffles or of Miss Clairol telling her that Blondes have more fun. What does the Black woman on welfare who has difficulty feeding her children have in common with the discontent of the suburban mother who has the luxury to protest washing the dishes on which her family's full meal was consumed.[12]

Even Black women who support the women's liberation movement admit that many of its goals are class-bound. Congresswoman Shirley Chisholm asserts that the women's liberation movement, with its emphasis on economic justice for women, must be viewed as a contributing factor to the overall economic improvement of Black women. As an example, she cites the national day care system advocated by the women's liberation movement as benefiting Black women.[13] At the same time, she says, she will not go out on a picket line to protest the exclusion of women from a males-only cocktail lounge. For her that is a white-middle-class virtue. She does not want to be in a lounge with men who do not want her there.[14]

Black women also come into conflict with the women's liberation movement on other issues. The demand for legalized abortions, for instance, goes against traditional Black values related to the status of children. As Ladner has noted, Black mothers have historically retained their children and raised them under the most severe circumstances. Abortions are strongly frowned upon among certain segments of the Black female population. Such an act is viewed as the murder of an unborn child.[15] However, more and more Black women are having abortions today.

At the root of the Black woman's rejection of the

women's liberation movement are the different historical experiences she has encountered and the fact that forms of oppression that the white woman has suffered are symbolic and have never applied to Black women. Many white women, for instance, are protesting the sheltered lives they have led—being put on a pedestal and being confined to suburbia with all its gadgetry. But Black women historically were the sex objects that white men used in order to preserve the white woman's place on that pedestal.

It is the white woman's desire to be emancipated from her home in suburbia that is most incomprehensible to Black women. One Black women comments that "white women have been do-nothing dolls and one gathers now that they want to be white men or something else."[16] Another one notes that the white woman wants out of her kitchen and the Black woman wants a decent one to go home to. Consequently, she says, the white woman's movement for liberation can never satisfy the needs of Black women.[17]

While white women may be oppressed as a group, they are still white. Many Black women feel that one of their greatest enemies has been the white woman who for hundreds of years underpaid and demeaned the Black woman in the kitchens of America.

The collaboration of white men and women in Black oppression is illustrated in this story of a female slave.

Her back bore the scars of a thousand stripes: not because she was backward in her work, nor because she was of an unmindful and rebellious spirit; but because it has fallen her lot to be the slave of a licentious master and jealous mistress. She shrank before the lusty eye of the one, and was in danger even of her life at the hands of the other, and between the two, she was indeed accursed.[18]

Although white women have argued that all other forms of exploitation are extensions of male supremacy, the memory of their treatment at the hands of "oppressed" white women remains clear in the minds of many Black women. As one retired and disabled domestic stated: "I never liked working for them (white women) when I was a domestic. Another thing is that white women don't respect you. I raised many of their children and slept with them and still they treated me like I was nothing."[19] In the words of another Black woman: "The faces of those white women hovering behind that Black girl at the Little Rock school in 1957 do not soon leave the retina of the mind."[20]

Some Black women go so far as to accuse white women of ulterior motives in their attempt to recruit Black women to the women's liberation movement. According to poetess Nikki Giovanni, it is:

> *Just another attempt of white people to find out what Black people are doing or to control what we are doing . . . . They (white women) want the equality to deal with Black women because they've certainly dealt with Black men. They're so upset about Black women not coming in because they're ultimately trying to control us. There aren't any other reasons why they could be upset. Black people consider their first reality to be Black and given that reality we know from birth that we are going to be oppressed—man, woman or eunuch.*[21]

One barrier to an effective coalition between Black and white women is their competition for Black men. As we have noted previously, Black men have become an object of much attention and competition from white women. This is particularly important in the light of the serious shortage of Black men available to Black women. A possible reason for the increased interest of white women in Black men is a shortage of white men. Although there is an excess of one million Black women in America, there is an even greater excess of white women, about four million.[22]

The sight of a Black man and white woman engaged in a romantic relationship has produced feelings of hostility and rage among Black women. Many Black women feel that Black men are being treated as stylish possessions or some "modish" prop of white women. Some Black men see white women as symbols of the white man's privileges. Black women tend to see them as symbols of the Black male's oppression and subjugation. As many Black women know, the majority of Black men held in death rows in various prisons are there for the alleged rape of a white woman.

At a recent conference of Black women in Chicago, it was reported that the women present could not move to other concerns of the liberation of Black people because of the issue of Black men and white women. The conference was bogged down because of the conflicting views of the participants that Black liberation must not freeze in its tracks because of white women or that the purported threat of white women was an issue of utmost importance and must be dealt with.[23]

A primary objection that many Black women have against involvement in the women's liberation movement is that it may estrange them from their men. As Ladner reports: This is the wrong time in American history for Black women to engage in competition against their men because women's lib comes at a time when Black men are asserting their masculinity in ways that have no precedent in recent history.[24] In the words of another Black female spokesman: "An organized effort to 'liberate' Black women is, at best, premature. Should we liberate her and leave Black men and children—the rest of the race—to their own salvation, each seeking his own road to freedom."[25]

The above statements reflect the belief of many Black women that Black men are not their enemy—it is the oppressive forces in the larger society that subjugate Black men, women, and children. One of the most obvious differences between Black and white women is that, while

Black women have suffered all the disabilities of their sex, they have seldom been afforded the protection accorded white women. Black men have never been allowed to protect their women. Thus, Black women have always been forced to take care of themselves.[26]

In the words of Congresswoman Shirley Chisholm, "I've been liberated a long time. There are some aspects of women's liberation that relate to Black women, but the rest of it is baloney."[27] As one Black woman looks at the question of Black male acceptance of women's liberation: "Black men are the one group accustomed to women who are able and assertive because their mothers and sisters were that way. And I don't think they reject their mothers and sisters and wives."[28]

The Black Male Perspective

Most men are conditioned through the socialization process to believe that they are endowed with qualities of leadership and that women should play a subordinate role in human affairs. This form of male chauvinism is most commonly found among white men in American society. But Black men cannot help but be affected by the stereotyped roles of men and women. To some degree they internalize male supremacy values as do white men. However, various social forces have prevented them from carrying out the suppression of Black women.

Black people have had little control over the enactment of their roles. Black males have not been overbearing with their women because white society has more severely restrained the behavior of Black men than Black women. This partly accounts for the very important role of Black women in American history. Women such as Harriet Tubman, Sojourner Truth, Ida B. Wells, and Hallie Q. Brown have no white female counterparts.

Historical records also reveal a number of Black male

chauvinists during that period. After the Civil War there were numerous cases of Black men demanding a superior position in the family. Even during slavery the freed Black male became a patriarch because he had purchased his wife and children from their slavemasters.[29] These examples only highlight the infusion of male chauvinist values throughout all of American society.

In reviewing the attitudes of Black male leaders, writers, and scholars toward Black women, one finds a mixture of affection, a recognition of their contribution to the Black struggle for liberation, and a desire to protect them from the ravages of white racism. All these elements have been exhibited in diverse ways by different Black men. One needs to understand how the times in which they lived shaped their attitudes on the woman question. Also, one finds a close correlation between the Black man's attitude on the role of women and his ideological position on the Black struggle.

Frederick Douglass, the abolitionist, was active during the days of slavery. Even today he would be considered a radical when measured by our society's ideological norms. Although his main concern was justice for Black people, he was one of the first males—Black or white—to advocate equal rights for women. When a conflict emerged between the rights of women and Blacks, he gave priority to obtaining justice for Blacks. Yet he firmly believed and so stated that "we are free to say that in respect to political rights, we hold woman to be justly entitled to all we claim for man."[30]

Even the conservative Black spokesman, Booker T. Washington, married women who were civic activists. He spoke fondly of the assistance of his wife in his work relating to his school and in her efforts to organize poor Black farm women of the South. But Washington's position on the woman question differed little from his stance on the Black question—both had an inferior role in society and should develop their character and moral sense before trying to elevate themselves on the level of men and whites. In his school, women were mostly taught subjects such as house-keeping, sewing, and dressmaking, all fields that fitted into the traditional roles of women.[31]

A twentieth-century Black male leader, W. E. B. Du Bois, was a consistent proponent of women's rights. His writings indicate the depth of his concern for the condition of women. At one point he declared that, "The uplift of women is next to the problem of the color line and the peace movement, our greatest modern cause."[32] Du Bois constantly extolled the virtues of Black women and once stated that he would forgive the white South much in its final judgment day but never the "wanton and continued and persistent insulting of the Black womanhood which it sought and seeks to prostitute to its lust."[33]

There may be some truth to the belief that being subject to oppression humanizes the oppressed. The case of Du Bois and Douglass indicates that a commitment to human justice transcends racial, religious, sex, and class boundaries. Both of them seemed to realize that until all people are free, nobody is free. A society cannot afford to subjugate a race of women and expect to be a just society. A person who has a sincere commitment to human justice should have ideas of human equality that can stand the test of time. Du Bois and Douglass have always been on the right side of the woman question.

When we analyze the views on women of the Black nationalist leaders, we find a return to the traditional male position that women should occupy a subordinate role. Most of these nationalist groups have based their position on the woman question on historical experiences. In particular, the Republic of New Africa advocates a return to the African patriarchal system where men make all the decisions. They also wanted a reinstatement of the system of polygyny in which Afro-American men could have more than one wife.[34]

The Nation of Islam (commonly known as the Black Muslims) also relates its present position on the role of women to past experiences when Black men could not support and protect their women, thereby abdicating any role of leadership. Also, Muslims base their attitudes toward the role of women on the Islamic religion. In traditional Moslem society, it is believed that men have a natural right to act as overseers of women. The Black Muslims teach that no marriage can succeed if the woman does not look up with respect to the man. A man must have something above and beyond the wife in order for her to be able to look to him for psychological security.[35]

When Malcolm X was a member of the Black Muslims, he echoed these same views. But he had a very close relationship with his wife. In his autobiography he states that he depended heavily upon his wife for strength to endure some of his crises. Malcolm believed that Islam was the only religion that gives both husband and wife a true understanding of love. According to him, in Western society when a woman loses her physical beauty, she loses her attraction. But Islam teaches individuals to look for the spiritual qualities in each other.[36]

The views of Malcolm X altered radically after he left the Nation of Islam. In his twelve years as a Muslim minister he preached so strongly on the moral issues that even Muslims charged him with being anti-woman. In retrospect, he admitted that every aspect of his teaching and all of his personal beliefs derived from his devotion to the Nation of Islam's leader, Elijah Muhammad. After Malcolm broke away from the Muslims in 1963 he steered away from morality and addressed himself to current events and politics.[37] His position on Black women just before he was assassinated is printed elsewhere in this book.[38]

Even revolutionary nationalist parties such as the Black Panther Party have held questionable views on the woman question. At one time the official position of the Black Panther Party was that the attempt to repeal the abortion laws was a genocidal plot. One of the former leaders of that party, Eldridge Cleaver, has stated that: "Black women take kindness for weakness. Leave them the least little opening and they will put you on the cross. . . . It would be like trying to pamper a cobra."[39]

At least Cleaver's view here is buttressed by his other tributes to Black women. The position of writer and cultural nationalist, Immamu Baraka (Leroi Jones), is a clear-cut call for Black female subordination. His organization has a doctrine concerning the Black woman's role in it. Women should not smoke, drink, wear slacks, or have abortions. They should not be involved in men's discussions except to serve refreshments. While the men are busy making decisions, women should occupy themselves with ironing, sewing, and cooking. The rationale for this sexual segregation of effort is the necessity for developing a unique Black culture that is bereft of all white concepts.[40]

If we look at how Black women have been written about by Black writers, we find that women are the chief protagonists. Men are rarely depicted as masterful male models. The fate of men is determined not by other men but by their female relatives.[41] However, despite the axiom that a writer's works reflect his own experiences, the writer rarely represents the normal individual in his environment. Perhaps Black male writers have certain personality traits that determine the significant persons in their works. One might read, for instance, Cleaver's critique of Black novelist James Baldwin.[42]

In reviewing some of the books written by Black men, one finds a certain ambivalence in them about Black women. Although the concept of the Black matriarchy emerged from the writings of E. Franklin Frazier, he held a generally favorable opinion of Black women. He saw the slave woman as the protectress of the race. Although he believed the matrifocal family to be undesirable, he was appreciative of the sacrifices Black women had made for their families over the years.[43] His most negative criticism of Black women was reserved for women of the middle class, a group he felt did not measure up to the intellectual and cultural abilities of middle-class white women.[44]

The more recent literature on Black women is very negative. One of the most virulent criticisms of Black women can be found in the book *Black Rage* by William Grier and Price Cobbs.[45] Their treatment of Black women led one Black female reviewer to label them ignorant and stupid. The book, she asserted, is "a clumsy but effective attempt to modernize old stereotypes to explain topics of current interest."[46] Basically, the thesis of the book is that the Black woman has been made to feel that she is not worth much and she arrives at this conclusion through the teachings of her mother who is also filled with self-hatred.

There are other questionable statements in the book such as, "Black women lack self-confidence, they are more skin color conscious, preferring those of light-skin, than Black men and they have abandoned any interest in their feminine appearance."[47] The authors go on to say that the Black woman aspires to the cosmetic beauty of white America. Since she lacks the qualities of attractiveness and feeling loved, her feeling of self-confidence is impaired. Instead of directing her hatred toward the object of her oppression, she directs it inward.[48]

Another Black writer, Calvin Hernton, has vacillated between his approbation of Black women and his rejection of them. At one point in his earlier works he asserts that Black women are just beginning to get the recognition they deserve as human beings.[49] Yet he claims that most Black women are obsessed with the idea of getting a white man. This accounts, he says, for their vociferous objection to Black men with white women. Black women are absolutely opposed to interracial mingling until they get a white man in their clutches. They are unattracted to white men until they get one.[50]

According to Hernton, the wave of the future will be

the Black woman and white man, because Black women have put a gap between themselves and their men. Black women are unable to transcend the conflicting emotions of self-love and self-hate for being Black. This hatred is transferred to the Black male. Most Black men have received from Black females that familiar hate stare that they commonly get from Southern whites. Black women cannot relate to the sexual nature of Black men. It is easier for them to interact with latent or known homosexuals than with masculine Black men.[51]

Most Black writers have summarily dismissed women's liberation as being irrelevant to Black women. Baraka calls it a part of America's contradictions, and any contradiction in America should be seen as a white against Black movement.[52] A Black male psychologist labels women's liberation as "a diversion, an activist way to ignore racism."[53] Another writer has charged that it is merely another white, middle-class self-hate and self-destruct mechanism. Many of the women in it, he says, are trying to substitute the latest revolutionary identity for an unfulfilling personality.[54]

The views of Grier and Cobbs and Hernton represent a few Black male opinions out of ten million. But they reach many people who feel compelled to respond. A Black female sociologist retorts that Black men are largely interested in liberation for themselves and are not sympathetic toward Black females. Indeed, she claims that Black female subordination is one of their chief goals. Black women should not be lulled into believing that the liberation of Black men is their greatest priority. Few Black men, she says, are their captives and fewer still seek to be their liberators.[55]

A similar, but less caustic, position is that of Frances Beale:

> *Since the advent of Black power, the Black male has exerted a more prominent leadership role in our struggle for justice in this country. He sees the system*

for what it really is for the most part, but where he rejects its values and mores on many issues, when it comes to women, he seems to take his guidelines from the pages of the Ladies Home Journal. *Certain Black men are maintaining that they have been castrated by society but that Black women somehow escaped this persecution and even contributed to this emasculation.*[56]

While the objects of oppression cite their various grievances against each other, their oppression continues. If women—Black and white—cannot unite, what is to become of the struggle of women to be liberated from sexist oppression? If Black men and Black women cannot get together, how will Blacks achieve liberation? We should not lose sight of the fact that a real revolution does not free only whites or men. It frees all of humanity because it attacks the basis of the exploitation of Blacks by whites and of women by men.

Summary

The women's liberation movement has signaled the birth of one more protest against the inequities in American society. Like Blacks and young people, women have become alienated from the value system of a country that denies them human dignity. Suddenly, they realize that they have been deluded into accepting their ascribed roles as sex objects and keepers of the hearth. The fact that they have intellectual and artistic skills has been ignored by a society that persists in depriving them of their freedom to express their creative abilities in most aspects of American life. As a result of the repression of their potential, women are forced into economic dependence on the male breadwinner, who brings in the family income and often decides its disposition.

Conceiving of the women's movement as only the

protest of suburban housewives against their lack of fulfillment in suburban households does a disservice to the revolutionary implications of this movement and belies the legitimate grievances of the female sex in this society. The exploitation of women does not involve just another oppressed minority but over half the population. Furthermore, changing the status of women will mean radical alterations in such sensitive areas as sexual relations, family ties, and other intimate personal matters. Their emancipation cannot help but dilute the power of the master race.[57]

Although this movement is currently dominated by middle-class women—and many have a low level of political consciousness—it is still in the beginning stage and has the same potential for ideological growth as the antiwar and Black liberation movements. Moreover, one's oppression is subjectively defined. Despite their middle-class status, white women may be pained deeply by their sex-related oppression. An older woman who loses her husband to a younger woman is grieved by this fact. Women whose value is primarily sexual face a certain malaise when they lose their beauty. The loneliness of widowhood and the rejection by society that elderly women face are hurts that go deep, even in the middle class.[58]

Another purpose of women's liberation is to free men. Instead of resenting the competition of women for traditionally male jobs, men may begin to question the necessity to compete at all. Men and women will be freed from the sexual games they play today—with men vying for sexual conquests and women enticing men into marriage by withholding their sexual favors. The emancipated women will share equally in family responsibilities and the male will be relieved of the awesome psychological burden that goes along with the exclusive responsibility for providing for the family.[59]

While the above elements are important in bringing about a fuller concept of humanity unrelated to sex-role distinctions, what is their relevance to Black women? For one thing, Black women suffer the most from every form of female oppression. They are most economically dependent on their husbands since they have even fewer job opportunities than white women. It is Black women who are affected most by the view of women as sex objects because they are forced into jobs such as waitress and secretarial work, where their sexual appeal is most emphasized.[60] When they work as domestic servants, they must daily confront or evade the sexual advances of their employers. Not only are Black women treated as sex objects, but they are inculcated with the society's exhortation to look like white women if they are to have any sense of self-worth.

Despite the necessity of their liberation from sexist as well as racist oppression, Black women have good cause for their cautious attitude toward the women's liberation movement. First, there is no reason to believe that the white woman would not take advantage of her racial status if allowed to openly compete with white men for the same jobs. Moreover, Black women suspect that the women's movement is a device to divert attention away from Black liberation movement and from the issue of racism.

One threat of the women's liberation movement is its potential for drawing a barrier between Black men and Black women. Many of the protests women make are against men in general—and deservedly so.[61] Yet, it is questionable if, at this stage of history, Black people can afford the luxury of having its female members in conflict with Black men over the limited resources available to either of them. Black males possess no political or economic power that Black women can obtain. That power is held by white males. And, a greater equalization of that power is a task for all Black people—not just women.

Still, there are unique problems Black women face because of their sex. In recent years they have begun to get together to work on some of those problems. They have organized separate organizations of Black women, but their organizations parallel and complement the existing Black movement. In this way they seek to make Black female liberation an essential part of the effort to free all Black people.

7

Voices of Black Womanhood

That man over there say that a woman needs to be helped into carriages, and lifted over ditches, and to have the best place everywhere. Nobody ever helped me into carriages, or over mud puddles, or gives me a best place. . . . And ain't I a woman? Look at me. Look at my arm! I have plowed and planted and gathered into barns, and no man could head me. . . . And ain't I a woman? I could eat as much as a man when I could get it, and bear the lash as well. . . . And ain't I a woman? I have borned thirteen children and seen them most all sold off into slavery. And when I cried out with a mother's grief, none but Jesus heard. . . . And ain't I a woman?

Sojurner Truth
Speech before the Woman's Rights Convention
at Akron, Ohio, in 1851

After reviewing the material on Black women for this book, I realized that there was little empirical research on the Black woman's concept of her role. A number of changes are taking place, concurrently and little recognized, that may have profound effects on the nature of Black family life. Adjustments in family arrangements and domestic patterns seem inevitable since more and more Black women are demanding an equalitarian status in the family. Concurrently, many Black men are demanding that Black women assume the traditional role of women. Black men, then, must be challenged to think in terms of sharing the family responsibility with Black women, adapting to the Black woman's new definition of the female role, and creating a spirit of democracy in the family.

Consequently, I decided to interview some Black women to find out about their concept of male and female roles as a supplement to the theoretical work completed for this book. Without the necessary research staff or facilities, nor the time, an extensive field research project could not be carried out. The main purpose of these interviews was more exploratory than definitive, more hypothesis generating than hypothesis testing. Therefore, there has been a greater concentration on the theoretical importance of the findings than the validity and reliability of the results.

By virtue of the small sample size and the research methodology employed, no statistical analysis will be made of the findings. This does not mean that there is no relationship between the variables investigated. It only means that no sweeping generalizations about Black women, based on this limited and biased sample, will be made. However, the results may be suggestive of possible new insights into the role of the Black woman. But, more importantly, this is a search for empirical generalizations that can be derived from the statements of the Black women interviewed which can be used to improve our understanding of the role of Black women in the family.

Purpose and Scope

The purpose of this study was to assess the Black woman's self-concept of her role in the family. This should provide a first-hand view of the problems she faces, and her reaction to those problems. Secondarily, an attempt was made to ascertain the Black female's view of the Black male's role and of how he has performed, or failed to perform, to her expectations. One problem that emerged from designing this study was that it only included women. This is a mistake common to researchers of family life. The reason for this oversight is commonly known: women are more easily located at home for interviews and they also invest more time in family affairs.

The Sample

The interviews consisted of ten Black women residing in the city of Washington, D.C. It was not a random selection and was overrepresented by middle-class Black women. Most of the women were members of a grass-roots antipoverty organization. The significance of their membership in an antipoverty group is that the women in this sample had a certain level of political consciousness and a commitment to uplifting the lower-income members of their race. Perhaps this had led to a heightened awareness of the problems Black women face in a racist and sexist society.

However, the women in this group are not representative of the prototypical Black woman. A scrutiny of their characteristics demonstrates a remote resemblance to the statistically average Black woman. The average number of years of schooling completed by the Black female interviewees was 14.7 years, compared to 9.2 for most Black women. Six of the subjects had college degrees, two had completed high school, and two had not completed high school. One of the biggest differences between the interviewees and the "typical" Black woman was the number of children they had. On the average, Black women have 3.9 children per family: the interviewees have only 1.10.

A slight bias is noted in the age range of the interviewees. The majority are in the twenty to thirty year range, the others are over fifty. This gives a profile of Black women in the early years of family life and after the completion of the childbearing stage of the family-life cycle. It is also possible that the youth of the female sample may be more indicative of changes in the Black female's concept of her role. The older age of other women in the sample may give us some idea of generational differences in the Black female role concept.

The middle-class bias in this sample does have some positive advantages. While the female interviewees are not representative of lower-class Black women, they are representative of middle-class Black women. Middle-class sectors of the Black community are too often ignored in family research, a practice that frequently highlights the deprivations that lower-class Blacks face and, in turn, their somewhat "negative" adaptations to those deprivations.

By studying middle-class Black women, it is easier to isolate out those elements in Black culture that are due to racism and sexism alone, and are not confounded by economic forces that are most peculiar to the Black lower class. Also, the female subjects had a link to the lower levels of Black life. Only one woman interviewed had less education than her mother or father. Thus, these women were upwardly mobile and have, at one time, been exposed to lower-class Black life.

Procedure

An unstructured interview schedule was the only research instrument. The questions were open-ended, but many of the responses have been edited, or condensed, for the sake of brevity or clarity. The interview schedule is one of the best research mechanisms for assessing social attitudes. It provides a way of uncovering more intricate relationships and nuances of meanings. Furthermore, and perhaps most important, the intimate face-to-face relationship in the interview situation helps the researcher develop a degree of insight into his subject's responses that cannot be achieved by the use of a written schedule or questionnaire.

Each interview session was conducted by the author and took approximately two and a half hours to complete. The setting for the interview was the respondent's home in a majority of cases. Questions were thoroughly explained by the investigator and no limit was placed on the time for response. The subjects were encouraged to elaborate at length on all questions and most statements have been condensed into a succinct answer that gives the essential meaning of their response.

Plan of Presentation

Six questions were put to the ten Black female subjects. These questions referred to the following phenomena: (1) the Black woman's satisfaction with her role performance; (2) her perception of intergenerational role continuity; (3) how the Black male perceived the role of Black women; (4) symmetry in the role expectations of Black men and Black women; (5) the Black female's definition of the Black male's role in the family; and (6) what changes in family relations the Black woman foresaw as a result of more and better employment opportunities for Black men.

The specific questions asked are placed before each interviewee's response. Because the writer guaranteed that the subject's identity would not be revealed in print, all ten women are referred to by their first initial on a continuous and consistent level in this study. Not all ten Black women are represented in the responses to each question since typical responses are put in extended quotes. Before presenting their answers to the six questions, a profile of our subjects and their family composition is presented.

A Profile of Ten Black Women

Mrs. A is a sixty-two-year-old, pleasantly plump woman. Her parents were middle class in background: her mother a physician, her father a professor. She was born in Oklahoma, graduated from college there, and worked as a school teacher all her life. Although married, she has no children. She is presently retired and lives off her pension and income from rental property. Her husband is now deceased but was still alive at the time of the interview. He was a sixty-four-year-old, very fair-skinned Black male. At the time of the interview he did not have a steady job because he drank heavily. The main source of his income was from royalties on some oil property leased by his family in Oklahoma. Mrs. A was the dominant figure in this family.

Mrs. B is a thirty-six-year-old, very obese woman. She is separated from her husband and currently works as a substitute teacher to supplement the meager child support payments she receives. Her husband is a postal employee in a nearby city who rarely visits her or the children. Two of her four children are presently living with her mother in Birmingham, Alabama. The subject has a college degree but finds it difficult to obtain steady employment because of her weight. She, of course, is the de facto head of her family.

Mrs. C is a fifty-nine-year-old, mild-mannered woman. She is a high school graduate who lived most of her life in Oklahoma. Most of her life she has been a housewife, although occasionally during hard times she did some housework. Her husband, who is seventy-one years old, has retired from his job as a railroad porter. No children were born to this marriage. Mrs. C is the daughter of a minister and her husband is definitely in control of this household.

Mrs. E is a fifty-one-year-old, dissipated-looking woman. She is a college graduate from West Virginia and works as a school teacher in one of the city elementary schools. Her parents were both working class people: the mother a household servant, the father a handyman. The subject's husband, also a school teacher, died three years ago in an automobile accident. While alive, he seemed to be in charge of all family decisions. Mrs. E has one child, a dentist in Ohio.

Mrs. H is a fifty-four-year-old, rather scatterbrained woman from Virginia. She is married, but is not living with her husband. Apparently, they still consider themselves man and wife although living apart. He is a purchasing agent for a department store in Philadelphia and has a college degree. She works as an elementary school teacher in the city. Her parents worked as household servants and laborers. Both the subject's children are grown: one is a teacher, the other a captain in the army. When living with her husband, it seems that he is the main decision-maker.

Mrs. I is a twenty-four-year-old, somewhat short and pretty woman. She has a masters degree in counseling psychology and is a counselor at one of the local high schools. Her husband has a Ph.D. in psychology and is a professor at one of the colleges in the city. The subject is originally from a suburb of Philadelphia where her mother worked as a registered nurse, her father as a civil service white collar employee. The subject's marriage would be characterized as equalitarian, although she appears to defer to him. They are the parents of a daughter, Lisa.

Mrs. K is a twenty-two-year-old, statuesque woman. She

is a college senior, majoring in child development. Her home is Chicago, where her father works in a steel factory, her mother does sewing in her home. The subject's parents both have less than an eighth-grade education. Her husband has a college degree in economics and is employed as an economist for a business firm. In this family our subject appears to be the primary decision-maker. They have one child.

Miss M is a twenty-year-old, hostility ridden female. She has two children, although not married, and is living in a common-law relationship with a man who is not the father of her children. He works as a mechanic at a service station. The subject dropped out of school in the tenth grade because she was pregnant. She has two sources of income: her common-law husband's salary and her welfare check. The subject is definitely in control of the household.

Mrs. R is a twenty-year-old, slim female. She is presently a social worker for the public welfare department. Her home is in Texas, where she attended college and received her degree in English. It was there that she met her husband, a college graduate who is an executive in a large corporation. The subject's mother is a housewife, her father a real estate agent. The interviewee and her husband have one child, a boy, and want one more, a girl. Her husband, by her own admission, makes most of the decisions in the family.

Miss S is a twenty-four-year-old, very attractive and articulate woman. She has a college degree in history but works as a secretary in one of the local colleges. Her home is in Southern California, where her mother was a civil service clerk, her father had his own car-washing business. She is extremely intelligent and well-read. However, she has experienced several personal difficulties due in part to her sexual liaison with a married man. At present she is going to group psychotherapy sessions.

Family Composition

1.	Mr. A* (64)	=	Mrs. A (62)		6.	Mr. I (28)	=	Mrs. I (24)
							Lisa (1)	
2.	Mr. B** (40)	=	Mrs. B (36)		7.	Mr. K (23)	=	Mrs. K (22)
	Joyce (12)		Willie (15)				Bertrand	
	Tony (4)		Terry (4)					
3.	Mr. C (71)	=	Mrs. C (59)		8.	Mr. M† (23)	=	Miss M (20)
						Corliss (3)		Arnisha (4)
4.	Mr. E* (55)	=	Mrs. E (51)		9.	Mr. R (27)	=	Mrs. R (20)
		John (30)					Martin (1)	
5.	Mr. H (54)	=	Mrs. H (54)		10.		−	Miss S (24)
	Roscoe (30)		Darlene					

*Deceased
**Separated
†Common-law Relationship

Question 1

How do you feel about your role as a Black woman? Are you satisfied, dissatisfied or both?

Mrs. A is satisfied. Her reasoning is, "I would rather be a Black woman with my education than be a poor uneducated white woman. As far as I am concerned, it is money that counts, not color."

Mrs. K is both happy and unhappy with her role. She comments that she likes being a wife and mother but would prefer more opportunity for leaving the house and enjoying cultural activities.

Miss M gives an uncertain response. She feels that a Black woman has it pretty good in life but it could be better. Particularly bitter is her evaluation of Black men. She states: "Black men should show more respect for their women. The first chance he gets, he drops her (the Black woman) and runs off with a white woman." Also acrimonious, or perhaps honest, is her attitude toward the white world. She comments that "a Black woman has to be twice as good as a white woman to get anywhere. But I like being a Black woman and wouldn't want to be any other color."

Mrs. C in contrast to Miss M is very satisfied with her role as a Black woman. In fact, she believes, some Black women are better off than white women. Here, at length, is what she said:

> *Yes, I am very satisfied with my role as a housewife. I always took care of the house while my husband was on the road. Housework has always been fun to me, and, besides, I also raised my niece and put her through high school.*
> *It doesn't feel any different being a Black woman.*

The only difference is white women don't have to do their own housework—the wealthy ones, that is. It depends on class. But, I feel that a white woman who isn't used to hard work has it harder than me. They're (white women) not trained to do proper housework. I have friends who do day work for white people, and they say that they (whites) keep a messy house.

Mrs. H is satisfied with her position as a Black woman. Her family is very close, she says, and they have never been on welfare. Also, she relates, a Black woman has more of a chance to do something in life today. Before, she knew there were certain limitations because she was Black and her goals in life were very restricted.

Some of the other women were not quite so satisfied with their role as a Black woman. Two of them gave the following reasons:

Miss S is unsure of what the role of a woman is, what the concept of femininity is, and how she should act out her role. The female role, she says, is subjectively defined, and each woman has to decide for herself what her role consists of. Men, she charges, don't know what they want in a woman—a mother figure, a sex object, or a slave. Women, she thinks, should have interests outside the home and a role other than just wife and mother.

Mrs. R feels that the Black man thinks of a Black woman as a sex object and that educated women resent this stereotype. Another reason she gives for being dissatisfied with her lot in life is that:

A Black woman has to prove that she's better than a white woman, even to her own men. Nothing infuriates me so much as to see all those Black entertainers married to white women. We Black women has two strikes against us—being female and Black.

Discussion: The responses of the Black women in this study reveal a continuum of satisfaction-dissatisfaction with their role as Black women. Several interesting factors stand out in their responses.

One salient difference in the responses was the tendency of the younger women to express dissatisfaction with their role. The older women appeared to be more contented with their position in life. One possible reason for this may be that as older, educated Black women they saw themselves as a relatively privileged group, especially in earlier times, in comparison to less educated and consequently poorer Black and white women.

Another curious result was that these Black women used as referents the status of white women. Unlike dissident white females who compare their status with that of men, Black women compare the quality of their lives to what they believe to be the advantaged or disadvantaged position of white women. There are some who would say that this is a case of social inferiors comparing themselves to other social inferiors.

However, the Black woman is also aware of the present inadequacies of her role as a woman. The young, educated Black woman wants more out of life than her predecessor. There is a current rebellion against the traditional concept of woman's role in the family and a desire to have a more clearly defined role that may be a combination of traditional and equalitarian.

Question 2
How do you feel that your role (as wife and/or mother) differs from that of your mother?
Three of the women interviewed felt that their roles are the same as their mothers' role, that they have the support of

their husbands, and that they have to perform essentially the same role functions as their mothers.

Mrs. E believes that her role is no different that her mother's role. She is convinced that:

> *My mother and I wanted the same things in life, a better life for our children. We both worked hard to prepare our children to get ahead in the world. The only difference I see is that I have more money than she did, and she worked on the farm.*

Seven of the subjects asserted that their role was different from that of their mothers. Some of the responses were:

Miss S feels that she is more aware of her environment and more capable of handling relationships with other people. A greater amount of education has equipped her with this capacity, she believes. She goes on to explain that she must also cope with a more complex society with fewer resources than her mother had. In essence, she says, this is an impersonal society in which each individual must learn mechanisms of survival, or they will perish.

Mrs. K states that her mother had more preparation for her role in the family. Her mother was also more dominant than she is in her household. She explains thus:

> *I can remember how, one time, my father told my mother that he was going out to play cards with some of his friends. My mother just took his hat and coat away from him and said quite decisively that he wasn't going nowhere until he fixed up that back porch. If I tried that with my husband, he would walk out the door over my fallen and bruised body.*

Mrs. B says that her mother was more thrifty, had more

strength, and was more capable of enduring crises. She says that she has been spoiled by modern conveniences and the push-button society, and that she might just fall apart emotionally if she faced a major crisis in her life.

Mrs. H reports that her family is more equal in making decisions and that her husband is more understanding and helpful in raising the children than her father was.

A final comment is the one by *Mrs. M*. She appeared to be expressing her resentment toward her mother in answering the question. She said:

> *I feel that my mother had different ideas when she grew up and then she tried to force them on me. But most of my friends didn't have the same ideas she tried to make me learn. She grew up in the depression, when times were hard, and believed that if you spared the rod, you spoiled the child. I am nicer to my kids than my mother was to me.*

Discussion: In answering this second question, most of the women give some indication that their role differs from their mothers' role in some aspect of their role functions. Some sensed that their lives are qualitatively better than their mothers' because they have more education and greater opportunities in life.

It is interesting to note that, despite the differences in educational achievements between the women interviewed and their mothers, they do not stress any particular gap in values. Perhaps their mothers, despite having less education, held values similar to the middle-class values of their daughters. This may account, in part, for the daughters' upward mobility in the class structure.

Other responses indicate that the interviewees felt that they were not as prepared for their roles as wives and mothers, as their mothers had been. Although technological advances have made their roles in the family easier, these women felt a lack of kinship ties and supports to help them through emotional crises that were available to their mothers.

The forces of social change will inevitably produce some alterations in the role expectations of wife and mother. One thing seems certain. The Black woman can no longer be the woman she used to be—the environment will not let her.

Question 3

How do you think your husband or boyfriend views the role of a woman?

Four of the women stated that their husbands feel that a woman should be a worker, wife, and mother. The incomes of some middle-class Black men are so marginal that the woman has to work and help contribute to the support of her family. When the wives work, the husbands frequently feel that everything in the family should be on an equal basis. One example was:

Mrs. H:

My husband feels that a woman should stay at home until the children enter school. After that she should get a job to help pay the bills. Of course, it's not that easy for us to make it on his salary alone. I like to help out with the bills and I also got tired of just staying at home and taking care of the children.

Six of the women stated that their husbands believed women should have a subordinate role in the family. Some of the comments went this way:

Miss S:

He feels women should be his slaves and devote themselves to his interests, whatever the cost to their own well-being. I do mean women, in the plural definition, since he also feels that he should not be restricted to just having one woman in his life, married or not. He believes, however, in strict fidelity for a woman.

Mrs. K reports that her husband is somewhat ambiguous about the role of a woman. He thinks she should work but that he should have the most authority in the family.

Mrs. B:

My husband felt that I was too domineering, and he wanted me to be submissive. However, he also believed that I should work and contribute to the support of the family.

Mrs. A thinks that her husband wants her to play the dominant role in the family. According to her, "He thinks I'm very efficient and knows I can do things better than he can. He appreciates my dominance and is satisfied."

Miss M related her feelings this way:

My old man likes to boss me all the time. He thinks a woman should wait on a man anytime he wants and always be loving and nice. But I have my own money, and I don't take nothing off no man. He likes to get money from me when he's broke.

Discussion: There is considerable conflict in the concept of the role of women between the majority of our interviewees and their husbands or boyfriends. It appears that many Black males adhere to the traditional concept of the submissive, passive role of women. At the same time they expect the female to be an equal breadwinner in the home. They expect women to remain in a subordinate position domestically while taking on a "male" role economically.

One positive aspect of the Black male's role expectation for the Black female is that women are not confined solely to the drudgery of housework and childrearing. However, this is a two-edged sword in many ways since Black women are forced to take on two roles: housewife and worker. Thus, they are faced with a unique brand of male chauvinist, one who wants the best of all possible worlds: a submissive wife and a working one.

Question 4

What is your reaction to your husband or boyfriend's view of your role?

Four of the women agree with their mate's perception of their role in the family. In all four cases, the husband/boyfriend believed the woman should have an equal or dominant role in the family. This agreement between the sexes is best summed up by:

Mrs. I:

We work together as a team. There's none of the attitude that this is my money because I earned it by working for it. Its understood that marriage is a two-way affair. I help out with the payment of all our bills, and he helps me with the housework. Likewise, when important decisions have to be made, we do it together.

Five of the women were in disagreement with their mate's view of the female role. In all five cases, his view of her role was that she was a subordinate member of the family and that male supremacy should reign. Some reactions to this attitude were:

Miss S:

His attitude is unrealistic and asinine. It absolutely infuriates me and I utterly refuse to accept his concept of the female role.

Mrs. B:

A husband and wife should be equal in everything. I don't think women should be subordinate.

Mrs. C:

He believes that a woman shouldn't make major decisions. When decisions have to be made, he usually wins his way but will ask me what I think. I don't agree with his view. Women should have an equal voice in decision making. After all, two heads are better than one.

If it's something really important that we disagree on, I just refuse to go along with what he wants. My mother always taught me to stand up for my rights.

One woman who felt that her husband was ambiguous about her role expressed her dissatisfaction thus:

Mrs. K:

His attitude leaves me in a state of chaos, because I don't know how to act. Because of society's changing values, both men and women are confused as to their respective role functions. Some men want authority to control things but don't want to take responsibility for the failures of decisions that they make.

Discussion: These women and their mates are in agreement on the role of the female if it is not placed on a subordinate level. The biggest problem arises among these educated Black women when their men take the traditional view that women should play a submissive role in their relationship. Black women who are educated, frequently co-breadwinners, take umbrage at the suggestion, or demand, that they have less than an equal voice in family matters.

At the same time one does not see the dominated, emasculated, Black male stereotype in the husbands of these women. In very few cases does the female have a clear-cut dominant role in the family. The mere fact that these Black women have to strongly assert their right to equality reflects a Black male dominance that much of the research on Black family life implies is missing.

However, the Black male's insistence on dominance, and the Black woman's resistance to being placed in a secondary position, may be the harbinger of much of the conflict and disharmony in many Black marriages. The Black male's claim to certain male prerogatives in decision-making is morally indefensible in the light of the Black woman's economic contribution to the family income. But, today, the Black woman's claim to absolute equality, a demand that seriously threatens fragile male egos, may make marriage less tenable.

Marital conflict does not have to emerge out of these perceived gaps in role definitions. It could be that the women in our study are being defensive about the attitudes of their husbands. They may feel that, in order to allay the concept of the overbearing Black matriarch, it is necessary to stress that they do not have an equal role in the family, and certainly not a dominant position.

There is no way to assess the impact of the attitudes of the women, as expressed in their complaints, on their marital relationships. Or, in other words, their mental resistance to the traditional concept of their role may be the only expression of their feeling.

Question 5

What do you think should be the male's role in the family?

Most of the subjects agreed that the man has primary responsibility for the support of the family. Some expressed the belief that he should take a more active role in the rearing of the children. An interesting response is that of:

Mrs. I:

The man should be a loving husband and father. He should take the responsibility for implementing all of the decisions in family matters. I feel there is also a need for him to communicate with the children so that they will know him better.

Another woman, *Mrs. K*, feels that both the man and woman should share responsibility for the support of the family and for doing household tasks. She thinks that the male has to participate on an equal basis in all family matters.

One woman has a conditional view of the man's role in the family.

Mrs. A:

A man's role is governed by his ability. All men are not capable of having authority in the family. If a man is capable, he should share the primary responsibility for the economic support of the family.

According to another respondent, the husband should be a helpmate in the household.

Mrs. E:

He's supposed to provide for his family, but the wife should help. He should help raise the children and work around the house.

One rather ambivalent statement is that of:

Mrs. C:

A man should be a loyal husband and father and the main provider in the family. He should look out for the family in general—make them feel secure. But he shouldn't handle the money, a wife should. Men don't have as good an idea of what's needed. They spend money foolishly. A woman is more levelheaded and more likely to save money for an emergency.

Discussion: The role concept that emerges from the subjects' view of the male's role in the family is a traditional one. By unanimous consent they agree that the male's primary role is to support the family. They seem to recognize no apparent contradiction in their expectation that the male take primary responsibility for the income maintenance of the family and their own desire for parity with the male in the decision-making processes.

Although they see themselves as helping with family support, they perceive this function as primarily a male one. Perhaps they feel that sex-role equality is their right because they perform the important task of taking care of the household and rearing the children. Or they may realize that the limited incomes permitted women do not enable them to take on a primary breadwinner status and also maintain the family's standard of living.

At the same time they expressed the belief that men should do more than provide economic support for the family, that he should take a more active role in household tasks, and especially in the socialization of children. The male viewpoint on this question would be valuable here since our female subjects definitely see contemporary Black men as not being adequate in this area.

Question 6

What influence do you think increased and better employment opportunities will have on the Black male's status in the family?

The author explained that the Black male has often been considered a subordinate, absent, or irresponsible member of the family and that this sometimes was attributed to his inability to find or keep a job, which, in turn, made it difficult for him to adequately support his wife and children.

Seven of the women felt that the Black male's status in the family would definitely improve as a result of the elimination of racist employment barriers. Three believed there would be no appreciable change in his status. Most of them were convinced that the Black man would be more responsible in fulfilling his husbandly and fatherly duties and that family relations would improve because of this.

They expressed their belief that the Black male's inability to find work has made him feel inferior and that he is often unable to perform effectively as a husband and father for this reason. They realize, also, that a fully employed Black husband/father will exert more control over family matters and subsequently receive more esteem in the eyes of the other family members. The opinions of the women on this subject are interesting enough to quote at length. Some of them follow:

Miss S:

As the Black man's status in the family increases, he will have more self-respect and relate more effectively to his wife and children. He will have to be more realistic about how he has related in the past and assume more responsibility in all areas of family activity.

Mrs. K:

When the male has more and better job opportunities, he may become more dominant and dogmatic in family matters. He will become more authoritarian and may try to restrict the freedom of other family members.

Mrs. A:

Black men have equal status now and don't need anymore. Increased job opportunities won't change his family status. How a man performs in the family depends on his home training.

Mrs. C:

If a man has a steady job, he wants more say-so in the family. It will be a problem because the woman will still be the boss in the family. But if two people love one another and sit down and reason together, they can make it all right.

Some men liked the past situation and were lazy and weak to some extent. The majority of Black men want their women to work for them. If they do get a job, they might not support their family. Of course, there are some exceptions. It depends on the individual.

Mrs. E:

The man's role as head of the household will be reestablished. He won't have any more power. It will take him a long time to get back that power. The woman has it (power) and she's going to keep it. He might as well be satisfied with what little power he has now.

I don't believe that the Black man will ask for more authority in the family. But if he does, there won't be any problems created. The woman may be so happy that he's working steady that she will let him make the decisions.

Mrs. H:

He will probably have more time to spend with his family. A good job will build up his ego—reestablish his self-respect. He will probably get more respect from his wife and children.

I don't know if he will have more power or not. Some unemployed men fling their power around anyway. He will be more pleasant and satisfied than before. He will probably stay home with his family more and be more stable. He will realize that the grass is no greener on the other side.

Discussion: The responses to this last question are important. Recent economic advances by Black men indicate that they will improve their socioeconomic status in this society. If Black women have achieved what degree of power they have in the family by virtue of their economic contributions, better jobs for Black men may require a reorientation of role and power relationships in the family. But the women interviewed do not see any conflict in this transitional stage.

One can detect some apprehension about what will take place on the part of some of our subjects. It could be that they do not see Black men as presently being a powerless group. Therefore, any increased economic advantage a Black man may gain from expanded job opportunities will only increase the power he already has and could restrict the woman's rights in the family.

At any rate, most of the women felt that racist employment practices have hindered Black men from carrying out their "normal" role in the family. Their general consensus was that as employment barriers based on race diminish, the Black male will take a more responsible and active role in the family.

In responding to this question, the women in this study may have been reacting to the society's stereotype of the irresponsible Black male. Most of these women have husbands who have had no problem finding employment due to their fairly high level of education. Consequently, these women may not have been responding to their own life situation but to what they assume or know to be true in the lower-class Black world.

Conclusion

These interviews were conducted to gain some insights into the Black woman's view of her role in the family and in the society. Certain questions asked were designed to reflect the endemic situation faced by Black women in this country. The question about changes in the Black male's status as a result of his occupational advancement reflect the author's view that racist employment practices have had a marked effect on role relationships in the Black family.

The responses of our subjects reveal several things. First, that Black men have been seriously handicapped by the society's denial to them of equal opportunity for employment. Secondly, if the Black male has better employment opportunities, he may become a more responsible family member but not necessarily a more powerful one. Whether true or not, the picture that emerges here is that Black women do not see themselves as all-powerful matriarchs reigning over castrated, supine Black men.

It could be that our female subjects saw their own economic independence as a liberating force that white women do not have to the same degree. Perhaps they realize that the white woman's economic dependence on the white man has led to the more subjugated role she has in the society. At any rate they do not see an increase in power as being an urgent need for Black men.

One positive change these women would like to see would be the Black male's assuming greater responsibility for his family and participating more in household tasks and child rearing. Apparently they feel that too much of the burden of household chores and child rearing has fallen on the woman's shoulders. Considering the fact that most of our interviewees were co-breadwinners in the family, this seems like a reasonable and fair request.

However, the discrepancies in their sex-role perceptions persists as a source of conflict for Black men and Black women. This difficulty is faced by men and women of all races in this constantly changing society and is an issue in need of solution. The failure to resolve the question of what is the appropriate, and equitable, role of each sex can only expand male-female conflict and increase the alienation of women from their family and the society at large.

One should note that while Black women may be presently dissatisfied with some aspects of the Black male's performance, they are by no means alienated from him. None of them, for instance, saw themselves as deprived of a career because they were tied to a home and children. Instead, they seemed not only content but happy with their roles as wives and mothers. It is also clear that although these women encountered male attitudes about the "proper" place of women, none of them had passively accepted such a male definition.

The small and biased sample used in this study limits its range of applicability. However, it gives us some insight into the responses of some Black women to their role vis-à-vis the Black man. In essence, it shows that pressures for changes in the role of Black women may become a part of the movement for changes in the status of Blacks in general. This means that Black men will have to make adjustments in their traditional mode of operation in the family. Historically, the Black man has risen to the occasion when necessary and has the potential to face the need for a redefinition of the situation. The Black man along with the men of other races must adapt to changes in family structure. The future of the family will be dependent upon their adaptation and adjustment.

Conclusions

One thing that I became aware of in my traveling recently through Africa and the Middle East, in every country you go to, usually the degree of progress can never be separated from the woman. If you're in a country that's progressive, the woman is progressive. If you're in a country that reflects the consciousness toward the importance of education, it's because the woman is aware of the importance of education. . . . One of the things I became thoroughly convinced of in my recent travels is the importance of giving freedom to the woman, giving her education, and giving her the incentive to get out there and put that same spirit and understanding in her children. And I frankly am proud of the contributions that our women have made in the struggle for freedom and I'm one person who's for giving them all the leeway possible because they've made a greater contribution than many of us men.

Malcolm X
in *By Any Means Necessary* (1970)

In the four hundred years that she has been on the American continent, the Black woman has faced many unique forces that have fashioned her sexual, marital, and familial roles. The peculiar institution of slavery was but one of those forces and should not be singled out as the sole determinant of the Black woman's role in contemporary society. Racism, capitalism, and male chauvinism have all contributed to the shaping of the Black woman's personality today.

We know that Black women were treated differently in precolonial African society than in the epoch of slavery in the United States. One result of this historical difference in Black female roles has been the tendency of some Black nationalist groups to glorify and seek to reincarnate the traditional family patterns of Africa. While we have described the important role of women in African political and social organization, there is little doubt that the patriarchal systems of most African tribes left men in firm control of the destiny and aspirations of its women.

To seek a return to a system of unchecked male supremacy for Black people runs counter to the trend toward the equalization of sex roles in American society. Blacks who advocate a reinstatement of the subordinate role of Black women seem to have unwittingly accepted the myth that Black men have been castrated by white society and that Black women collaborated in their emasculation. Such an assumption only serves to create sex-role antagonisms in the Black community that will pit Black women and men against each other, thus furthering the cause of white racism. But a house divided against itself cannot stand, an axiom that some Blacks have yet to learn.

We should not lose sight of the fact that it is white racism that is responsible for the oppression of Black people: man, woman and child. It was white racism that kidnapped Black men from their African homeland and brought them to the shores of America as slaves. The impact of slavery was much greater for Black men in light of their previous roles in their families and communities. They were stripped of all masculine rights and responsibilities, sometimes not permitted to form families, other times being arbitrarily separated from them. In essence, there was no life satisfaction for them under the system of slavery.

But Black women benefited little from the suppression of their men. It only left them exposed to all the atrocities a society can perpetrate on defenseless women. The only analogy for the status of Black women in colonial America can be found in societies where enemy troops have successfully occupied a defeated opponent's home territory. Women in those situations are subject to all sorts of dehumanizing experiences because they exist beyond the pale of human consideration.

It is out of those experiences that the independent and courageous role of Afro-American women has been fashioned. And it is the spirit of Black women that was literally responsible for the survival of Black people in the postbellum South. Few Black women have exercised their self-reliant role in any effort except that in behalf of Black men and children. Anybody that thinks otherwise does not know his history or is motivated by something other than a commitment to the liberation of Black people. To make Black women villains in the Black-white scenario is to serve the cause of Black oppression.

One cannot examine the role of Black women except in relationship to Black men. Although we have stressed the unique efforts of Black women in the maintenance of Black peoplehood, the contributions of Black men should not be understated. Except for the period of slavery, there is no evidence to show that the majority of Black men were not present in their homes and supporting their families. When Frazier described the Black matriarchy, it was one of several forms of Black families extant during the postslavery period. As far as we know, female-headed households in the Black community have always been in the minority. Furthermore, they are largely concentrated in the lower-class, the group that has been most victimized by a pervasive racist social structure and a chaotic and irresponsible economic system.

The primary problems Black women have faced with their men is that there are not enough of them and that the ones available have not been permitted to provide adequate support for their families. If white women understood this reality of the Black woman's history, they might better comprehend why some Black women are more concerned with the elevation of their men than in liberation for themselves. Since white society has deprived Black men of equal job and educational opportunities, many Black women know what it is to be equal to men. For years they have shared the equal oppression of Black men, and they see no need to seek ascendancy over them now.

Thus, Black liberation is seen as Black women's liberation. It will liberate Black women from the labor market they have been thrust into by the unemployment and under-employment of their men. It will liberate them from the sole responsibility for their families and for making decisions that they will gladly leave to men. It will liberate them back to their homes, where they can spend a leisurely amount of time in the kitchen or raising their children themselves instead of having them socialized in the streets or by surrogate parents.

Women's liberation may be the wave of the future, but what will it mean to Black women? There are Black women who wonder whether they will be used in the effort to liberate white women. Many white women want to be freed from the chores of household chores and child rearing. But who will take care of the household tasks and the little white children while white women begin meaningful jobs? We know who has done it for them in the past—Black women.

The future will probably bring new challenges to Black women. Just as some Black men are beginning to find their manhood, other social forces may halt this process. In this society manhood is closely identified with the ability to do productive work and provide for one's family. But what will happen when new technology renders the labor of men valueless? Today machines can do the work of human hands. The process of automation is complemented by cybernetics where machines correct their own mistakes. What then is to happen to men whose whole self-image is wrapped up in jobs taken by unfeeling and cheaper machines? The technological advances that we speak of encroach on the jobs of the skilled and unskilled first—the kinds of jobs most Black men have.

It is possible that Blacks will continue to have role integration, whereby Black men and women interchange their household and economic roles. We already know that the number of Black female-headed households (as well as white female-headed households) is increasing. Much of this is due to the problems of racism and poverty. But some of it relates to the problems increasingly related to marital maladjustments. While we can pinpoint many factors that figure in marital dissolution, the freedom of women is a signficant one. In the past the stability of marriage was based on the subordination of women. It is simply easier to have harmony under a dictatorship than in a democracy. If the answer to stabilizing marriage is to suppress the female personality, then most women may opt for the disease rather than the cure.

White women are just beginning to question the rigid definitions of roles in this society. For years Black women have practiced the interchanging of roles. One problem that arises from their role integration is the one-sided nature of it. Too many Black men have taken refuge in the society's segregation of male and female roles to escape sharing in what are labeled female tasks. They have not participated equally in the responsibilities of raising children and in domestic chores.

Those Black men, then, will have to be resocialized in their attitudes toward women and women's work. For too long the society has imposed dual roles on the Black woman—she has had to raise children and support them too. All this time she has accepted her role and maintained her faith in Black men. While some Black men have abdicated their responsibilities, deserted their families, and abandoned Black women for white women, Black women have generally kept the faith. But there may come a time when wells run dry, patience runs thin, and Black men may overdraw on the supply of the Black woman's goodwill.

That time is not yet near. One finds in the Black community a closeness between men and women that is not that common among whites. It is quite clear that many white women in the women's liberation movement are very bitter toward all men. While it should not distract from the goals of female liberation, the problem of lesbianism is one that many sectors of women's lib are grappling with. These attitudes of male-hostility are not found in their same intensity or magnitude among Black women. The Black woman is still very much committed to heterosexual relations.

There are no definitive answers to the questions of what the future will bring to the sexual, marital, and familial relationships of Black women. We know that the sexual exploitation of Black women in the past has led to a more healthy attitude toward sex than her more restrained white counterpart. She has avoided the guilt-ridden attitudes so many white women have toward sexual relations. As a consequence Black women have experienced a greater degree of pleasure in sexual activities. Many white women hope to achieve the same kind of pleasure.

The Black woman's historical role as a mother was but one testimony to her courage and sacrifice during the harshest years of Black oppression. She raised her children to be able to withstand all the destructive forces in their environment. Motherhood was the one aspect of the Black woman's life that she could receive some satisfaction from.

White society did not make motherhood easy for the Black woman. As a slave she experienced the ordeal of pregnancy while laboring in the fields. Subsequently, she was forced to share the time for raising children with her time in the labor market. She often had to raise her child with the knowledge that his humanity was constricted by his race, that his abilities to achieve were curtailed by white racism, and that the negative forces in the ghetto might ultimately consign him to the destination of so many Black men—the street corners, prison, or a early grave.

All these forces have helped to shape the form of Black womanhood in America. From these historical and contemporary experiences, she has developed the resiliency to fight for the survival of her people. We can only understand Black womanhood if we study the interaction of the historical and contemporary social forces she has faced. Once we gain insight into the reality of the lives of Black women, we shall know what white racism has wrought and what Black womanhood has overcome. The future may bring serious challenges to us all. But, in the past as in the present, Black womanhood represents the finest of the human spirit in overcoming the obstacles encountered in the search for freedom.

Notes

Foreword

1. Daniel P. Moynihan, *The Negro Family: The Case for National Action* (Washington, D.C.: U.S. Department of Labor, 1965).
2. Andrew Billingsley, *Black Families in White America.*
3. Toni Cade, ed., *The Black Woman.*
4. Jay David and Melvin Walkins, *To Be A Black Woman: Portraits in Fact and Fiction* (New York: William Morrow, 1971).
5. Mari Evans, *I Am a Black Woman* (New York: William Morrow, 1970).
6. Inez Reid, *Together Black Women* (New York: Emerson-Hall, 1972).
7. Joyce Ladner, *Tomorrow's Tomorrow.*
8. Black Woman's Community Development Foundation, Washington, D.C.
9. W. E. B. Du Bois, *Darkwater* (New York: Shocken Books, 1969), p. 185.

Introduction

1. Jean Bond and Pat Perry, "Has the Black Man Been Castrated," p. 5.

1. Black Womanhood: Myth and Reality

1. Annie M. D. Lebeuf, "The Role of Women in the Political Organization of African Societies," in Nancy Reeves, ed., *Womankind* (Chicago: Aldine, 1971), pp. 321-331.
2. *Ibid.*
3. *Ibid.*
4. Eric Williams, *Capitalism and Slavery* (Chapel Hill: University of North Carolina Press, 1944), pp. 19-20.
5. E. Franklin Frazier, *The Negro Family in the United States*, pp. 17-19.
6. Kenneth Stampp, *The Peculiar Institution* (New York: Vintage Books, 1956), pp. 345-354.
7. Frazier, *Negro Family*, p. 53.
8. Angela Davis, "Reflections on the Black Woman's Role in the Community of Slaves," p. 13.
9. *Ibid.*
10. Maurice Davie, *Negroes in American Society* (New York: McGraw-Hill, 1949), p. 207.
11. Pierre Van Den Berghe, *Race and Racism* (New York: John Wiley and Sons, 1967), pp. 87-88.
12. *Ibid.*
13. W. E. B. Du Bois, "The Servant in the House," in *Darkwater* (1920; New York: Schocken Books, 1969), p. 116.
14. *Ibid.*
15. John Dollard, *Caste and Class in a Southern Town* (1927; New York: Doubleday Anchor Books, 1957), p. 152.
16. Jacquelyn Jackson, "Black Women in a Racist Society."

17. Hortense Powdermaker, *After Freedom*, p. 145.
18. C. F. Paul Lewison, *Race, Class, and Party: A History of Negro Suffrage and White Politics in the South* (New York: Grosset and Dunlap, 1965).
19. Cf. Gunnar Myrdal, *An American Dilemma* (New York: Harper and Bros., 1944), pp. 182-201.
20. Frazier, *Negro Family*, p. 105.
21. Joyce Ladner, *Tomorrow's Tomorrow*, p. 241.
22. U.S. Department of Commerce, Bureau of the Census, Current Population Reports: *Special Studies*, Series P-23, no. 37 (Washington, D.C.), table 8, 1970.
23. *Ibid.*
24. U.S. Department of Health, Education and Welfare, Research and Statistics Note no. 23 (Washington, D.C., December 1965).
25. *Ibid.*
26. Frazier, *Negro Family*, pp. 209-224.
27. Daniel P. Moynihan, "Employment, Income and the Ordeal of the Negro Family."
28. The majority of Black women on welfare were not deserted by their husbands. Only 20 percent of Black families receiving public assistance had been deserted by the husband-father. See U.S. Department of Health, Education and Welfare, National Center for Social Statistics, Aid for Dependent Children Study (unpublished data, 1969).
29. *Ibid.*
30. "Welfare—The Shame of a Nation," *Newsweek*, February 8, 1971, p. 24.
31. Cf. Robert Hill, *The Strengths of Black Families*, p. 10.
32. U.S. Department of Commerce, Bureau of the Census, *1970 Census of Population, Advance Report*. Series PC (V 2) -1 (Washington, D.C., 1971).
33. Jacquelyn Jackson, "Aged Negroes and their Cultural Departures from Stereotypes and Rural-Urban Differences," No. 10 *Gerontologist*, 1970, pp. 140-145.

34. James Boudouris, "Homicide and the Family," *Journal of Marriage and the Family*, November 1971, pp. 671-672.
35. *Ibid.*, p. 675.
36. E. James Lieberman, "American Families and the Vietnam War," *Journal of Marriage and the Family*, November 1971, p. 711.
37. U.S. National Advisory Commission on Selective Service, *Who Serves When Not All Serve* (Washington, D.C.: U.S. Government Printing Office, 1967), p. 26.
38. All Black people in the nation's prisons are considered political prisoners because the political state has dealt with them differently than with whites. Although most Black crimes are committed against other Blacks, they are usually judged by whites, whose interests as a group are not necessarily to further the welfare of the Black population.
39. Robert Chrisman, "Black Prisoners—White Law," *Black Scholar*, April-May 1971, pp. 44-46.
40. Jacquelyn Jackson, "But Where are the Men," pp. 36-38.
41. *Ibid.*
42. Daniel P. Moynihan, *The Negro Family: The Case for National Action* (Washington, D.C.: U.S. Department of Labor, 1965), pp. 31-32.
43. Jackson, "But Where are the Men," pp. 30-31. In 1970, the percentage of Black women completing college increased again, while that of Black males declined. However, at the top of the educational ladder, Black males were still more numerous, as was the case for white males. (Personal communciation from Jacquelyn Jackson, November 1971.)
44. Jackson, "Black Women in a Racist Society," pp. 38-39.
45. While this has generally been true in the twentieth century, there have been eras prior to 1900 when Black men were more educated than Black women. But with

more education, Black women have consistently earned less than Black men.

46. Jackson, "Black Women in a Racist Society," p. 46.
47. Hill, *Strengths of Black Families*, pp. 14-15.
48. Jean Noble, *The Negro Woman College Graduate* (New York: Columbia University Press, 1956), p. 64.
49. U.S. Department of Labor, Bureau of Labor Statistics, *Employment and Earnings*, vol. 16, no. 7 (Washington, D.C., January 1970), table A-1.
50. Tobia Bressler and Nampeo McKenney, "Negro Women in the United States" (Paper presented at the Annual Meeting of the Population Association of America, Boston, 1968), p. 17.
51. Findings of the Twentieth Century Fund Task Force, quoted in *Washington Post*, November 30, 1971, p. 1.
52. Sonia Fuentes, "Job Discrimination and The Black Woman," *Crisis*, March 1970, pp. 103-108.
53. Moynihan, *The Negro Family*, p. 17.
54. Robert Blood and Donald Wolfe, *Husbands and Wives* (New York: Free Press of Glencoe, 1960), p. 35.
55. Russel Middleton and Snell Putney, "Dominance in Decisions in the Family: Race and Class Differences," p. 607.
56. Delores Mack, "Where the Black Matriarchy Theorists Went Wrong," pp. 86-88.
57. Herbert Hyman and John Reed, "Black Matriarchy Reconsidered," *Public Opinion Quarterly*, Fall 1969, pp. 346-354.
58. Joyce Ladner, *Tomorrow's Tomorrow*, p. 35.

2. The Sexual Life of Black Women

1. Calvin Hernton, *Sex and Racism in America*, p. 136.
2. E. Franklin Frazier, "Sex Life of the African and American Negro," p. 769.
3. Boris DeRachewitz, *Black Eros: Sexual Customs of*

Africa from Prehistory to the Present Day (New York: Lyle Stuart, 1964).

4. Melville Herskovits, *Dahomey*, pp. 280, 283.
5. Frazier, "Sex Life," pp. 770-771.
6. *Ibid.*, p. 771.
7. E. Franklin Frazier, *The Negro Family in the United States*, p. 17.
8. *Ibid.*, pp. 18-19.
9. *Ibid.*, pp. 53-54.
10. Angela Davis, "Reflections on the Black Woman's Role in the Community of Slaves," p. 13.
11. Frazier, *Negro Family*, p. 53.
12. Kenneth Stampp, *The Peculiar Institution* (New York: Vintage Books, 1956), p. 360.
13. Quoted in Louis Wirth and Herbert Guldhammer, "The Hybrid and the Problems of Miscegenation" in Otto Klineberg, ed., *Characteristics of the American Negro* (New York: Harper and Row, 1944), pp. 263-264.
14. Hernton, *Sex and Racism in America*, p. 124.
15. W. J. Cash, *The Mind of the South* (New York: Vintage Books, 1960), p. 87.
16. John Dollard, *Caste and Class in a Southern Town* (Garden City, New York: Doubleday Anchor Books, 1957), p. 139.
17. Cf. Gunnar Myrdal, *An American Dilemma* (New York: Harper and Bros., 1944), pp. 60-61.
18. Jessie Bernard, *Marriage and Family Among Negroes*, p. 75.
19. Maude Katz, "The Negro Woman and the Law," *Freedomways*, vol. 22, no. 3, p. 283.
20. Hernton, *Sex and Racism in America*, p. 128.
21. John Joward Griffin, *Black Like Me* (New York: Signet, 1963), p. 100.
22. Frazier, *Negro Family*, p. 214.
23. Dollard, *Caste and Class*, p. 147.

24. Frazier, "Sex Life," p. 774.
25. Allison Davis and John Dollard, *Children of Bondage* (1940; New York: Harper and Row, 1964), p. 272.
26. Lee Rainwater, *Behind Ghetto Walls*, p. 56.
27. Charles S. Johnson, *Growing up in the Black Belt*, p. 230.
28. Davis and Dollard, *Children of Bondage*, p. 276.
29. Robert Staples, "Sex and Games in the Black Community" (unpublished manuscript, 1970, based on a study of 250 Black male and female college students in Florida and California).
30. Davis and Dollard, *Children of Bondage*, p. 272.
31. Boone Hammond and Joyce Ladner, "Socialization into Sexual Behavior in a Negro Slum Ghetto," p. 46.
32. *Ibid.*
33. *Ibid.*, pp. 44-45.
34. Paul Gebhard, et al., *Pregnancy, Birth and Abortion*, p. 155.
35. Alan Bell, "Black Sexuality: Fact and Fancy," pp. 11-12.
36. David Schulz, *Coming Up Black*, pp. 46-47.
37. Joyce Ladner, *Tomorrow's Tomorrow*, pp. 51-52.
38. Schulz, *Coming Up Black*, p. 49.
39. Staples, "Sex and Games."
40. Rainwater, *Behind Ghetto Walls*, pp. 301-304.
41. Ira L. Reiss, "Premarital Sexual Permissiveness Among Negroes and Whites."
42. Cf. Robert Bell, *Premarital Sex in a Changing Society* (Englewood Cliffs, New Jersey: Prentice-Hall, 1966), pp. 124-132.
43. *Ibid.*, pp. 13-16.
44. Charles S. Johnson, *Growing up in the Black Belt*, p. 135.
45. Calvin Hernton, *Coming Together*, p. 17.
46. Ladner, *Tomorrow's Tomorrow*, p. 200.

47. *Ibid.*, p. 202.
48. Lee Rainwater, "Some Aspects of Lower Class Sexual Behavior," *Journal of Social Issues*, April 1966, pp. 104-105.
49. Rainwater, *Behind Ghetto Walls*, p. 57.
50. Elliott Liebow, *Tally's Corner*, p. 152.
51. Staples, "Sex and Games."
52. Frazier, "Sex Life," p. 769.
53. Bernard, *Marriage and Family Among Negroes*, p. 76.
54. Clemont Vontress, "The Black Male Personality," p. 15.
55. Liebow, *Tally's Corner*, p. 143.
56. Schulz, *Coming Up Black*, pp. 136-146.
57. Nathan Hare and Julia Hare, "Black Women 1970," p. 66.
58. Alan Bell, "Black Sexuality," pp. 11-12.
59. James K. Skipper and Gilbert Nass, "Dating Behavior: A Framework for Analysis and an Illustration," *Journal of Marriage and The Family*, November 1966, pp. 412-420.
60. U.S. Department of Commerce, Bureau of the Census, *1970 Census of Population, Advance Report: General Population Characteristics.* Series PC (V 2) - 1 (Washington, D.C., 1971).
61. Bernard, *Marriage and Family Among Negroes*, p. 70.
62. Pauli Murray, "The Negro Woman in the Quest for Equality" (paper presented at Leadership Conference, National Council of Negro Women, Washington, D.C., November 1963), pp. 11-12.
63. Willard Waller, *The Family: A Dynamic Interpretation* (New York: Cordon Company, 1938), pp. 275-276.
64. Staples, "Sex and Games."
65. Rainwater, *Behind Ghetto Walls*, p. 284.
66. Bernard Rosenberg and Joseph Bensman, "Sexual Patterns in Three Ethnic Subcultures of an American Underclass."
67. Johnson, *Growing up in the Black Belt*, p. 226.
68. Staples, "Sex and Games."

69. Alan Bell, "Black Sexuality," pp. 11-12.
70. Alvin Poussaint, "Blacks and the Sexual Revolution," p. 118.
71. Personal communication from Wardell Pomeroy, former associate director of the Kinsey Institute for Sex Research, November 1971.
72. James M. Stephens, Jr., "Two Women Plan to Be Married; File Suit; Make It Federal Case," *Jet*, November 4, 1971, pp. 20-24.
73. D. I. A. Burch, director of the Divorce and Concilliation Service of Cook County Circuit Court, quoted in *Jet*, August 5, 1971, p. 12.
74. Cf. Emmett George, "Role of Blacks and Group Sex," *Jet*, August 5, 1971, p. 12.
75. Menachem Amir, "Forcible Rape," *Sexual Behavior*, November 1971, pp. 24-36.
76. *Newsweek*, November 22, 1965, p. 42.
77. Amir, "Forcible Rape," pp. 24-26.
78. Poussaint, "Blacks and the Sexual Revolution," p. 114.
79. Hare and Hare, "Black Women 1970," p. 67.
80. *Ibid*.
81. Frank A. Petroni, "Teen-age Interracial Dating," September 1971, p. 54.
82. "Black Women Prefer Black Men," *San Francisco Chronicle*, December 3, 1970, p. 24.
83. Hans Sebald, "Patterns of Interracial Dating and Sexual Liaison of White and Black College Men," pp. 7-8.
84. Staples, "Sex and Games."
85. Kenneth Clark, *Dark Ghetto*, p. 68.
86. Sebald, "Patterns of Interracial Dating," p. 6.
87. Petroni, "Teen-age Interracial Dating," pp. 54-55.
88. Jacquelyn Jackson, "Black Women in a Racist Society," p. 16.
89. *Ibid*.
90. Mrs. Anna J. Cooper, quoted in Eleanor Flexner, *Century of Struggle: The Woman's Rights Movement in*

the *United States* (Cambridge, Massachusetts: Harvard University Press, 1959), p. 128.

3. Bodies for Sale: Black Prostitutes in White America

1. Simone de Beauvoir, *The Second Sex* (New York: Bantam Books, 1961), pp. 82-83.
2. Boris DeRachewiltz, *Black Eros: Sexual Customs of Africa from Prehistory to the Present Day* (New York: Lyle Stuart, 1964), p. 18.
3. *Ibid.*, pp. 110-111.
4. *Ibid.*, pp. 279-280.
5. *Ibid.*
6. Arthur J. Calhoun, *A Social History of the American Family*, vol. 2 (New York: Barnes & Noble, 1960), p. 229.
7. *Ibid.*, pp. 296-297.
8. Ben Ames Williams, *A Diary from Dixie* (Boston: Houghton-Mifflin, 1949), pp. 21-22.
9. E. Franklin Frazier, *The Negro Family in the United States*, , pp. 60-61.
10. Calhoun, *Social History of the American Family*, p. 304.
11. *Ibid.*, p. 310.
12. Fernando Henriques, *Prostitution in Europe and the Americas* (New York: Citadel Press, 1965), p. 262.
13. *Ibid.*, p. 254.
14. John Dollard, *Caste and Class in a Southern Town* (1937; New York: Doubleday Anchor Books, 1957), p. 152.
15. *Ibid.*, p. 153.
16. *Ibid.*
17. *Ibid.*
18. *Ibid.*, pp. 158-159.
19. Allison Davis, Burleigh B. Gardner, and Mary Gardner, *Deep South*, p. 32.

20. Calhoun, *Social History of the American Family*, p. 297.
21. Dollard, *Caste and Class*, p. 143.
22. Frazier, *Negro Family*, pp. 50-69.
23. Hortense Powdermaker, *After Freedom*, p. 182.
24. Walter Reckless, *Vice in Chicago* (Chicago: University of Chicago Press, 1933), pp. 26-28. Of course, some women became prostitutes after they got to Chicago.
25. Gunnar Myrdal, *An American Dilemma* (New York: Harper and Bros., 1944), p. 974.
26. Paul Gebhard et al., *Pregnancy, Birth and Abortion* (New York: Harper & Row, 1958), p. 187.
27. Harold Greenwald, *The Call Girl* (New York: Ballantine Books, 1958), pp. 15-27.
28. Harold Gasnell, *Negro Politicians* (Chicago: University of Chicago Press, 1935), pp. 120-121.
29. Greenwald, *The Call Girl*, p. 15.
30. Myrdal, *An American Dilemma*, p. 974.
31. St. Clair Drake and Horace Cayton, *Black Metropolis* (Chicago: University of Chicago Press, 1945), p. 596.
32. Myrdal, *An American Dilemma*, p. 974.
33. Judge John Murtagh and Sarah Harris, *Cast the First Stone* (New York: McGraw-Hill, 1957), p. 89.
34. *Ibid.*, pp. 14-15.
35. Alfred Kinsey et al., *Sexual Behavior in the Human Male* (Philadelphia: W. B. Saunders Company, 1948), p. 604.
36. Reckless, *Vice in Chicago*, p. 278.
37. Elliot Liebow, *Tally's Corner*, pp. 143-144.
38. Charles Winick and Paul Kinsie, *The Lively Commerce: Prostitution in the United States* (New York: Quadrangle Books, 1971).
39. Wardell Pomeroy's remarks at Conference on Religion and Human Sexuality, St. Louis, November 1971.
40. Greenwald, *The Call Girl*, p. 162.
41. Murtagh and Harris, *Cast the First Stone*, p. 103.

42. *Ibid.*, p. 182.
43. Greenwald, *The Call Girl*, p. 163.
44. Murtagh and Harris, *Cast the First Stone*, p. 104.
45. Drake and Cayton, *Black Metropolis*, p. 595.
46. Ulf Hannerz, *Soulside*, p. 55.
47. Greenwald, *The Call Girl*, p. 27.
48. David Schulz, *Coming Up Black*, p. 82.
49. Iceberg Slim is the author of *Pimp* (Los Angeles: Holloway Publishing Company, 1967). He made this observation on the television program "Black Journal: The Black Pimp," January 29, 1972.
50. Murtagh and Harris, *Cast the First Stone*, p. 159.
51. Reckless, *Vice in Chicago*, p. 278.
52. Murtagh and Harris, *Cast the First Stone*, p. 137.
53. Greenwald, *The Call Girl*, p. 148.
54. Karl Abraham, *Selected Papers on Psychoanalysis* (New York: Basic Books, 1953), p. 36.
55. Abram Kardiner and Lionel Oversey, *The Mark of Oppression* (New York: W. W. Norton, 1951), p. 230.
56. Drake and Cayton, *Black Metropolis*, p. 598.
57. *Ibid.*, p. 597.
58. Reckless, *Vice in Chicago*, p. 27. However, many Black women with this background do not enter prostitution.
59. Kingsley Davis, "Sexual Behavior," in *Contemporary Social Problems*, ed. Robert K. Merton and Robert A. Nisbit, 3rd edition (New York: Harcourt, Brace and Jovanovich, 1971), p. 347.
60. "Harlem," *Fortune*, July 1939, p. 170.
61. *Report of the National Advisory Commission on Civil Disorders* (New York: Bantam Books, 1968), pp. 307-308
62. *Jet*, September 28, 1971, p. 29.
63. "8 D.C. Vice Squad Policemen Indicted," *Washington Post*, January 22, 1972, p. 1.
64. "A. S. Doc Young, The Subject Is," *Los Angeles Sentinel*, December 9, 1971, p. A7.

65. *Jet*, May 26, 1966, p. 44.
66. "Black Journal: The Black Pimp," (television program, January 29, 1972).
67. Winick and Kinsie, *The Lively Commerce.*
68. Murtagh and Harris, *Cast the First Stone*, p. 191.
69. Gebhard, et al., *Pregnancy, Birth and Abortion*, p. 186.
70. "V.D.: The Epidemic," *Newsweek*, January 24, 1972, pp. 46-47.
71. de Beauvoir, *The Second Sex*, p. 524.
72. Quoted in *Newsweek*, December 20, 1971, p. 42.

4. Being Married — and Black

1. William Goode, *World Revolution and Family Patterns* (Glencoe, Illinois: Free Press, 1962), p. 380.
2. A. R. Radcliffe-Brown and Daryll Forde, *African Systems of Kinship and Marriage* (London: Oxford University Press, 1967), pp. 43-72.
3. John Hope Franklin, *From Slavery to Freedom* (New York: Alfred A. Knopf, 1967), pp. 28-31.
4. George Peter Murdock, *Social Structure* (New York: Free Press of Glencoe, 1948), pp. 30-31.
5. Melville J. Herskovits, *The Myth of the Negro Past*, pp. 170-172.
6. E. Franklin Frazier, *The Negro Family in the United States*, p. 17.
7. B. A. Botkin, *Lay My Burden Down* (Chicago: University of Chicago Press, 1945), p. 159.
8. Frazier, *Negro Family*, pp. 17-32.
9. Stanley Elkins, *Slavery: A Problem in American Institutional and Intellectual Life* (Chicago: University of Chicago Press, 1968), p. 53.
10. Frazier, *Negro Family*, pp. 17-32.
11. Sarah Bradford, *Harriet Tubman, the Moses of Her People* (New York: Corinth Press, 1961), p. 27.
12. Arthur J. Calhoun, *A Social History of the American*

Family, vol. III (New York: Barnes & Noble, 1919), pp. 39-40.
13. Henderson H. Donald, *The Negro Freedman* (New York: Abelard-Schuman, 1952), pp. 57-62.
14. Frazier, *Negro Family*, pp. 73-88.
15. Charles S. Johnson, *Shadow of the Plantation*, p. 83.
16. *Ibid.*, p. 75.
17. Sister Frances Woods, *The Cultural Values of American Ethnic Groups* (New York: Harper and Brothers, 1956), p. 223.
18. Gunnar Myrdal, *An American Dilemma* (New York: Harper and Bros., 1944), p. 931.
19. Eric Josephson, "The Matriarchy: Myth and Reality," *Family Coordinator*, October 1969, pp. 268-276.
20. Charles Johnson, *Growing up in the Black Belt*, p. 225.
21. Lee Rainwater, *Behind Ghetto Walls*, p. 179.
22. Lee Rainwater, "The Crucible of Identity," p. 180.
23. St. Clair Drake and Horace Cayton, *Black Metropolis*, p. 583.
24. *Ibid.*, p. 586.
25. *Ibid.*
26. Rainwater, *Behind Ghetto Walls*, pp. 179-180.
27. Jualynne Dodson, *To Define Black Womanhood*, pp. 22-23.
28. Frazier, *Negro Family*, pp. 320-321.
29. Thomas Pettigrew et al., "Color Gradations and Attitudes Among Middle-Income Negroes."
30. C. S. Anderson and Joseph Himes, "Dating Values and Norms on a Negro Campus."
31. U.S. Department of Commerce, Bureau of the Census, *1970 Census of Population, Advance Report: General Population Characteristics, United States* (Washington, D.C., February 1971).
32. Donald S. Akers, "On Measuring the Marriage Squeeze," *Demography* 1 (1967), pp. 907-924. For example, in 1969 nearly a third of all Black women 24 years old

were still single, compared with less than a quarter in 1960.

33. Carlfred Broderick, "Social Heterosexual Development Among Urban Negroes and Whites."

34. Elliot Liebow, *Tally's Corner*, p. 110.

35. Rainwater, *Behind Ghetto Walls*, pp. 48-54.

36. "Black Women Prefer Black Men," *San Francisco Chronicle*, December 3, 1970, p. 24.

37. Calvin Hernton, *Sex and Racism in America*, p. 61.

38. Joyce Ladner, *Tomorrow's Tomorrow*, p. 280.

39. Phylliss Hallenbeck, "An Analysis of Power Dynamics in Marriage," *Journal of Marriage and the Family*, May 1966, p. 201.

40. Reuben Hill and Howard Becker, eds., *Family, Marriage and Parenthood* (Boston: D. C. Heath, 1955), p. 790.

41. Leland J. Axelson, "The Working Wife," pp. 457-464.

42. Robert Hill, *The Strengths of Black Families*, pp. 13-14.

43. Abram Kardiner and Lionel Ovesey, *The Mark of Oppression*, p. 71.

44. David Schulz, "Some Aspects of the Policeman's Role as It Impinges Upon Family Life in a Negro Ghetto."

45. Charles E. King, "The Sex Factor in Marital Adjustment."

46. Lee Rainwater, *Family Design*, p. 66.

47. Robert Blood and Donald Wolfe, *Husbands and Wifes* (Glencoe, Illinois: Free Press, 1960), pp. 66, 172.

48. Robert Bell, "The Related Importance of Mother and Wife Roles Among Black Lower Class Women," in *The Black Family: Essays and Studies*, ed. Robert Staples (Belmont, California: Wadsworth, 1971), pp. 253-254.

49. *Ibid.*

50. *Ibid.*, p. 254.

51. Karen Renne, "Correlates of Dissatisfaction in Marriage."

52. Rainwater, "The Crucible of Identity," p. 255.

53. Ladner, *Tomorrow's Tomorrow*, p. 37.

54. Personal communication from William Yancey, Vanderbilt University, February 1971.
55. Robert Bell, "Comparative Attitudes about Marital Sex Among Negro Women in the United States, Great Britain, and Trinidad."
56. Rainwater, "The Crucible of Identity," pp. 62-63.
57. Bell, "Comparative Attitudes about Marital Sex."
58. Liebow, *Tally's Corner*, p. 116.
59. Drake and Cayton, *Black Metropolis*, p. 587.
60. Jean Noble, *The Negro Woman College Graduate* (New York: Columbia University Press, 1956), p. 108.
61. *Ibid.*
62. Julius Roth and Robert Peck, "Social Class and Social Mobility: Factors Related to Marital Adjustment." *American Sociological Review* 16 (1951): pp. 478-487.
63. Pauli Murray, "The Negro Woman in the Quest for Equality" (Paper presented at Leadership Conference, National Council of Negro Women, Washington, D.C., November 1963), pp. 11-12.
64. Cf. Jacquelyn Jackson, "Black Women in a Racist Society."
65. Kardiner and Ovesey, *The Mark of Oppression*, p. 69.
66. Goode, *After Divorce*, pp. 54-55.
67. The proportion of middle-class spouses living together is higher than the corresponding proportion for lower-class Blacks. There is very little variance in the prevalence of divorce. Cf. Reynolds Farley, "Trends in Marital Stability Among Negroes," in *The Family Life of Black People*, ed. Charles Willie (Columbus, Ohio: Charles E. Merrill, 1970), pp. 178-179.
68. U.S. Department of Commerce, Bureau of the Census, *Social and Economic Variations in Marriage, Divorce and Remarriage* (Washington, D.C., 1967), pp. 1-2.
69. *Ibid.*, p. 8.
70. Goode, *After Divorce*, p. 139.
71. U.S. Public Health Service, *Vital Statistics of the United*

States, 1965-1968. Given in Hill, *The Strengths of Black Families*, appendix.
72. Rainwater, *Behind Ghetto Walls*, p. 778.
73. David Heer, "Negro-White Marriage in the United States," pp. 262-273.
74. Frazier, *Black Bourgeoisie*, p. 218.
75. Nathan and Julia Hare, "Black Women 1970", p. 67.
76. Hernton, *Sex and Racism in America*, p. 137.
77. *Ibid.*, p. 139.
78. Nathan Hare, "Will the Real Black Man Stand Up," *Black Scholar*, June 1971, p. 33.
79. Robert Merton, "Intermarriage and the Social Structure: Fact and Theory," *Psychiatry*, August 1941, pp. 361-374.
80. Todd H. Pavela, "An Exploratory Study of Negro-White Intermarriage in Indiana," *Marriage and Family Living*, May 1964, p. 209.
81. Jessie Bernard, "Note on Educational Homogamy in Negro-White and White-Negro Marriages," *Journal of Marriage and the Family*, August 1966, pp. 274-276.
82. *Los Angeles Sentinel*, February 4, 1971.
83. Constantine Panunzio, "Intermarriage in Los Angeles, 1924-33," *American Journal of Sociology*, March 1942, p. 690.
84. Joseph Washington, Jr., *Marriage in Black and White*, p. 303.
85. Joseph Golden, "Patterns of Negro-White Intermarriage," *American Sociological Review*, April 1954, p. 146.
86. Randall Risdon, "A Study of Interracial Marriages Based on Data for Los Angeles County."
87. Hugo G. Beigel, "Problems and Motives in Interracial Relationships," pp. 192-193.
88. Chuck Stone, *Tell It Like It Is* (New York: Bantam Books, 1970), pp. 43-44.
89. Nancy Sirkis, *One Family* (Boston: Little, Brown and Company, 1970), p. 27.

234   *Notes*

5. The Joy and Pain of Motherhood

1. Shulamith Firestone, *The Dialectic of Sex* (New York: Bantam Books, 1970), p. 72.
2. Caroline Bird, *Born Female* (New York: Pocket Books, 1971), p. 208.
3. E. Franklin Frazier, *The Negro Family in the United States*, p. 33.
4. *Ibid.*, p. 34.
5. *Ibid.*
6. Meyer Fortes, "Kinship and Marriage among the Ashanti," in A. R. Radcliffe-Brown and Darryl Ford, eds., *African Systems of Kinship and Marriage* (London: Oxford University Press, 1950), p. 252.
7. *Ibid.*
8. Sheila Hobson, "The Black Family," p. 14.
9. George P. Murdock, *Africa: Its People and Their Culture* (New York: McGraw-Hill, 1959).
10. Frazier, *Negro Family*, p. 37.
11. Kenneth Stampp, *The Peculiar Institution* (New York: Vintage Books, 1956), p. 343.
12. *Ibid.*, pp. 316-317.
13. Arna Bontemps, *Great Slave Narratives* (Boston: Beacon Press, 1969), p. 198.
14. Stampp, *The Peculiar Institution*, p. 343.
15. B. A. Botkin, *Lay My Burden Down* (Chicago: University of Chicago Press, 1945), pp. 55, 154, 189.
16. Benjamin Quarles, ed., *Narrative of the Life of Frederick Douglass, an American Slave* (Cambridge, Mass.: Harvard University Press, 1960), pp. 35-36.
17. Frazier, *Negro Family*, p. 37.
18. Quoted in Frazier, *Negro Family*, p. 41.
19. Melville J. Herskovits, *The Myth of the Negro Past*, pp. 170-172.
20. Frazier, *Negro Family*, pp. 15-16.
21. Maurice Davie, *Negroes in American Society* (New York: McGraw-Hill, 1949), p. 207.

22. Frazier, *Negro Family*, pp. 73-88.
23. *Ibid.*
24. Personal communication from Talmadge Anderson, director of Black studies, Washington State University, November 1970.
25. Hortense Powdermaker, *After Freedom*, p. 145.
26. *Ibid.*
27. Frazier, *Negro Family*, pp. 268-280.
28. Reynolds Farley, *Growth of the Black Population*, pp. 1-4.
29. *Ibid.*
30. U.S. Department of Commerce, Bureau of the Census, *Fertility Indicators 1970*, Series P-23, no. 26 (Washington, D.C., April 1971), p. 1.
31. Farley, *Growth of the Black Population*, pp. 104-117.

32. Adelaide Cromwell Hill and Frederick Jaffe, "Negro Fertility and Family Size Preferences: Implications for Programming of Health and Social Services," in *The Negro American*, eds. Talcott Parsons and Kenneth Clark (Boston: Beacon Press, 1966), p. 208.
33. U.S. Department of Commerce, Bureau of the Census, *1960 Census of Population: Women by Number of Children Ever Born*, PC (2)-3A (Washington, D.C., 1964), table 8.
34. Frazier, *Negro Family*, p. 330.
35. Jeanne Noble, *The Negro Woman College Graduate* (New York: Columbia University Press, 1956), pp. 39-42.
36. Clyde Kiser and Myrna Frank, "Factors Associated with the Low Fertility of Nonwhite Women of College Attainment," *Millbank Memorial Fund Quarterly*, October 1967, p. 427.
37. *Ibid.*, pp. 427-449.
38. U.S. Department of Commerce, Bureau of the Census, *Population Characteristics: Fertility Variations by*

Ethnic Origin, Series P-20 (Washington, D.C., November 1971).

39. Phillip R. Kunz and Merlin B. Brinkerhoff, "Differential Childlessness by Color."
40. Leslie Westoff and Charles Westoff, *From Now to Zero* (Boston: Little, Brown and Company, 1971), p. 248.
41. Franklin Watson, "A Comparison of Negro and White Populations: 1940-1960," *Phylon*, Summer 1968, p. 152.
42. Alphonso Pinkney, *Black Americans* (Englewood Cliffs, New Jersey: Prentice-Hall, 1969), p. 51.
43. Westoff and Westoff, *From Now to Zero*, p. 248.
44. E. Franklin Frazier, "The Negro and Birth Control," *Birth Control Review*, March 1933, pp. 68-70.
45. W. E. B. Du Bois, "Black Folk and Birth Control," *Birth Control Review*, May 1938, p. 90.
46. Carolyn Anspacher, "Why Birth Control Frightens Blacks," *San Francisco Chronicle*, April 10, 1969, p. 4.
47. Dr. Charles Willie, position paper presented to the President's Commission on Population Growth and the American Future, June 1971.
48. The Committee on Human Development of the National Conference on the Status of Health in the Black Community, Nashville, Tennessee, December 1971.
49. Daniel Watts, "Birth Control," *Liberator*, May 1969, p. 3.
50. Robert Staples, ed., *The Black Family*, p. 183.
51. Dr. Andrew Billingsley, in a speech delivered before the Annual Conference of Planned Parenthood-World Population, in San Francisco, October 1971.
52. Wylda B. Cowles, summary of an interview with Malcolm X, May 1962.
53. Dick Gregory, "My Answer to Genocide," *Ebony*, October 1971, p. 66.
54. Joyce Ladner, *Tomorrow's Tomorrow*, p. 256.

55. William A. Darity and Castellano B. Turner, "Family Planning, Race Consciousness and the Fear of Race Genocide" (Paper presented at the Workshop on Research Approaches to Sex Education, Contraception, Family Planning and Morality, at Bethesda, Maryland, September 1970).

56. Toni Cade, "The Pill: Genocide or Liberation," in *The Black Woman*, ed. Toni Cade (New York: Signet, 1970), p. 164.

57. Linda Larue, "The Black Movement and Women's Liberation," p. 42.

58. These figures are reported in Westoff and Westoff, *From Now to Zero*, pp. 251-254.

59. *Ibid.*

60. *Ibid.*

61. Lee Rainwater, *Family Design*, p. 220.

62. Westoff and Westoff, *From Now to Zero*, p. 257.

63. *Ibid.*, pp. 255-256.

64. *Ibid.*, pp. 257-258.

65. Rainwater, *Family Design*, pp. 293-296.

66. Ladner, *Tomorrow's Tomorrow*, pp. 262-263.

67. Paul Gebhard et al., *Pregnancy, Birth and Abortion*, p. 164.

68. "Annual Report of the New York City Department of Health," June 1971.

69. Report of the Population Council of the United States, 1971.

70. Marvin Wanetick, "Most Blacks Favor Legal Abortion," *Michigan Chronicle*, June 5, 1971, p. 1.

71. Westoff and Westoff, *From Now to Zero*, p. 268. Approximately one out of every three Black births in the years 1960-65 was not wanted.

72. Cf. Christy Ashe, "Abortion or Genocide," *Liberator*, August 1970, pp. 4-9. The typical argument against Black birth control is that children are needed to fight in the Black Liberation struggle.

73. Florynce Kennedy, quoted in *The Militant*, October 29, 1971, p. 10.
74. Charles S. Johnson, *Shadow of the Plantation*, p. 58.
75. Robert Bell, "The Relative Importance of Mother and Wife Roles Among Negro Lower-Class Women," in Robert Staples, ed., *The Black Family: Essays and Studies* (Belmont, California: Wadsworth, 1971), pp. 248-256.
76. *Ibid.*
77. Robert Blood and Donald Wolfe, "Negro-White Differences in Blue Collar Marriages in a Northern Metropolis."
78. Zena Smith Blau, "Exposure to Child Rearing Experts."
79. Robert Hess and Virginia Shipman, "Early Experiences and the Socialization of Cognitive Modes in Children."
80. E. Franklin Frazier, *Negro Youth at the Crossways*, p. 204.
81. Allison Davis and John Dollard, *Children of Bondage* (1940; New York: Harper & Row, 1964), p. 267.
82. *Ibid.*
83. David Schulz, *Coming up Black*, p. 145.
84. Johnson, *Shadow of the Plantation*, p. 100.
85. Schulz, *Coming up Black*, p. 145.
86. Staples, ed., *The Black Family*, p. 186.
87. Allison Davis and Robert J. Havighurst, "Social Class and Color Differences in Child Rearing," pp. 710-714.
88. Davis and Dollard, *Children of Bondage*, p. 265.
89. Thomas Lee Gillete, "Maternal Employment and Family Structure as Influenced by Social Class and Role" (Ph.D. dissertation, University of North Carolina, 1961).
90. Davis and Dollard, *Children of Bondage*, p. 275.
91. *Ibid.*
92. Schulz, *Coming up Black*, pp. 21-42.
93. Fortes, "Kinship and Marriage among the Ashanti," pp. 274-276.

94. Robert Hill, *The Strengths of Black Families*, p. 5.
95. Frazier, *Negro Family*, p. 114.
96. John Dollard, *Caste and Class in a Southern Town* (New York: Doubleday Anchor Books, 1957), p. 159.
97. Ira Iscoe et al., "Age, Intelligence, and Sex as Variables in the Conformity Behavior of Negro and White Children."
98. Lee Rainwater, *Behind Ghetto Walls*, p. 219.
99. Schulz, *Coming up Black*, pp. 42-48.
100. Rainwater, *Behind Ghetto Walls*, p. 65.
101. Hortense Powdermaker, *After Freedom*, p. 215.
102. Robert Coles, *Children of Crisis* (New York: Little, Brown and Company, 1964), p. 66.
103. Robert Coles, "In the South These Children Prophesy," *Atlantic Monthly*, March 1963, pp. 111-112.
104. Schulz, *Coming up Black*, p. 155.
105. Erik Erikson, "The Concept of Identity in Race Relations: Notes and Queries," *Daedalus*, Winter 1966, pp. 145-171.

6. Black Women and Women's Liberation.

1. Karl Marx and Friedrich Engels, *Manifesto of the Communist Party* (New York: International Publishers, 1922).
2. Caroline Bird, *Born Female* (New York: Pocket Books, 1971), pp. 110-125.
3. Ellen Keniston and Kenneth Keniston, "The American Anachronism: The Image of Women at Work," *American Scholar*, Summer 1964.
4. Inge Powel Bell, "The Double Standard," *Transaction*, November-December 1970, p. 80.
5. *Ibid.*, p. 78.
6. William Raspberry, "A Vicious Form of Bias," *Washington Post*, February 7, 1972, p. A19.
7. Jessie Bernard, letter to *American Sociologist*, November 1970, pp. 374-375.

8. Bird, *Born Female*, p. 124.
9. Helen Hacker, "Women as a Minority Group," *Social Forces*, October 1951, pp. 60-69.
10. Benjamin Quarles, "Frederick Douglass and the Women's Rights Movement," *Journal of Negro History*, January 1940, p. 35.
11. Linda Larue, "The Black Movement and Women's Liberation," p. 36.
12. *Ibid.*
13. Helen King, "The Black Woman and Women's Lib," p. 74.
14. Ronald Kisner, "Shirley Chisholm Kicks Off Campaign for U.S. President," *Jet*, February 10, 1972, p. 14.
15. Joyce Ladner, *Tomorrow's Tomorrow*, pp. 265-267.
16. King, "Black Woman and Women's Lib," p. 75.
17. Mary Dennison, "Total Liberation Comes Before New Roles," *N.Y. Amsterdam News*, November 6, 1971, p. A7.
18. Gilbert Osofosky, *The Burden of Race* (New York: Harper & Row, 1967), p. 328.
19. King, "Black Woman and Women's Lib," p. 76.
20. Toni Morrison, quoted in *Jet*, January 27, 1972, p. 32.
21. Quoted in King, "Black Woman and Women's Lib," pp. 74-75.
22. U.S. Department of Commerce, Bureau of the Census, *1970 Census of Population, Advance Report: General Population Characteristics, United States*, PC (V 2) -1 (Washington, D.C.).
23. Brenda Butler, "Black Man-White Woman Rap Snarls Confab," *Jet*, February 10, 1972, pp. 24-25.
24. Joyce Ladner, "Sexism of Racism," unpublished paper, p. 10.
25. Dennison, "Total Liberation," p. A7.
26. Ladner, *Tomorrow's Tomorrow*, p. 283.
27. Kisner, "Shirley Chisholm," p. 14.
28. Charlayne Hunter, "Many Blacks Wary of Women's

Liberation Movement in the U.S.," *New York Times*, November 17, 1970, p. 41.

29. E. Franklin Frazier, *The Negro Family in the United States*, pp. 127-141.
30. Quoted in Booker T. Washington, *Frederick Douglass* (Philadelphia: George W. Jacobs and Company, 1906), p. 136.
31. Cf. Booker T. Washington, *Up From Slavery* (New York: Doubleday, 1901), p. 222.
32. W. E. B. Du Bois, *Darkwater* (New York: Harcourt, Brace & World, 1920), p. 181.
33. *Ibid.*, pp. 171-172.
34. Theodore Draper, *The Rediscovery of Black Nationalism* (New York: Viking Press, 1969), p. 138.
35. C. Eric Lincoln, *The Black Muslims* (Boston: Beacon Press, 1961).
36. Alex Haley, *The Autobiography of Malcolm X* (New York: Grove Press, 1955), pp. 232, 305.
37. *Ibid.*, p. 294.
38. Quoted from *By Any Means Necessary*, ed. George Breitman (New York: Pathfinder Press, 1970), p. 179.
39. Eldridge Cleaver, *Soul on Ice* (New York: McGraw-Hill, 1968), p. 158.
40. Sisters For Black Community Development, "Black Woman's Role in the Revolution" (Newark, New Jersey, 1971). This publication reflects Jones's views.
41. Abram Kardiner and Lionel Ovesey, *The Mark of Oppression*, p. 341.
42. Cleaver, "Notes on a Native Son," in *Soul on Ice*, pp. 97-111.
43. Frazier, *Negro Family*, pp. 33-49.
44. E. Franklin Frazier, *Black Bourgeoisie*, pp. 195-212.
45. William Grier and Price Cobbs, *Black Rage*.
46. Cf. Janet Saxe's book review in *Black Scholar*, March 1970, p. 58.
47. Grier and Cobbs, *Black Rage*, pp. 39, 80.

48. *Ibid.*, p. 33.
49. Calvin Hernton, *Sex and Racism in America*, p. 166.
50. *Ibid.*, p. 150.
51. Calvin Hernton, *Coming Together*, pp. 53, 59.
52. Quoted in King, "Black Woman and Women's Lib," p. 76.
53. *Ibid.*, p. 74.
54. William Banks, Jr., "Women's Lib: A New Cop-out on the Black Struggle," *Liberator*, September 1970, pp. 4-5.
55. Jacquelyn Jackson, "Black Women in a Racist Society," pp. 72-73.
56. Frances Beal, "Double Jeopardy: To Be Black and Female," in *The Black Woman: An Anthology*, ed. Toni Cade (New York: Signet, 1970), pp. 114-116.
57. George Novack, "Revolutionary Dynamics of the Struggle for Women's Liberation," *Militant*, October 17, 1969, pp. 7-9.
58. Bell, "The Double Standard," p. 80.
59. Warren T. Farrell, "The Resocialization of Men's Attitudes Towards Women's Role in Society" (Paper presented before the American Political Science Association, Los Angeles, September 1970).
60. Elizabeth Barnes, "Sisterhood is Powerful," *Militant*, October 23, 1970, p. 9.
61. Of course, Black men have been somewhat disadvantaged by the increased emphasis on equal rights for women. Some white employers now prefer hiring Black women for his positions, thus getting two minorities for the price of one.

Bibliography

Aldous, Joan. "Wives' Employment Status and Lower-Class Men as Husband-Fathers: Support for the Moynihan Thesis." *Journal of Marriage and the Family* 31 (August 1969): 469-476.

Anders, Sarah. "New Dimensions in Ethnicity and Child Rearing Attitudes." *American Journal of Mental Deficiency* 73 (1969): 505-508.

Anderson, C.S., and Himes, Joseph. "Dating Values and Norms on a Negro College Campus." *Marriage and Family Living* 21 (April 1959): 227-229.

Andrew, Gwenn. "Determinants of Negro Family Decisions in Management of Retardation." *Journal of Marriage and the Family* 30 (November 1968): 612-617.

Axelson, Leland J. "The Working Wife: Differences in Perception Among Negro and White Males." *Journal of Marriage and the Family* 32 (August 1970): 457-464.

Baughman, Earl, and Dahlstrom, W. Grant. *Negro and White Children: A Psychological Study in the Rural South.* New York: Academic Press, 1968.

Beal, Frances. "Double Jeopardy: To Be Black and Female." *New Generation* 51 (Fall 1969): 23-28.

Beigel, Hugo G. "Problems and Motives in Interracial Relationships." *Journal of Sex Research* (November 1966): 185-205.

Bell, Allan. "Black Sexuality: Fact and Fancy." Paper presented in *Focus: Black America* Series at Indiana University, Bloomington, Indiana, 1968.

Bell, Robert. "Comparative Attitudes about Marital Sex among Negro Women in the United States, Great Britain, and Trinidad." *Journal of Comparative Family Studies* 1 (Autumn 1970): 71-81.'

———. "The Lower Class Negro Family in the United States and Britain: Some Comparisons." *Race* 11 (October 1969).

———. "Lower Class Negro Mothers and Their Children." *Integrated Education* 2 (December-January 1965): 23-27.

———. "The One Parent Mother in the Negro Lower Class." Paper presented to the Eastern Sociological Society, April 1965.

Bernard, Jessie. "Marital Stability and Patterns of Status Variables." *Journal of Marriage and the Family* 28 (November 1966): 421-439.

———. *Marriage and Family Among Negroes.* Englewood Cliffs, New Jersey: Prentice-Hall, Inc., 1966.

Biller, Henry. "A Note on Father Absence and Masculine Development in Lower-Class Negro and White Boys." *Child Development* 39 (1968): 1004-1006.

Billingsley, Andrew. "Black Families and White Social Science." *Journal of Social Issues* 24 (Summer 1970): 127-142.

———. "Family Functioning in the Low-Income Black Community." *Social Casework* 50 (1969): 563-572.

——— and Billingsley, Amy T. "Illegitimacy and Patterns of Negro Family Life." In *The Unwed Mothers,* edited by Robert W. Roberts, New York: Harper & Row, Publishers, 1966, 131-157.

——— and Billingsley, Amy Tate. "Negro Family Life in America." *Social Service Review* 39 (September 1965): 310-319.

—— and Giovannoni, Jeanne. *Children of the Storm.* New York: Harcourt, Brace-Jovanovich, 1972.

Blau, Zena Smith. "Exposure to Child Rearing Experts: A Structural Interpretation of Class Color Differences." *American Journal of Sociology* 69 (May 1964): 596-608.

Blood, Robert, and Wolfe, Donald. "Negro-White Differences in Blue Collar Marriages in a Northern Metropolis." *Social Forces* 48 (September 1969): 59-63.

Bond, Jean C., and Perry, Pat. "Has the Black Man Been Castrated?" *Liberator* (May 1969): 4-8.

Bowie, C.C. "The Meaning of the Marriage Contract to 674 Negro Male Veterans." *International Journal of Sexology* 2 (1948): 42-43.

Brodber, Erna, and Wagner, Nathaniel. "The Black Family, Poverty, and Family Planning: Anthropological Impressions." *Family Coordinator* (April 1970): 168-172.

Broderick, Carlfred. "Social Heterosexual Development Among Urban Negroes and Whites." *Journal of Marriage and the Family* 27 (May 1965): 200-203.

Brody, Eugene B. "Color and Identity Conflict in Young Boys: Observations of Negro Mothers and Sons in Urban Baltimore." *Psychiatry* 26 (May 1963): 188-201.

Brown, Thomas Edwards. "Sex Education and Life in the Negro Ghetto." *Pastoral Psychology* (May 1968).

Cade, Toni, ed. *The Black Woman: An Anthology.* New York: Signet Publishing Company, 1970.

Campbell, Arthur. "Fertility and Family Planning Among Non-White Married Couples in the United States." *Eugenics Quarterly* 12 (September 1965): 124-131.

Carper, Laura. "The Negro Family and the Moynihan Report." *Dissent* (March-April 1966).

Cavan, Ruth Shone. "Negro Family Disorganization and Juvenile Deliquency." *Journal of Negro Education* 28 (Summer 1959): 230-239.

Chisholm, Shirley. "Racism and Anti-feminism." *Black Scholar,* (January-February 1970): 40-45.

Clarizio, Harvey. "Maternal Attitude Change Associated

with Involvement in Project Head Start." *Journal of Negro Education* 37 (1968): 106-113.

Clark, Kenneth. *Dark Ghetto.* New York: Harper & Row, Publishers, 1965.

Coles, Robert. "Children and Racial Demonstrations." *American Scholar* vol. 34, no. 1 (Winter 1964-65): 78-92.

Comer, J.P. *The Black Family: An Adaptive Perspective.* New Haven: Child Study Center, Yale University, 1970.

Cox, O.C. "Sex Ratio and Marital Status Among Negroes." *American Sociological Review* 5 (1940): 937-947.

Curtis, Thomas, and Archibald, Billy. "On Revering the Black Woman." *Negro Digest* 76 (May 1967): 94-98.

Darity, William A., and Turner, Castellano B. "Family Planning, Race Consciousness and the Fear of Race Genocide." Paper presented at the Workshop on Research Approaches to Sex Education, Contraception, Family Planning and Morality, September 1970, at Bethesda, Maryland.

Davies, Vernon. "Fertility Versus Welfare: The Negro American Dilemma." *Phylon* 27 (1967): 226-232.

Davis, Allison, and Havighurst, Robert. "Social Class and Color Differences in Child Rearing." *American Sociological Review* 11 (1946): 698-710.

———; Gardner, Burleigh B.; and Gardner, Mary. *Deep South.* Chicago: University of Chicago Press, 1941.

——— and Havighurst, Robert J. *The Father of Man: How Your Child Gets His Personality.* Boston: Houghton Mifflin Company, 1947.

Davis, Angela. "Reflections on the Black Woman's Role in the Community of Slaves." *Black Scholar* (December 1971): 2-16.

Deasy, Leila C., and Quinn, Olive W. "The Urban Negro and Adoption of Children." *Child Welfare* (November 1962).

Dodson, Jualynne. *To Define Black Womanhood.* Institute of the Black World, Atlanta, Georgia (February 1971).

Drake, St. Clair, and Clayton, Horace. *Black Metropolis.* Chicago: University of Chicago Press, 1945.

Du Bois, W.E.B. *The Negro American Family.* Atlanta: Atlanta University Press, 1908.

Duncan, Beverly, and Duncan, Otis Dudley. "The Family and Occupational Success." *Social Problems* 16 (Winter 1969): 273-285.

Ebony. "That Black Man-White Woman Thing." August 1970, 130-133.

Edwards, G. Franklin. "Marital Status and General Family Characteristics of the Non-white Population of the United States." *Journal of Negro Education* 22 (Summer 1953): 280-290.

———. "Marriage and Family Life Among Negroes." *Journal of Negro Education* 22 (Fall 1963): 451-465.

Edwards, Harry. "Black Muslim and Negro Christian Family Relationships." *Journal of Marriage and the Family* 30 (November 1968): 604-611.

Erikson, Erik. "Memorandum on Identity and Negro Youth." *Journal of Social Issues* 20 (October 1964): 29-42.

Farley, Reynolds. *Growth of the Black Population.* Chicago: Markham Publishing Company, 1970.

——— and Hermalin, Albert. "Family Stability: A Comparison of Trends Between Blacks and Whites." *American Sociological Review* 36 (February 1970): 1-17.

Feagin, Joe R. "The Kinship Ties of Negro Urbanites." *Social Science Quarterly* 49 (December 1968).

Fischer, Ann, et al. "The Occurrence of the Extended Family at the Origin of the Family of Procreation: A Developmental Approach to Negro Family Structure." *Journal of Marriage and the Family* 30 (May 1968): 290-300.

Franklin, Robert M. "Attitude of Negro College Students Toward Intrafamily Leadership and Control." *Marriage and Family Living* 16 (August 1954): 252-253.

Frazier, E. Franklin. *Black Bourgeoisie.* 1957. New York: Free Press of Glencoe, 1965.

———. "Ethnic Family Patterns: The Negro Family in the United States." *American Journal of Sociology* 54 (May

1948): 433-438.

———. *The Free Negro Family.* Nashville, Tenn.: Fisk University Press, 1932.

———. *The Negro Family in Chicago.* Chicago: University of Chicago Press, 1932.

———. *The Negro Family in the United States.* 1939. Chicago: University of Chicago Press, 1966 (revised edition).

———. "The Negro Slave Family." *Journal of Negro History* 15 (April 1930): 198-206.

———. *Negro Youth at the Crossways.* Washington, D.C.: American Council on Education, 1941.

———. "Problems and Needs of Negro Children and Youth Resulting from Family Disorganization." *Journal of Negro Education* 19 (1950): 261-277.

———. "Sex Life of the African and American Negro." In *The Encyclopedia of Sexual Behavior,* edited by Albert Ellis and Albert Abarbanel, pp. 769-775. New York: Hawthorn Books, 1961.

Furstenberg, Frank F. "Premarital Pregnancy among Black Teenagers." *Transaction* 7 (May 1970): 52-55.

——— et al. "Birth Control Knowledge and Attitudes Among Unmarried Pregnant Adolescents." *Journal of Marriage and the Family* 31 (February 1969): 34-42.

Gallagher, Ursula. "Adoption Resources for Black Children." *Children* 18 (March-April 1971): 49-53.

Gans, Herbert. "The Negro Family." *Commonweal* (October 1965): 47-51.

Gass, G. Z., et al. "Family Problems in Upgrading the Hardcore." *Family Coordinator* 18 (October 1969): 99-106.

Gebhard, Paul, et al. *Pregnancy, Birth and Abortion.* New York: Harper and Brothers, 1958.

Geismar, Ludwig, and Gerhart, Ursula. "Social Class, Ethnicity and Family Functioning: Exploring Some Issues Raised by the Moynihan Report." *Journal of Marriage and the Family* 30 (August 1968): 480-487.

Glazer, Nona Y., and Creedon, Carol F., eds., *Children and Poverty*. Chicago : Rand McNally, 1968.

Golden, Joseph. "Social Control of Negro-White Intermarriage." In *Selected Studies of Marriage and the Family*, edited by Robert Winch et al. New York: Holt, Rinehart and Winston, 1953.

Goode, William. *After Divorce*. New York: Free Press of Glencoe, 1956.

———. "Illegitimacy in the Carribean Social Structure." *American Sociological Review* 25 (February 1960): 21-30.

Gordon, Joan. *The Poor of Harlem: Social Functioning in the Underclass*. New York: Office of the Mayor, 1965.

Gottlieb, David, and Tenhouten, Warren D. "Racial Composition and the Social System of Three High Schools." *Journal of Marriage and the Family* 27 (May 1965): 204-212.

Grier, William, and Cobbs, Price. *Black Rage*. New York: Bantam Books, 1968.

Hammond, Boone, and Ladner, Joyce. "Socialization into Sexual Behavior in a Negro Slum Ghetto." In *The Individual, Sex and Society*, edited by Carlfred Broderick and Jessie Bernard, pp. 41-52. Balitmore: Johns Hopkins Press, 1969.

Hannerz, Ulf. *Soulside*. New York: Columbia University Press, 1969.

Hare, Nathan. "The Frustrated Masculinity of the Negro Male." *Negro Digest* (August 1964): 5-9.

——— and Hare, Julia. "Black Women 1970." *Transaction* (November-December 1970): 65-68.

Harrison, Danny, et al. "Attitudes of Rural Youth Toward Premarital Sexual Permissiveness." *Journal of Marriage and the Family* 31 (November 1969): 783-787.

Hart, H. "Differential Negro Fertility." *American Sociological Review* 18 (June 1953): 192-194.

Hartnagel, Timothy. "Father Absence and Self-Conception Among Lower-Class White and Negro Boys." *Social Problems* 18 (Fall 1970): 152-163.

Heer, David. "Negro-White Marriage in the United States." *Journal of Marriage and the Family* 28 (August 1966): 262-273.

Henderson, George. "Role Models for Lower-Class Negro Boys." *Personnel and Guidance Journal* 46 (1967): 6-10.

Henton, C. L. "The Effect of Socio-Economic and Emotional Factors on the Onset of Menarche Among Negro and White Girls." *Journal of Genetic Psychology* 98 (1961): 255-264.

Hernton, Calvin. *Sex and Racism in America.* New York: Doubleday & Company, Inc., 1965.

——. *Coming Together.* New York: Random House, 1971.

Herskovits, Melville J. *The American Negro.* New York: Harper and Brothers, 1928.

——. *Dahomey: An Ancient West African Kingdom.* New York: J.J. Augustin, 1938.

——. *The Myth of the Negro Past.* Boston: Beacon Press, 1958.

Hertz, Hilda, and Little, Sue Warren. "Unmarried Negro Mothers in a Southern Urban Community." *Social Forces* 23 (October 1944): 73-79.

Herzog, Elizabeth. "Is There a Breakdown of the Negro Family?" *Social Work* (January 1966): 1-8.

——. "Why So Few Negro Adoptions?" *Children* 12 (1965): 3-10.

—— et al. *Families for Black Children.* Washington, D.C.: U.S. Department of Health, Education, and Welfare, Office of Child Development, 1971.

Hess, Robert, and Shipman, Virginia. "Early Experience and the Socialization of Cognitive Modes in Children." *Child Development* 36 (1965): 869-885.

Hetherington, E. Mavis. "Effects of Parental Absence on Sex-typed Behaviors in Negro and White Pre-adolescent Males." *Journal of Personality and Social Psychology* 4 (1966): 87-91.

Hill, Mozell, et al. "Research on the Negro Family." *Marriage and Family Living* 19 (February 1957): 25-31.

Hill, Robert. *The Strengths of Black Families.* New York: Emerson-Hall, 1972.

Himes, Joseph S. "The Factor of Social Mobility in Teaching Marriage Courses in Negro Colleges." *Social Forces* 30 (May 1962): 439-443.

———. "Interrelation of Occupational and Spousal Roles in a Middle Class Negro Neighborhood." *Marriage and Family Living* 22 (November 1960): 262-263.

———. "Some Reactions to a Hypothetical Premarital Pregnancy by 100 Negro College Women." *Marriage and Family Living* 26 (August 1964): 344-349.

——— and Edwards, R. E. "Hair Textures and Skin Color in Mate Selection Among Negroes." *Midwest Journal* 4 (1952): 80-85.

——— and Hamelett, Margaret. "The Assessment of Adjustment of Aged Negro Women in a Southern City." *Phylon* 23 (1962): 139-147.

Hobson, Sheila. "The Black Family: Together in Every Sense." *Tuesday* (April 1971): 12-14, 28-32.

Iscoe, Ira, et al. "Age, Intelligence, and Sex as Variables in the Conformity Behavior of Negro and White Children." *Child Development* 35 (1964): 451-460.

Jackson, Jacquelyne. "Black Women in a Racist Society." In *Racism and Mental Health,* edited by Charles W. Willie et al. Pittsburgh: University of Pittsburgh Press, forthcoming.

———. "But Where Are the Men?" *Black Scholar* (December 1971): 30-41.

———. "Marital Life Among Older Black Couples." *Family Coordinator* 21 (January 1972): 21-28.

———. "Negro Aged Parents and Adult Children: Their Affective Relationships." *Varia* 2 (Spring 1969): 1-14.

Jeffers, Camille. *Living Poor.* Ann Arbor, Michigan: Ann Arbor Publishers, 1967.

Johnson, Charles S. *Shadow of the Plantation.* Chicago:

University of Chicago Press, 1934.

———. *Growing Up in the Black Belt.* Washington, D.C.: American Council on Education, 1941.

Kamii, Constance, and Radin, Norma. "Class Differences in the Socialization Practices of Negro Mothers." *Journal of Marriage and the Family* 29 (May 1967): 302-310.

Kardiner, Abram, and Ovesey, Lionel. *The Mark of Oppression.* New York: W. W. Norton & Company, Inc., 1951.

King, Karl. "Adolescent Perception of Power Structure in the Negro Family." *Journal of Marriage and the Family* 31 (November 1969): 751-755.

———. "A Comparison of the Negro and White Family Power Structure in Low-Income Families." *Child and Family* 6 (1967): 65-74.

King, Charles E. "The Sex Factor in Marital Adjustment." *Marriage and Family Living* 16 (August 1954).

King, Helen, "The Black Woman and Woman's Lib." *Ebony* 26 (March 1971): 68-76.

Kleinerman, Gerald, et al. "Sex Education in a Ghetto School." *Journal of School Health* (January 1971).

Kunz, Phillip R., and Brinkerhoff, Merlin B. "Differential Childlessness by Color: The Destruction of a Cultural Belief." *Journal of Marriage and the Family* 31 (November 1969): 713-719.

Ladner, Joyce. *Tomorrow's Tomorrow: The Black Woman.* Garden City, New York: Doubleday & Company, Inc., 1971.

Larue, Linda. "The Black Movement and Women's Liberation." *Black Scholar* 1 (May 1970): 36-42.

Lewis, Hylan. *Blackways of Kent.* Chapel Hill: University of North Carolina Press, 1955.

———. "The Changing Negro Family." In *The Nation's Children,* vol. 1, edited by Eli Ginzberg. New York: Columbia University Press, 1960.

———. "Culture, Class and Family Life Among Low-Income Urban Negroes." In *Employment, Race, and Poverty,* edited by Arthur Ross and Herbert Hill. New York: Harcourt, Brace & World, Inc., 1967.

Liebow, Elliot. "Attitudes Toward Marriage and Family Among Black Males in Tally's Corner." *Milbank Memorial Fund Quarterly* 4 (1970): 151-180.

———. *Tally's Corner.* Boston: Little, Brown and Company, 1966.

Lincoln, C. Eric. "The Absent Father Haunts the Negro Family." *New York Times Magazine* (November 28, 1965).

———. "A Look Beyond the Matriarchy." *Ebony* (August 1966): 111-116.

Lystad, M. H. "Family Patterns, Achievements, and Aspirations of Urban Negroes." *Sociology and Social Research* 45 (1961): 281-288.

McBroom, Patricia. "The Black Matriarchy: Healthy or Pathological?" *Science News* 94 (October 19,1968): 394.

Mack, Delores. "Where the Black Matriarchy Theorists Went Wrong." *Psychology Today* 4 (January 1971): 24.

McDowell, Sophia. "Black-White Intermarriage in the United States." *International Journal of Sociology of the Family* 1 (May 1971).

McQueen, Albert. "Incipient Social Mobility Among Poor Black Families." Paper presented at the National Council on Family Relations Meeting, August 1971, at Estes Park, Colorado.

Maxwell, J. W. "Rural Negro Father Participation in Family Activities." *Rural Sociology* 33 (1968): 80-93.

Meadow, Kathryn P. "Negro-White Differences Among Newcomers to a Transitional Urban Area." *Journal of Intergroup Relations* 3 (1962): 320-330.

Mercer, Charles V. "Interrelations Among Family Stability, Family Composition, Residence and Race." *Journal of Marriage and the Family* (August 1967): 456-460.

Middleton, Russel, and Putney, Snell. "Dominance in Decisions in the Family: Race and Class Differences." *American Journal of Sociology* 29 (May 1960): 605-609.

Miller, Elizabeth W. *The Negro in America: A Bibliography.* Cambridge, Mass.: Harvard University Press, 1966.

Monahan, Thomas. "Interracial Marriage in the United States: Some Data on Upstate New York." *International Journal of Sociology of the Family* 1 (March 1971).

Moynihan, Daniel Patrick. "Employment Income and the Ordeal of the Negro Family." *Daedalus* 94 (Fall 1965): 745-770.

National Conference of Black Social Workers. *The Black Family.* Philadelphia, Pa.: MMS Public Relations, 1971.

Noble, Jean, "The American Negro Woman." In *The American Negro Reference Book,* edited by John P. Davis, pp. 522-547. Englewood Cliffs, New Jersey: Prentice-Hall, 1964.

Parker, Seymore. "Social and Psychological Dimensions of the Family Role Performance of the Negro Male."*Journal of Marriage and the Family* (August 1969): 500-506.

—— and Kleiner, Robert J. "Characteristics of Negro Mothers in Single Headed Households." *Journal of Marriage and the Family* 28 (November 1966): 507-513.

Petroni, Frank. "Teenage Interracial Dating." *Transaction* (September 1971): 52-59.

Pettigrew, Thomas. *A Profile of the Negro American.* Princeton, New Jersey: D. Van Nostrand Company, Inc., 1964.

—— et al. "Color Gradations and Attitudes Among Middle Income Negroes." *American Sociological Review* 31 (June 1966): 365-374.

Pierce, Chester. "Problems of the Negro Adolescent in the Next Decade." In *Minority Group Adolescents in the United States* edited by Eugene Brady. Baltimore: Williams and Wilkins Company, 1968.

Pope, Hallowell. "Negro-White Differences in Decisions Regarding Illegitimate Children." *Journal of Marriage and the Family* 31 (November 1969): 751-755.

Poussaint, Alvin. "Blacks and the Sexual Revolution." *Ebony* (October 1971): 112-122.

Powdermaker, Hortense. *After Freedom: A Cultural Study in the Deep South.* New York: Viking Press, 1939.

Radin, Norma, and Glasser, Paul H. "The Use of Parental Attitude Questionnaires with Culturally Disadvantaged Families." *Journal of Marriage and the Family* 27 (August 1965): 373-382.

Radin, Norma, and Kamii, Constance K. "The Child-Rearing Attitudes of Disadvantaged Negro Mothers and Some Educational Implications." *Journal of Negro Education* 34 (Spring 1965): 138-146.

Rainwater, Lee. *Behind Ghetto Walls: Negro Families in a Federal Slum.* Chicago: Aldine Publishing Company, 1970.

———. "The Crucible of Identity: The Lower-Class Negro Family." *Daedalus* 95 (Winter 1966): 258-264.

———. *Family Design.* Chicago: Aldine Publishing Company, 1964.

——— and Yancey, William. *The Moynihan Report and the Politics of Controversy.* Cambridge, Mass.: Massachusetts Institute of Technology Press, 1967.

Reed, Julia. "Marriage and Fertility in Black Female Teachers." *Black Scholar* 1 (January-February 1970): 22-28.

Reid, Ira D. A. *In a Minor Key: Negro Youth in Story and Fact.* Washington, D.C.: American Council on Education, 1940.

Reiner, Beatrice. "The Real World of the Teenage Negro Mother." *Child Welfare* 47 (1968): 391-396.

Reiss, Ira L. "Premarital Sexual Permissiveness Among Negroes and Whites." *American Sociologist Review* 29 (October 1964): 688-698.

Renne, Karen. "Correlates of Dissatisfaction in Marriage." *Journal of Marriage and the Family* 32 (February 1970): 54-67.

Risdon, Randall. "A Study of Interracial Marriages Based on Data for Los Angeles County." *Sociology and Social Research* (1954-1955): 91-95.

Rosen, Lawrence. "Matriarchal and Lower Class Negro Delinquency." *Social Problems* 17 (Fall 1969): 175.

Rosenberg, Bernard, and Bensman, Joseph. "Sexual Patterns in Three Ethnic Subcultures of an American Underclass." *Annals of the American Academy of Political and Social Science* (March 1968): 61-75.

Ryan, William. "Savage Discovery: The Moynihan Report." *Nation* November 22, 1965.

Scanzoni, John. *The Black Family in Modern Society.* Boston: Allyn and Bacon, Inc., 1971.

Schulz, David. *Coming Up Black: Patterns of Ghetto Socialization.* Englewood Cliffs, New Jersey: Prentice-Hall, Inc., 1969.

———. "Some Aspects of the Policeman's Role as It Impinges upon Family Life in a Negro Ghetto." *Sociological Focus* (September 1969): 63-71.

———. "Variations in the Father Role in Complete Families of the Negro Lower Class." *Social Science Quarterly* 49 (December 1969): 651-659.

Schwartz, M. "Northern United States Negro Matriarchy: Status versus Authority." *Phylon* 261 (Spring 1961): 18-24.

Sebald, Hans. "Patterns of Interracial Dating and Sexual Liaison of White and Black College Men." Unpublished paper, 1971.

Smith, Howard P., and Abramson, Marcia. "Racial and Family Experience Correlates of Mobility Aspirations." *Journal of Negro Education* 31 (Spring 1962): 117-124.

Smith, Mary. "Birth Control and the Negro Woman." *Ebony* (March 1968): 29-37.

Smith, Raymond. "The Nuclear Family in Afro-American Kinship." *Journal of Comparative Family Studies* 1 (Autumn 1970): 55-70.

Sommerville, Rose. "Contemporary Family Materials— Black Family Patterns." *Family Coordinator* 19 (July 1970): 279-286.

Staples, Robert. "The Black Prostitute in White America." In *The Black Family: Essays and Studies,* edited by Robert

Staples, pp. 366-377. Belmont, Calif.: Wadsworth Publishing Company, 1971.

———. "The Black Woman's Burden: Racism and Sexism." *Zena* (1972).

———. "Childhood in a Black Ghetto: A Case Study." In *The Black Family: Essays and Studies,* edited by Robert Staples, pp. 271-277. Belmont, Calif.: Wadsworth Publishing Company, 1971.

———. "Educating the Black Male at Various Class Levels for Marital Roles." *Family Coordinator* 19 (April 1970): 164-167.

———. "Ideological Conflict in Family Analysis." *Black Scholar* (November 1971): 42-45.

———. "The Influence of Race on Reactions to a Hypothetical Premarital Pregnancy." *Journal of Social and Behavioral Science* (Spring 1972): 32-36.

———. *The Lower Income Negro Family in Saint Paul.* St. Paul: St. Paul Urban League, 1967.

———. "The Matricentric Family: A Cross-Cultural Examination." *Journal of Marriage and the Family* 34 (February 1972): 156-165.

———. "Reconstruction of the Black Lower Class Family: The Role of the Social Worker." *Bayviewer* 5 (July 1969): 14-18.

———. "Mystique of Black Sexuality." *Liberator* 7 (March 1967): 8-10.

———. "The Myth of the Black Matriarchy." *Black Scholar* (January-February 1970): 9-16.

———. "The Myth of the Impotent Black Male." *Black Scholar* (June 1971): 2-9.

———. "Negro-White Sex: Fact and Fiction." *Sexology* 35 (August 1968): 46-51.

———. "Research on Black Sexuality: Its Implications for Family-life, Education, and Public Policy." *Family Coordinator* 21 (April 1972): 183-188.

———. "Research on the Negro Family: A Source for Family Practitioners." *Family Coordinator* 18 (July 1969): 202-210.

———. "Sex Behavior of Lower Income Negroes." *Sexology* 34 (October 1967): 52-55.

———. "Sex Life of Middle-Class Negroes." *Sexology* (September 1966): 86-89.

———. "Sexual Attitudes, Values and Knowledge in the Black Subculture." In *Religion and Human Sexuality.* New York: Siecus, forthcoming.

———. "The Sexuality of Black Women." *Sexual Behavior* June 1972, 4-15.

———. "Some Comments on Black Women and Women's Liberation." *Black Scholar* 1 (June 1971): 53-54.

———. "Towards a Sociology of the Black Family: A Decade of Theory and Research." *Journal of Marriage and the Family* 33 (February 1971): 19-38.

———. "What's Wrong with the Negro Family?" *Progressive World* 20 (October 1966): 32-37.

———, ed. *The Black Family: Essays and Studies.* Belmont, Calif.: Wadsworth Publishing Company, 1971.

Steinman, Anne, and Fox, David I. "Attitudes Toward Women's Family Role Among Black and White Undergraduates." *Family Coordinator* 19 (October 1970): 363-367.

Stokes, Gail. "Black Woman to Black Man." *Liberator* 8 (December 1968): 17.

Sussman, Marvin, and Yeager, H. C., Jr. "Mate Selection Among Negro and White College Students." *Sociology and Social Research* 35 (1950): 46-49.

Teele, J. E., and Schmidt, W. M. "Illegitimacy and Race, National and Local Trends." *Milbank Memorial Fund Quarterly* 48 (April 1970): 127-150.

Teicher, Joseph. "Some Observations on Identity Problems in Children of Negro-White Marriages." *Journal of Nervous and Mental Disease* 146 (1968): 249-265.

Teitz, C., and Levit, S. "Patterns of Family Limitation in a Rural Negro Community." *American Sociological Review* 18

(1953): 563-564.

Tenhouten, Warren. "The Black Family: Myth and Reality." *Psychiatry* (May 1970): 145-173.

Thursz, Daniel. *Where Are They Now?* Washington, D.C.: Health and Welfare, Council of the National Capital Area, 1966.

Tulkin, Steven. "Race, Class, Family and School Achievement." *Journal of Personality and Social Psychology* 9 (1968).

Udry, Richard. "Marital Instability by Race, Sex, Education, Occupation, and Income Using 1960 Census Date." *American Journal of Sociology* 72 (September 1966): 203-209.

U.S. Department of Labor. *The Negro in the West: The Negro Family.* Washington, D.C.: Government Printing Office, 1971.

Valien, Preston, and Fitzgerald, Alberta. "Attitudes of the Negro Mother Toward Birth Control." *American Journal of Sociology* 55 (1949): 279-283.

Vincent, Clark. "Ego Involvement in Sexual Relations." *American Journal of Sociology* 65 (November 1959): 287-296.

—— et al. "Familial and Generational Patterns of Illegitimacy." *Journal of Marriage and the Family* 31 (November 1969): 659-667.

Vontress, Clement. 'The Black Male Personality." *Black Scholar* 2 (June 1971): 10-17.

Washington, Joseph, Jr. *Marriage in Black and White.* Boston: Beacon Press, 1970.

Watkins, Mel, and David, Jay. *To Be A Black Woman: Portraits in Fact and Fiction.* New York: William Morrow and Company, 1970.

Westoff, Charles F. "Contraceptive Practice Among Urban Blacks in the United States, 1965." *Milbank Memorial Fund Quarterly* 48 (April 1970).

Willie, Charles V., ed. *The Family Life of Black People.* Columbus, Ohio: Charles E. Merrill Books, Inc., 1970.

Index

Competition of white women
for Black males, 58,
107, 118, 119, 120,
170, 192, 193-94
Concubines, 66, 76, 78, 80,
124
Consciousness raising, 162
Crummell, Alexander, 35

D

Dating, 105
behavior, 57-62
interracial, 118-19, 120-21
Davis, Angela, 13
Day care, 149, 159, 163, 168
Dellard, John, 15, 154
Discrimination, *see* Racism
Divorce, 5, 96, 97, 101,
116-17
Dodson, Jualynne, 104
Domestic employment,
15-16, 25, 27, 41, 42,
78, 169, 170, 181
Double standard, 41, 69,
75, 94
Douglass, Frederick, 132,
167, 173, 174
Drake, St. Clair, 103, 114
Dual oppression, *see* Sexism
and racism
DuBois, W. E. B., 1, 15-16,
139, 174

E

Economic deprivation, 96,
111, 112, 186

and sex, 46, 78, 88,
92-93, 138, 151
Economic exploitation, 14,
40, 92-93, 213, *see also*
Employment; Racism
Economic independence,
100, 101, 102, 207
Education, 15, 24-27, 105,
114-15, 185, 186, 196,
212
Emancipation Proclamation,
14
Employment
captive labor force, 11-12
discrimination in, 14, 15,
25, 163, 203, 206
male's instability of, 17,
19, 24, 32, 46, 112,
113, 125, 135,
203-206, 212
opportunities for women,
26-27
surplus labor supply, 17
see also Domestic
employment; Racism
Erikson, Erik, 158-59
Extended family system,
130, 150
Extra-marital sex, 44, 75,
99, 103, 113-14, 197

F

Family organization, 184,
188-90, 197-203,
207-208
bi-parental, 18, 189

marital, 106-107
see also Role of female
Income, median, 19, 25, 27
Infant mortality rate, 139
Infanticide, 12, 132
Inferiority, ideology of, 3,
11-12, 36, 80, 85, 164,
165, 166
Interracial relations
dating, 58, 67-69
marital, 12, 41, 58,
118-24, 193-94
sexual, 39, 65-69, 76,
177-78
Interview study
conclusion, 206-208
family composition
chart, 191
procedure, 186-87
profiles, 188-90
purpose and scope, 185
questions, 187
responses, 192-205
sample, 185-86

J

Jackson, Jacquelyn, 24, 25
Johnson, Charles, 147-48

K

Kardiner, Abram, 109, 115
Keniston, Ellen and
Kenneth, 165
King, Charles, 110

King, Martin Luther, 139
Kinsey Institute for Sex
Research, 45, 62-63,
82, 84, 145
Kinsie, Paul, 84
Kiser, Clyde, 137

L

Ladner, Joyce, 30, 44, 46,
52, 108, 112, 141, 145,
164, 168, 171
Larue, Linda, 142, 167
Laws, unfairness of, 40, 65,
89-90, 98, 118, 145,
163
Lesbians, 63-64, 91, 178, 214
Liebow, Elliot, 53, 56, 84,
106, 114

M

Mack, Delores, 29
Malcolm X, 92, 140, 175
Male chauvinism, 32, 69,
162, 269, 172-73, 199,
210, *see also* Women's
liberation movement
Male-headed households, 18,
189, 190, *see also*
Patriarchy
Male virility cult, 55-57
Marriage
African forms of, 97, 126
as sexist institution, 93

Ovesey, Lionel, 109, 115

P

Patriarchy, 27, 30, 33, 101,
174, 210
Petroni, Frank, 62
Pimp, 86-87, 91
Planned Parenthood
Organization, 140
Polygyny, 64, 97-98, 132,
174
Postemancipation era, 14-17
Poverty, *see* Economic
deprivation
Powdermaker, Hortense, 16,
135, 156
Power relationships in
families, 28-31, 108-10,
205, 207
Pregnancy, 24, 45, 46, 52,
57, 106, 157
Premarital sex, 45, 48, 52,
75, *see also* Male
verility cult
Promiscuity, 38, 56, 100,
197
Prostitutes, 66
arrests of, 81-82
attitudes toward, 74-75,
79-80, 87, 89, 93
motivation of, 76, 78,
79, 88
perversion and, 85
problems of, 90-92
semiprostitutes, 85-86

unstable backgrounds of,
88-89
VD and, 91-92
see also Pimp
Putney, Snell, 29

R

Racism, 5-6, 10, 11, 20, 21,
22, 25, 31, 40, 43, 46,
94, 96, 102, 111, 113,
138, 155, 156-57, 158,
162, 167, 203, 206,
210, 211, 213, 215
Racism and sexism, *see*
Sexism and racism
Rainwater, Lee, 43, 53,
59-60, 103, 106, 112,
114, 117, 145, 155
Rape, 23, 39, 46, 64-65, 66,
163, 171
Rapping, 59-60
Reconstruction Acts, 99-100
Reed, John, 29
Reiss, Ira, 50
Remarriage, 117
Renne, Karen, 111
Role, female, 183-208
during slavery, 11, 12, 31,
38-40, 43, 131, 132,
133
historical, 10-11, 172
new definition of, 184,
185, 186, 193,
194-97, 200, 207-208

ROBERT STAPLES is an associate professor in the Department of Sociology at the University of California, San Francisco.

Noted for his family studies in the area of human sexual behavior,
Dr. Staples is the author of *The Lower Income Negro Family in St.
Paul* and editor of *The Black Family: Essays and Studies*.